Climbing for Causes:

A Personal Story

By

Nick B. Comande

authorHOUSE™
1663 Liberty Drive, Suite 200
Bloomington, Indiana 47403
(800) 839-8640
www.AuthorHouse.com

First published by AuthorHouse 01/20/05

ISBN: 1-4208-0792-7 (sc)
ISBN: 1-4208-0793-5 (dj)

Printed in the United States of America
Bloomington, Indiana

This book is printed on acid free paper

For Rachel, because there is no greater challenge for a father than to raise a daughter

And to all the people that supported, encouraged and climbed with me.

Table of Contents

Prologue

Someone once said that a picture is worth a thousand words. Being more than an amateur photographer, I could always appreciate the phrase; still, I never believed that a single picture could or would change my life, but change it, it did.

My eyes were opened to a whole new world, to something I had never considered. I became aware that mountains are more than just something to view, and I was shown the road to adventure. Never did I think that I would be on my way, seeing remote places of the world, and helping different charities at the same time. It was indeed, a turning point in my life.

The year was 1988; my 30th birthday was nearing and I needed something new – a different way to celebrate. I wanted an exotic vacation. My last adventure had been three years earlier when I traveled on a cruise ship to see Halley's Comet. I had gone as far south as Curicio and Caracas, Venezuela. It was time again to travel to some far away place.

After several weeks of looking at travel brochures and listening to others tell about their distant journeys, I decided to go to Europe; Germany, Switzerland and Austria. I thought that a couple of weeks with a rental car would give me a chance to see some of the more scenic parts of these countries.

My father, who is a wonderful person, did not share my enthusiasm or excitement of European travel; he didn't think it was a good idea. The Achille Lauro affair was still fresh in his mind and terrorism in Europe was on the rise. The thought of my going overseas made him nervous. Strange, considering I ran into burning buildings for a living. I, on the other hand, thought that everything would be fine and wonderful, and all

I had left to do was set the dates and go. It was almost October, and I was planning my trip for early December.

Some people may call it fate, a draw of the cards, or even the luck of the Irish; I called it "a turning point."

Carol Duncan, my travel agent for some time, in whom I had often entrusted all my travel arrangements, was busy talking on the phone to another client. Over the past few weeks she had been helping me find interesting places to see and visit in Europe.

Since I dealt only with her, I didn't mind waiting for her to finish whatever she was doing. It was during that time that everything changed. While Carol was busy talking on the phone, I was killing time by looking at the travel brochures of Europe.

I don't know why I looked at those brochures of Africa, but I picked one up – maybe to look at the animals. Then, I stopped to look at a picture of a mountain; it was Kilimanjaro, although I didn't know that until I read the caption at the bottom of the picture. All I knew was that Ernest Hemingway had written a book about the mountain, but now, I knew something else about it: I knew that I wanted to go see it! In the seconds that passed into minutes, and in the minutes that passed into longer minutes while I waited for Carol, my wanting to see Kilimanjaro in person increased more and more, until I decided that not only did I want to see it, but I wanted to climb it.

When Carol finished with her phone call, she asked me if I was ready to go to Europe. I didn't hesitate to say that we were going to scrap all her hard work. I simply handed her the travel brochure, opened to the picture of Kilimanjaro, and said, "I want to go here, instead." She looked at me and asked if I was kidding. I wasn't. Before I left the travel agency, Carol had looked through a number of specialty travel books until we found one that would serve my purpose. Once again, I was in the planning stages of a vacation that would beat all vacations, but it was more than that; it was the start of an adventure. Actually, it was beginning to feel more like a quest.

I left the travel agency and stopped by my parents' house. I gently broke the news to Dad that I was going to Africa to climb a mountain. He was startled, and he paused before he replied, "What's wrong with Austria, Germany and Switzerland?" From his reaction, I felt my newest vacation idea must be the greater of the two evils.

The outfit that would help me get to the mountain was called Mountain Travel of California. They sent me a catalog; I called it my wish book, because I wished that I could travel to half of the places it listed. There were trips in there that would take active, expedition-like travelers all over the world, ranging from the Sahara to the Antarctic. Before this, I had never realized that there were such vacations available.

My trip was still several months away; I had much plotting and planning to do. I needed a new passport, and there were shots to consider, but most importantly, I had to get into shape. Not that I was terribly out of shape, mind you, but I could have been in better shape. I was an eight-year veteran of the Racine Fire Department. My job helped me stay in shape, but not for what I was planning to do. I had to train for my climb and I didn't know where to begin. At the time, I started to think that I was putting the proverbial cart before the horse; I thought more about what I was going to do and how very little I knew about it. I had signed up for a trip, and I wasn't even sure of what I was getting myself into. How could I train for a mountain climb? I didn't know the first thing about it. I knew a little bit about ropes, and I had done a little hiking; I had camped out in my life, but I had never backpacked anywhere. I was getting myself into something without really knowing what I was doing, and for some strange reason, it was terribly exciting!

Something else I would learn—about half way into the climb – was high altitude. I had never experienced that before. I had no concept of thin air, pulmonary edema or their effects on a climber. Living in Racine was like living at sea level; there were no mountains, not even any big hills. The only altitude I had ever experienced was in an airplane, and that didn't count. Regardless, I plunged into a makeshift training schedule, used a treadmill and a Stair Master to prepare for the climb.

According to Mountain Travel, my trip featured a photo safari of several game preserves before the climb. Since I loved using a camera, I found this opportunity as exciting as the climb. I also received the trip itinerary and an equipment list, telling what I was responsible for. I would have a week to spend in Africa before we actually reached Mt. Kilimanjaro. I would get to see African countryside, and animals living in their natural habitat. I would eat exotic foods, and take more pictures than I ever had taken before. To prepare myself for the rest of the trip, I did a little research. Sure, I bought a book on Africa, but I should have done more. I spent too much time researching Mt. Kili. To me it was the main reason for the trip, but I should have paid more attention to the rest of the country I would be in.

Mt. Kilimanjaro is 19,340 feet high, and located near the equator in the country of Tanzania. I figured it must be pretty warm, so all I would need would be a winter jacket and a good windbreaker to wear when we made our play for the frozen summit. I had never even heard about Gortex at the time.

Throughout the planning, enthusiasm grew and grew as the deadline to my adventure drew nearer. It was still two months away and it seemed like time was dragging on. I even read *The Snows of Kilimanjaro* by Hemingway. The book talked, not about the mountain, but what happened to a hunter/writer who was at its base. Some of my fellow firefighters thought I was a bit misguided for wanting to travel all the way to Africa to climb a mountain. Some thought that I should be going somewhere to lie out on a beach. Others thought it was an opportunity of a lifetime.

But my climb was to take a serious twist, and I owe James King for that. James is another Racine firefighter; we were stationed together while I was planning my trip. He had an extra ticket to an appreciation dinner sponsored by the Milwaukee Chapter of the Muscular Dystrophy Association and asked me if I would like to go with him. It would not be overly fancy, but it would be fun. Here many groups and organizations were praised for all their hard work in raising funds for the MDA. When it came to fire departments, the MDA read off the names and amounts of money raised by each particular fire department.

For as long as I could remember, firefighters had always raised money for the MDA. Over the years, our department had held bed races, blood pressure checks, and filled the boot on street corners during the Jerry Lewis Telethon. We had fund drives, basketball games, and other ways of raising money for Jerry's Kids. Even when I was much younger, I had Muscular Dystrophy carnivals in my back yard. I only raised $19, but I remember being proud when I sent it in.

Donations at the banquet were read according to the amount raised, with the least amount read first. It started with the City of Racine. Our department only had a little more than $200. Apparently, our department hadn't done a very good job at fund raising that year. James and I talked about what we did to raise money, and what we should have done, and how it would be nice to come up with a new way to raise money for the MDA.

We talked about the bed races. We had done several in the past but they were dangerous – pushing beds down busy streets, and collecting money in old pairs of our bunker boots. Several times some of our people had been almost hit by cars. This may not have been a wise move on our part. After all, weren't firefighters supposed to promote safety, and not set poor examples? One thing I did learn while filling the boot was that most people who stopped to donate money had old or beat up cars – filled with kids. They didn't mind pulling over to donate a buck while those in the newest sports cars, and who probably had more money than they knew what to do with, wouldn't stop to give so much as a wooden nickel or the time of day.

James and I tried to think about new types of sporting events and marathons. He thought of things like walks, bike rides and hula-hoop contests had been used way too much. Then he said half jokingly, "Too bad we couldn't turn your climb into a fund raising event." We laughed it off, but it sat and festered inside our minds.

Next thing we knew, it wasn't funny anymore. It was feasible. In the course of 20 minutes, James and I figured that if people pledged a nickel for each 100 feet I would climb, and I made it to the top of Kilimanjaro, they would then owe $9.65. A dime pledge would raise $19.34. Since I was already going to Africa to climb Kilimanjaro, there would be no overhead – just my time and the cost of getting the pledge sheets made. By the end of the conversation, both James and I were fired up, and I felt there was more purpose in the climb. If it worked, others would then benefit by what I was doing. I could hardly wait to bring it up to Lynn Deedering. She was presently the head of the MDA, Milwaukee Chapter.

After the ceremony – when James and I approached Lynn – I was more than enthusiastic about telling her what James and I had planned. When we told her, she did something that I did not expect: she laughed. She also thought that our idea would never work. Her response hurt me, briefly, but I kept my head held high. I told her I thought it was worth a try. We talked for a few more minutes before James and I said good-bye. We left the ceremony and drove the 24 miles home from Milwaukee. During the ride home we mostly discussed my climb and how we could successfully turn it into a fund raising event. The more I thought of Lynn laughing at me, the more eager I became to prove her wrong. The idea would work. The more I thought of Lynn saying that it wouldn't work, the more I thought of it as a challenge. There in the car – on the way home – I decided that I would turn my climb into a fund raising event, with all proceeds going to the Muscular Dystrophy Association. Without realizing it, I was getting myself into something else that I had never done before: organizing a fundraiser.

The idea of my climbing for a cause seemed to take off. The first thing I needed was a pledge sheet to record the pledges and donations. With the help of a couple of other firefighters, Jim Schmitz and Mark Geisler, pledge sheets were drawn up and printed in less than a week. On short notice, Schmitz and Geisler gave me what I needed. The top half of the pledge sheet had a picture of a rock climber using a rope to go up a steep pitch. They added a fire helmet to the climber and then printed a description of what I was doing and where. The bottom half of the sheet was marked off with lines for people to place their name, address and amount they were willing to pledge per foot.

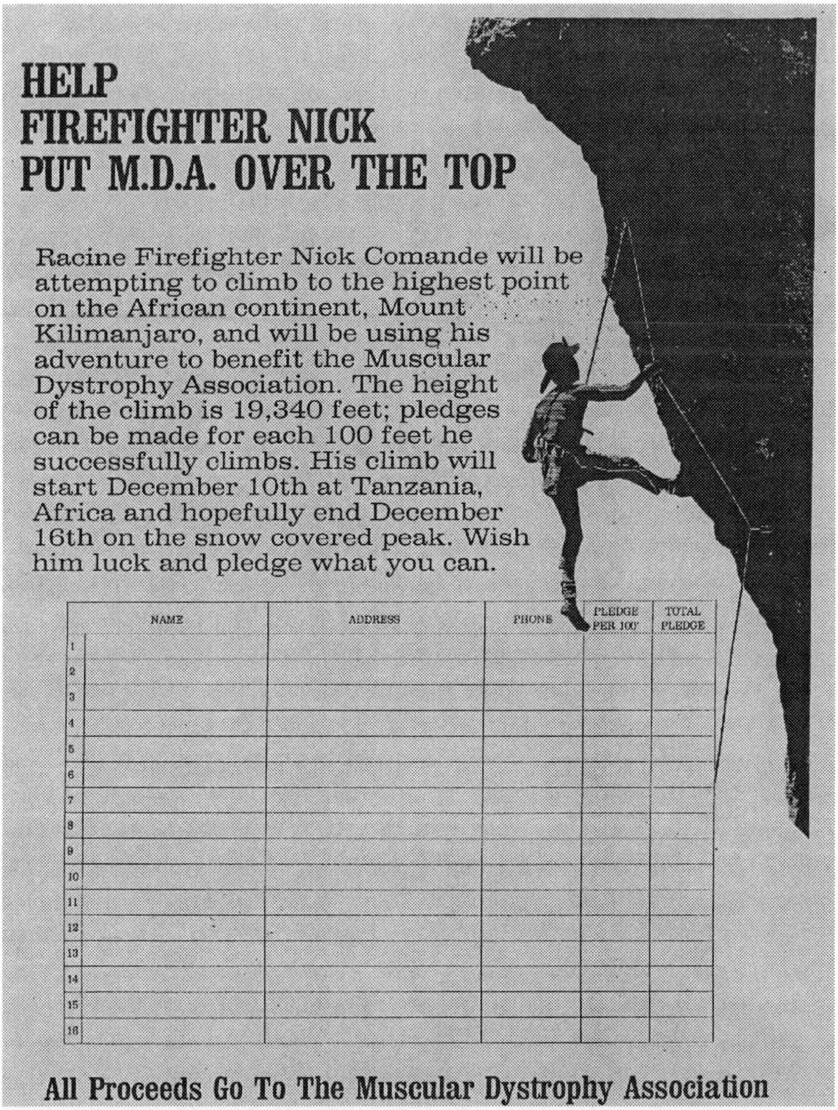

HELP FIREFIGHTER NICK PUT M.D.A. OVER THE TOP

Racine Firefighter Nick Comande will be attempting to climb to the highest point on the African continent, Mount Kilimanjaro, and will be using his adventure to benefit the Muscular Dystrophy Association. The height of the climb is 19,340 feet; pledges can be made for each 100 feet he successfully climbs. His climb will start December 10th at Tanzania, Africa and hopefully end December 16th on the snow covered peak. Wish him luck and pledge what you can.

	NAME	ADDRESS	PHONE	PLEDGE PER 100'	TOTAL PLEDGE
1					
2					
3					
4					
5					
6					
7					
8					
9					
10					
11					
12					
13					
14					
15					
16					

All Proceeds Go To The Muscular Dystrophy Association

I hung pledge sheets in the seven fire stations in the city; I gave them to family members and friends to help me get them filled with pledges. Eventually, the local newspaper learned of my activities and wanted to do an article on my climb; it was the first real publicity my climb had gotten.

It also was the first time I learned that one just doesn't go out to raise money for an organization.

Several days later I received a phone call from Lynn at the MDA office in Milwaukee. She told me that what I was doing was wrong. What I didn't know was that the MDA has to OK anything that has their name on it. I had used their name during the interview with the Racine Journal Times, and on every one of my pledge sheets. Lynn wasn't very happy with me because my climb was not sanctioned by the MDA; it was not yet recognized as a legal function. Lynn was also concerned with the liability aspect of the climb. She worried that if something unfortunate happened to me while on the climb, my family or I would come back to the MDA with a lawsuit.

I quickly learned some of the legal aspects of fund raising. I didn't realize that permission was needed to raise money for an organization. I told Lynn about everything I had done since that night in Milwaukee; I told her about the pledge sheets that I had made and how I had already started to collect pledges and donations. Lynn said that it was too late to do anything about it. She knew that I was sincere in what I was doing and that I meant no harm. To settle the matter about liability, I sent a copy of the pledge sheet and a letter to her, which she forwarded to her superiors saying that I had started my fundraising climb without knowing the particulars, and that the MDA would not be held responsible. That seemed to satisfy the MDA because I didn't hear anything else from them, so my climb for a cause would go on.

I admit that I was a bit offended by the experience. Here I was taking my vacation and trying to turn it into something that would benefit others. The trip expenses were coming from my pocket, and I wasn't asking for any kind of reimbursement from anyone. After all, the entire trip to Africa was planned before I decided to make it a fundraising event. The pledge sheets had been donated, so there was no cost there; the only other expenditure would be my time in getting pledges, and the time it would take to collect them. I didn't think about starting over and choosing a different charity, or starting from the beginning so as not to cause anyone problems. I didn't have the time to do so; mostly, because firefighters raise money for Muscular Dystrophy. They had done it for years and were great contributors. The President of the International Association of Fire Fighters had been presenting checks for millions of dollars to Jerry Lewis at his telethons – millions which had been raised by firefighters across the country. It felt good to know that I would be part of that in next year's figure.

I needed a target figure to raise, so I set my goal at $2,000 for the MDA. When I wasn't out looking for pledges, I was spending my spare time getting ready for the climb. I had to get into better shape; I spent more time working out and riding my bike, but not once did I think that I would have to train for altitude. I spent mornings on a treadmill which I had set on a steep incline to simulate going uphill; it was a poor substitute for the real thing, but I believed that it was helping me. Being in good shape was important to Mountain Travel; along with my packet containing the rest of the trip information and an equipment list, came a doctor's release form. I would have to pass (a physical examination), have the form filled out, and returned before I could get their final OK.

Passing the physical was the easy part; filling the equipment list was going to take some doing; I had virtually no equipment, not even a sleeping bag; I ended up having to borrow one.

Chapter One
Mt. Kilimanjaro

(*With apologies to Ernest Hemingway*)

I call this trip, my trip of firsts – my first time climbing, my first time traveling to some new and exciting countries, and my first time with certain new experiences. Never before had I traveled so far away from home, and never had I traveled so far alone. I flew from Chicago to Nairobi, Kenya, Africa, on December 2, 1988, with stops in New York and Frankfurt, Germany, to change planes. The layover in Frankfurt was short – too short to do anything (I would have enjoyed sightseeing). It was here, at this airport, that I had my first encounter with a washroom attendant. I remember standing, washing my hands, when suddenly, out stepped a lady from somewhere behind me and handed me a towel. Well, I thought to myself, different countries – different customs.

The flight to Nairobi was as long as the flight to Frankfurt, and I was getting extremely bored spending so much time on an airplane; I couldn't sleep or relax. So when I landed in Nairobi, it was nighttime and all I wanted to do was get some serious sleep – in a bed.

It didn't take long to go through customs and hail a cab. During the 25-minute ride to the hotel, I looked out the cab window into the darkness. It was hard for me to believe that I was actually in Africa. I had visions of seeing vast herds of wildlife such as those in the brochures, but it was dark, and I could barely see the side of the road. Later, I checked into the hotel; my room was ready and waiting. I still hadn't slept, but by now I was very excited; I could feel the adrenaline flowing through me. Sleeping was going to be difficult, but I forced myself into bed, if for no other reason than to fight off the jet lag that I was certain to experience later. Tomorrow, I was to meet the other members of the climb.

I awoke and called home to tell my family that I had arrived safely, and to put my father more at ease. Later, I met our guide and the other people who would be on the trip with me. Everyone was friendly and looking forward to all the upcoming sights and wildlife we were scheduled to see. Before starting our climb, we would tour the game preserves of Lake Manyara and the Ngorongoro Crater. I took a short day-tour outside the city to Karen Blitzen's house, feeling thankful that I had seen *Out of Africa*; otherwise, I would not have understood why it was famous. On the way back to Nairobi, the driver saw some giraffes, and he pulled over so we could photograph them. I had never seen animals in the wild before, especially exotic ones; I was quite impressed.

Later that day, I exchanged three twenty dollar bills. Because of the exchange rate, I was given a pile of money so big that I had to split it up between my pockets. For the next several days we toured game preserves south of the Kenyan border in Tanzania. This time, I saw animals living in the wild. There were lions, elephants, herds of water buffalo and hippos. I decided that even if I never climbed the mountain, my coming to Africa would be well worth the trip just to see these sights.

During my stay at Lake Manyara, Tom Ripilino our guide from Mountain Travel, was planning to go jogging to loosen up for the Kilimanjaro climb. The rest of the party was invited to go along. Since I did not enjoy jogging and did very little, if any, I was reluctant to go, but in order to stay with the rest of the group, I joined them. I was the youngest member of the party, and I felt that I was in just as good a shape as anyone else on the climb, but I learned a new lesson that day: age has nothing to do with being in shape. In the three miles or so that we jogged, I was able to keep up with everyone for the first half of the run.

Then it hit me. Suddenly, I had no strength, and it was difficult to catch my breath. I hadn't realized that I was running almost 5,000 feet higher in altitude than what I had been used to. I started to slow down. Eventually, everyone passed me by, leaving me behind. Soon all I could see in the distance was the cloud of dust being kicked up as they ran ahead of me. I managed to walk back to the resort half-an-hour later – still trying to catch my breath. It was my first experience with thin air.

On the 9th of December, our group arrived at the Kibo Hotel in Marangu. The mountain was covered with clouds, so we could not see it as we drove in to the hotel. Again, my adrenaline was on the rise. We would start our climb!

The hotel wasn't as neat and clean as those back in the states, but this was a third world country; it was better than I had expected. Little did I know that after a week of camping out with no modern accoutrements, the Kibo soon would seem like a five-star hotel.

December 8, 1988 Ngorongoro Crater

Basically, I'm keeping this journal for myself, but for those who may read this, I'll try to be explicit. I'm writing with a fountain pen to simulate what it would have been like to put thoughts to paper as writers did long ago.

It has been a long day here at the Ngorongoro Crater; I photographed lions, wildebeest, giraffes, hippos and rhinos. I'm sitting in the main hall of the lodge; it is one of the few heated places – meaning it is the only room with a fireplace. Tomorrow my seven companions, our guide and I will leave for the city of Marangu, and the starting point of our climb up Kilimanjaro – Kili for short.

I'm using this time to write some facts about the mountain. Though I've been in Africa over a week, the real adventure is just beginning. Most of the facts I've learned about Kili are from our host Tom Ripilino. He has climbed the mountain before and has taught the group some of the ins-an-outs of climbing this mountain. Using Tom as a reference, and a book I purchased here in Africa, I will try to give some background.

Kilimanjaro is roughly 200 miles south of the equator in the country of Tanzania; it is the tallest mountain on the African continent. Kili is made up of three extinct volcanoes: Shira at 13,000 feet, Mawenzi at 16,896 feet, and Kibo at 19,340 feet. The inner crater of Kibo is almost a mile wide; its two highest peaks are called Gilman's Point at 18,760 feet. Uhuru Peak at 19,340 feet, is the ultimate goal of my trip. Kilimajaro is also one of the world's highest freestanding mountains with a length of 36 miles; its greatest width is 24 miles.

The country is truly beautiful; one really has to see it to believe it. Our climb to the top will take roughly six days, with a one-day rest to acclimatize to the thinner air. I'm a bit anxious to see and photograph the mountain; photos can be wonderful, but sometimes they just don't capture the true essence of the subject.

It is almost midnight, but I don't mind staying up. Most of tomorrow will be spent traveling to the city of Marangu, an 8-hour or so drive. I'll be able to sleep in the van, if the roads smooth out for a while. The generator that provides all the light on the premises is used only between 6 p.m. and midnight and it will soon be turned off. The fireplace will not give off enough light to write by, and I'll have to use my flashlight to find my way back to my room.

December 9, 1988 Kibo Hotel, Marangu Elevation: about 5,000 feet

As predicted, this has been a long day, just less than eight hours by van to the Kibo Hotel. The roads are extremely rough in places; I call them the spice roads because the dust kicked up by autos or trucks looks like paprika or cinnamon. I needed a shower to get several layers of it off me once we got here. (A scarf to cover my mouth would have been beneficial; it might have kept me from breathing in the dust as we drove along). As we neared the city of Marangu, I could see Kilimanjaro in the distance; it was mostly hidden by clouds, and though the summit was still 30 miles away, it looked huge. I was beginning to wonder if I had bitten off more than I could chew. I checked into my room; my roommate for the trip is Blake Sherrod, from Alabama (I could tell by his accent). Blake has a touch of what we're calling Kilimanjaro's Revenge. I've been more fortunate, and have suffered no problems here with the water.

After checking in, Blake, two other group members (Hugh Grove, a college professor and his wife Nancy, a microbiologist), and I went for a side excursion to a nearby waterfall. We paid a local to lead us. It was a humid walk, about two-thirds of a mile, through some low-lying rainforest, but well worth the walk. The waterfall was a beautiful sight, over 80 ft. tall, and the water was cold and clear and tasted good; but I still plan to purify my drinking water with iodine pills.

I began to wonder what it would be like to climb up the mountain. During and after dinner tonight, with Tom's direction, we will plan our final strategies for our trip up the side of Kilimanjaro. Though we've been doing it all through the trip, this time it seems so much more important; probably because tomorrow the climb really begins. I have learned that we are taking the Marangu route. This is an easier route than the one I originally was told we would take. I thought we were going up the Umbre route, a much steeper climb. Now, I'm glad we're not; I cracked two bones in my right foot playing racquetball two days before I left the States. I've kept it well-taped and it hasn't really bothered me; if it gets too bad, I have something for the pain. I've given Blake some of my other medicines to help him with his "Revenge."

I packed three times tonight because of all the stuff I brought; the less weight the better. I don't know how many porters we have yet, but they will carry our community gear up the mountain. The rest of us will only carry daypacks. I will be carrying the first aid kit, since I'm an E.M.T. (Emergency Medical Technician), and because Tom said so. It added another five to six pounds to my pack, and includes everything from band-aids to a suture kit. If all goes well, we won't have to use any of it; this group seems pretty well-rounded, and no one seems careless – but accidents do happen.

We all seem a bit anxious to get started, since none of us have ever climbed anything like this before. I, for one, can't wait to get started. Sleep may be difficult tonight, but I'll try because I may need my strength tomorrow. I have the same feeling I had as a kid long ago: it's like going to bed on Christmas Eve, knowing that when I wake up in the morning there will be presents under the tree. I should try to sleep; seven o'clock breakfast will come soon enough. I only wish I had my Walkman with me; I could listen to some music to relax. Music is something I really miss. I guess that I should do without it. When traveling to another country, "one should do as the Romans do." I see that Blake is having no trouble sleeping; I hope I can sleep that sound, as well.

December 10, 1988 Madara Hut Elevation: 9,000 feet

So far so good! I'm presently in an A-frame hut with two floors; the upper floor has bunk beds with foam-rubber mattresses. There are enough beds to sleep 18 people, but there are nine of us, so there is room to spare. The lower floor is a main hall with six large picnic tables and benches; it also has a wood stove for heat. There is no electricity – a modern convenience I learned to take for granted back home. Since there are no lights, I have the honor of writing this by the light of a kerosene lamp and two candles. Some of the others are reading their books on Mt. Kili. Nancy is writing in her journal. The weather is tolerable yet – not at all cold – and somewhere in the mid- fifties.

Les, a computer engineer from Ohio, has a thermometer, but he isn't here right now. It's nearly 8 p.m. and it has been a long day; I'm sure I will sleep well tonight. Anticipation of the climb kept me from falling asleep early last night – and to make matters worse – the city of Mandara (where we stayed last night), was observing a local custom: some joker rings a church bell to awaken the rest of the town.

I was up by 5:30 a.m. I took a long hot shower, knowing that this would be the last one I would take until I returned to the Kibo Hotel next week. I met the rest of the group for breakfast at 7 a.m., and we left via bus to the park gate where we started our long walk up Mt. Kili. Tom collected our passports and other valuables and locked them in the hotel safe. Everything else that we wouldn't need while on the mountain was locked up in a storage room. I left one of my two cameras behind; I was cutting down on the weight I carried and it made sense to take only one camera.

Tom, our guide from Mountain Travel, was in charge. Joining our group of eight tourists from the States, were 19 locals; they included three assistant guides and a cook; the rest were porters, bringing our total complement to 27. We all rode the same small bus – each of us hanging on to it wherever we could. Still, we managed to make it to the park gate safely; at least we had everyone we'd started out with.

It was here that we hoped to see our first real glimpse of Kilimanjaro; unfortunately there was heavy cloud cover. We had to sign in at the park gate. The registrar asked for name, age, country and occupation. I was the only firefighter on the page I was signing. Also, I was the youngest climber; most of the people listed on the page were just a few years older than me.

I looked around the area; all the park rangers carried rifles. There were leopards in the area, but the rangers assured us that we wouldn't see any; leopards are night feeders, and we would be out of the area long before nightfall.

A local approached me about exchanging some U.S. currency; this was clearly the black market we often had been warned about since entering Tanzania. Regular exchange was about 750-to-one, but black market was 1000-to-one. I was carrying a little unclaimed cash on me, but I declined. First, I didn't need it; second, I didn't want to carry it all the way up the mountain. I also figured there would be very little to buy on the mountain.

Once given the go ahead, we started the climb. At first, we walked up a slanted path that was not very steep, but wide enough to let six or seven people walk side by side. It became evident from the start that we would walk at our own pace. After the first 20 minutes we already had split up and the path narrowed. Blake and John (a real estate developer from Colorado) and I took the lead; Tom, having done this before, took his time.

The walk was beautiful. The first part took us through a hot and humid rain forest that looked like something out of a Tarzan movie; there were even vines to swing on – yes, I did swing on one of them. I soon lost sight of Blake and John; I stayed in the rain forest and explored it a bit. I heard monkeys in the distance, but I couldn't get close enough to photograph any of them. There were birds of many sizes and colors. Les, the bird watcher of the group, was having a field day.

Halfway up to Madara Hut I ran into John and Blake again; they had stopped to take pictures and relieve themselves. Tom had pointed out during our pre-climb briefings that people burn off more moisture at higher altitudes, so we were required to drink up to six quarts of water a day. We soon learned what I called the "flow-through process": what goes in – must come out. I notched my canteen each time I emptied it so I could more easily keep track of my daily intake.

From our stopping point, looking through the breaks in the clouds, we could see the top of Mt. Kili; the summit – covered with patches of snow – was still very far away.

Though wearing shorts, I was sweating profusely; even my hat was soaked with sweat. This is why we drank so much water—to keep from dehydrating. The air – here and farther up the trail—smelled so fresh. I saw flowers – more beautiful than I had ever seen, but I silently hoped they wouldn't affect my allergies.

Our brief photo-stop ended and we moved on. I couldn't keep pace with Blake and John, and though I wasn't having trouble breathing, I had begun to slow down. I realized this could be a problem later on in the climb; only time will tell. I made it to Mandara Hut in two hours and six minutes. Average length of time, according to the chart, is three hours. Based on those standards, I was better than average.

The Mandara camp consisted of one main hut – which we had to ourselves – a number of smaller one-room huts that slept four people each, and a cookhouse. At the park gate, Tom gave us all a small lunch consisting of two sandwiches, a hard-boiled egg, and a bar of chocolate (which didn't taste very good). I also finished off my second quart of water. I was really glad that I had brought along enough powdered Tang and Crystal Light to spike it with flavor. Others in the group had the same foresight, except for Blake; I shared mine with him.

Within the next 2 ½ hours, the rest of the caravan made it to Mandara Hut. Since dinner would be a long while yet, Hugh, Nancy, John and I decided to do something to break up the afternoon. We hiked over to a nearby place called Maundi Crater which took us only another 30 minutes. It was a big crater (50 yards across and nearly perfectly bowl shaped). It was simply gorgeous! I wished I'd brought my camera with me; in fact, not a single one of us was carrying one. We had left everything behind at the hut except our water. We all had a canteen, and the question of the day was: "What number quart are you on?"

From the crater, I got my first real glimpse of Kili; it was impressive. Behind some closer hills stood a large dark slab of earth pushing itself into the sky; patches of white snow and ice were on the upper rims. I was amazed to think that I was going to climb that [mountain], or at least I would try! Again, I wished I'd brought my camera to record this wonderful view that lay before me. The sky was clear and blue, but to the west clouds were coming that would soon block out our view of the mountain. When we finished our walk around the crater, we met up with two more members of our group: Martin, a lawyer from Washington, DC and his wife, Rose Anne – a consultant for a senator. Our walk around the crater was so beautiful the first time, we repeated it before we went back to camp together.

Dinner was brought to us and we ate together on one of the picnic tables. It was well received, though I don't recall what it was; maybe I had just been hungry from the day's hike. After dinner, while discussing the day's events, Tom relayed to us some distressing news; he informed us of a death on the mountain. A 45-year-old man had died of a possible heart attack or pulmonary edema. Tom didn't want to alarm us, but he did want to warn us of the possibility that we would pass by the body as we climbed up the mountain the next day. It really put a damper on the evening, but that's life – or more precisely, death.

The rest of the day consisted of exploring the area and finishing our quota of water. As the sun went down, everything became very quiet and peaceful; stars filled the sky, although the high trees kept me from seeing only those directly above me.

I've been writing here awhile. The candles have burnt down quite a bit, and everyone is in bed – except for Tom, who is reading. I have finished my six quarts of water, and for the last time tonight I will use the flush toilet (a convenience we won't have when we leave here tomorrow).

December 11, 1988 Horombo Hut Elevation: 12,500 feet

It has been another long day. I'm presently at or about 12,360 ft. and more than halfway there, but the worst is yet to come. I made the walk up here in 3 hours 48 minutes, which according to the park guides is still under the usual five hours; I'm ahead of the average. I didn't fair as well as yesterday, falling from third person to reach camp, to sixth. Not that it makes any difference which number you are when coming into camp, but I thought I would do better than I did. I slept well last night; actually, I had no trouble, whatsoever, falling asleep, but I did have a headache when I awoke. Some in our group were using Diamox, a medicine that helps prevent altitude sickness. Those using it have been on it for the last week. I've borrowed some, but by the time it starts to work, the climb will be over. I do feel the change in altitude; partly because I live in Racine, Wisconsin, which is so close to sea level. I feel it much, much more! The day I go to the summit will prove to be a real challenge, providing I make it that far.

The climb today was both beautiful and exciting. We woke and ate breakfast around 7:00 a.m. We all had a healthy appetite and drank a lot of tea and coffee (just tea for me); all the liquids we consumed counted toward our six quarts.

The sky was a deep shade of blue with just a few scattered clouds, but what made it so wonderful was the sight of clouds floating below us – partially down the mountain. With the exception of being in an airplane, this was the first time I had ever encountered clouds below me.

I started out wearing shorts again. It was hot in the sun, but it got cold if you went into the shade. I thought to myself, how can it be cold so close to the equator? Then it hit me; there was snow on the top of Kilimanjaro. How can there be snow here? Then I realized – the higher we go, the colder it gets.

I was slowly learning about mountain climbing and the surrounding conditions. I knew that I had brought all this cold weather gear here for a reason, but now I understood why.

Being a firefighter doesn't allow me to wear a beard, so I like to grow one whenever I get the chance. I had stopped shaving even before I left the States, and I had a good start of a beard.

Now, the other male members of the group have stopped shaving. It only made good sense; we had to purify all our water for drinking, so why take the time to purify it for washing? We knew that the water was clean and supposedly germ free, but no one wanted to take the chance of getting "Kilimanjaro's Revenge;" besides, hot water was now very scarce. The wood we brought was used for cooking, not washing.

I had some difficulty adjusting to the thinner air today. I was unable to keep up with the faster members of the group. Since Hugh, Nancy and John came from Colorado where the elevation was 8,000 ft., they didn't feel the change in altitude like I did.

Once again, we were given bag lunches before starting out, so we could stop and eat along the way. All I could think about was getting to the next stop. I must have walked alone for at least three hours. It was so peaceful that I didn't mind not talking to anyone; it gave me time to think.

Today's hike took me out of the rain forest and into the area that is called heath and moorland, or according to the Kili book I bought, Zone 3.

Zone 1 is called cultivation where farming is done; Zone 2 is the rain forest where I was yesterday. I soon left the rain forest. As I walked, I saw lots of low grasslands with grass no higher than three feet.

I was passing other climbers as they were coming down the mountain. Everyone says "Jambo" as they pass by; this means hello in Swahili. Everyone I've met along this beaten path – porters or, whoever we meet along the way – has been very friendly. I kept looking and moving forward, not pausing to take photographs; I was wrapped up in a personal uphill battle and decided to take photos on the way down. I also wanted to make sure I had enough film for the summit; I had only three rolls of 36 exposures left.

I felt so at ease in my climb to our second night's stop – mentally that is. Physically, this part of the climb was somewhat demanding. Again, I was sweating buckets, having finished one of my canteens halfway up the trail. I was rationing my second canteen filled with tea until I found a stream where I could refill it.

I began to have a little difficulty breathing; I was not gasping for air, but I was taking deeper than usual breaths. (By the end of the hike, my lungs were hurting more than my legs.) There were a number of valleys and gorges that I walked up and down. It felt like I had walked much longer than the 3 hours 48 minutes that my stop watch said I had; it felt more like three days. By the time I reached Horombo Hut, I finally had managed to slow my pace down and stop exerting myself; otherwise, I would've been really hurting and completely exhausted.

Though I did very little of any kind of climbing and just walked up to Horombo Hut, I didn't mind that I was alone during most of this hike. With the exception of a few porters coming down the mountain, there was no one. The wind and the sound of my own footsteps on the loose gravel were the only sounds I heard; I couldn't remember the last time I had been this alone. Not only was it very peaceful, but I felt at peace with myself, as well. Without the outside distraction of a Walkman – which I only wished for occasionally – I found my mind wondering about many things. I thought about times and events that I hadn't thought of in years. I even thought of things that I had never thought of before. Maybe by the time I get off this mountain, I'll have my act together. It would be nice to know, for instance, what I will do with the rest of my life. After all, I owe it to myself, and realistically thinking, no one else is going to do it for me.

I was relieved when I reached Horombo Hut; it looked very similar to the Mandara Hut complex, except there were no trees in the area. We were now above the tree line and nothing more than grass and small bushes would grow here. The only real sign of technology was a solar powered wireless with which to contact the ranger station in case of an emergency.

Since our group was the largest, we would have the opportunity to sleep in the main hut again; it was identical to the one in the Mandara campsite. I could see the peak of Kilimanjaro still far off in the distance, and off to my right, I could see the peak of Mawenzi. I was not totally exhausted when I reached Horombo, but I was in need of a rest. I sat down on some rocks next to my fellow climbers who had finished before me and ate lunch. For someone who hates cold sandwiches, I ate them gladly. Even the bad chocolate bar hit the spot, and I finished up with two of the many granola bars I had brought with me. While talking to my friends, I learned that the fat yucca plants and cactuses that I had passed along the way were really called Lobelias and Sencious plant; they are unique to this area. There are also many other plants indigenous to the area, but their names have already slipped my mind.

After lunch and a lengthy rest in the sun and another quart of water to replace what I'd sweated out, Hugh, Nancy, John and I decided to walk up to the next ridge about one-third of a mile away – all uphill, of course. From the top of the ridge we could see clouds coming up the side of the mountain toward us. Clouds were quickly covering up the sun, and the temperature was dropping. Once the sun was covered and the colder temperature reached us, so did something else – the bad news from last night. I spotted the crew of porters bringing down the body of the climber who had died yesterday. They were about 75 yards away, and I watched them through the telephoto lens of my camera. I took a picture, not to be morbid, but because it was part of my trip. Five porters guided a cart with two large wheels. On the cart and wrapped in what may have been a sleeping bag, was the body of a man, who – for whatever reason – had died doing the same thing we were about to do.

I'm sure from this point on the four of us will think about him. We joked about it to lighten the situation; it made things seem not so bad. We called him Uncle Henry for lack of a better name. Because of my past work with the fire department and rescue squad, I was accustomed to seeing dead bodies, but the others admittedly had not. John made the comment, "This is just like another day at the office for you, Nick." In some respects he was right, but the four of us were about to do the same thing that this man died trying to do, but we felt smarter than him. We had trained hard; we weren't going to push ourselves, and we didn't have asthma or a heart condition that he apparently had. Because we saw a body carried down the side of the mountain, we would be very aware of what could happen.

After Uncle Henry had passed us by, we sat on some rocks – talking and joking – until the temp had fallen well into the 40's. Afterwards, we returned to camp and unpacked. We are going to be here for two nights to get acclimatized to the thinning air; I know I will need it! I have a slight headache now, but it was worse earlier in the day. Dinner was welcome tonight because we were all hungry. Despite all I'm eating, I feel like I'm losing weight; at this rate, I really should be looking good for Christmas.

With the flow-through process still continuing, I walked out to the edge of a nearby lava flow with a 70-foot drop off. From there I saw a remarkable sunset through the clouds. Again, I wished I'd had my camera, but now I'm glad I didn't photograph it. It was a special moment for me; there I was – halfway around the world – sitting by myself watching the sun set in Africa. It was a special, private moment, the way the sun was shining through the clouds. It was very serene; but then, something else special happened. As I sat on the edge of the lava flow, a cloud came right up the side of the mountain and over me. It was the first cloud I had ever touched; hopefully, it won't be the last. As it started to get darker, I walked back to our hut. The men who were bringing Uncle Henry down the mountain were getting ready to leave. I was glad; they had placed his body right next to our hut. I didn't relish the feeling of getting up and walking outside on a hopefully sunny day, then finding a body next to our door step. His body is gone now, but the memory lingers on.

It is nearly 10 p.m. now. I was interrupted from writing by the flow-through process, but now, I'm sitting by candles and a kerosene lamp. Once again, Tom is reading; Nancy is writing. The rest of the group is in their bunks reading, sleeping, or talking to each other. It is pitch black outside, so we have to use a light to get around. The sky has cleared of the clouds that arrived during sunset, and now it is loaded with stars. I can even see the Southern Cross; I hadn't seen that since the time I went to South America to see Halley's Comet back in 1986. From here, the stars look eternally brilliant and seem to go on forever. From the edge of the lava flow we can see the lights of the city of Moshi; perhaps tomorrow I'll try to take a picture of it. One last thing before I retire for the night. (I bring it up hesitantly because we're not absolutely sure of this yet.) Tom told us after dinner tonight that two other climbers may have fallen to their deaths on the other side of the mountain. If this is true, it means there have been three deaths in all.

We were all quiet for awhile after we heard the news; then we talked about what we were doing here, asking ourselves if it was really worth it. To me, this has become more than a hike. I told the others that I was doing this not only for myself, but also as a fundraiser for Muscular Dystrophy.

They said what I was doing was a good thing; they supported me in my quest to the top. I showed them the flag I planned to leave on the top of the mountain. It was not very ornate, it was square, bright yellow with black embroidered lettering. Donated to me by Ruth, the owner of Letter Perfect embroidery.

Now, I am tired and I must get some sleep, but I'll probably read some before I go to bed. I still have a slight headache and my neck is sore from carrying my backpack; I hope it isn't sore tomorrow. We will be here one more night to acclimatize (something Uncle Henry didn't do). We will take a 10-mile (round trip) hike to the base of Mt. Mawenzi tomorrow; it is the second highest peak on Kilimanjaro. It also will be a preview of what lies ahead.

December 12, 1988 Horombo hut second night Elevation: 12,500 feet

It has been another long day. Again, I write by candlelight on the lower floor of our hut. Most of the group is upstairs reading, resting, or whatever. As for myself, I feel it is more important to write, and to keep track of events and commit them to paper before they are lost to memory. I was outside earlier, on the edge of the lava flow, writing a letter to a friend back home. I couldn't finish it though; it was cooling down too fast. While I sat on a rock, I watched another cloud come straight up the side of the mountain and hang right over me. It was cold and damp, but I was getting up close to something which was usually so very far away. I was touching a cloud, and the mere thought of it made me shiver on the outside, but as I shivered, my heart grew warm, as well. It became too cold to finish my letter, so I left the edge of the lava flow, and came back to the main hall. (When a cloud comes up the mountain and stays during the twilight hours, the temperature drops very quickly.) It can't be much more than 35 degrees out now. The metal of my Cross pen now feels like ice. (Once I had finished my letter home, I traded in my Cross pen for the fountain pen I've been using to record these events.)

We arose early and had a warm breakfast; then we prepared to hike to the base of Mt. Mawenzi. Tom told us it was a 10 to 11- mile roundtrip. Rose Anne, Hugh, John, Blake and I have headaches; I took some Anaprox for mine and it seemed to help. Rose Anne and her husband, Martin, will not be coming with us today; they are saving their strength for the push up to our next higher camp. I think that Rose Anne is feeling a bit more ill than the rest of us, but even now I'm holding doubts of making it myself. Martin is staying to keep her company.

Tom and I, along with two guides and five other climbers started our hike to Mawenzi. Our destination is Tarn Hut, which is a place climbers can stay before they try for the summit of Mawenzi. Tarn is little more than a very small A-frame sheet metal structure with a door on it. It isn't even tall enough to stand up in, yet it sleeps four. I suppose being that close together at night would help conserve body heat.

We started out on the same trail we had taken yesterday when the four of us ran into Uncle Henry. While crossing this part of the path, John asked if I saw a lot of death on my job. I had the feeling he was reminded of Uncle Henry and we were having the same thoughts. I answered, "yes" to his questions, and without going into much detail, I told him that I had seen heart attacks, shootings, stabbings, and car accidents. I explained that firefighters can get used to seeing death, but it still bother us.

Speaking for myself, it still bothers me to see infants and young children die. I guess I feel sorry for them, knowing that they will never have the opportunity to see and experience life like it should be. By that, I mean we take the good with the bad. I don't know how someone can really know what is good until they feel the bad.

I was able to keep up a good pace during the hike today. We will gain some altitude during the day's hike, but we will lose it when we return to Horombo Hut. This will help us acclimatize or get used to the thinner atmosphere – something Uncle Henry didn't do. This is all part of the process of reaching the summit, and the way I'm feeling now, I will need all the help I can get. An hour into the walk, I lost the lead and started to fade back. By the end of the second hour I was at least 100 yards behind the rest of the group. I was having trouble breathing, but I kept pushing on. It would have been so easy to turn around and head back down to Horombo Hut. Each step down would make it that much easier on me, but if I stopped, I would never make it to the top of Kilimanjaro. There was too much riding on this, but it wasn't just the fact that I was doing this to raise money for MD; I was doing it for myself. It's been a long time since I've had a goal, and even though this goal may be short-lived, it is still all I have right now.

The trail was not steep; its incline was hardly noticeable except in a few places where you could actually see a rise in the gradient. Needless to say, I pushed on. As long as I was moving I was getting closer to the base of Mawenzi. Moving also kept me warm. The temperature was somewhere between 40 and 50 degrees. I was in the sun the whole time, but when that wind blew, I could feel the chill. Since there was no way to get out of it, I just made the best of it. All I was wearing was a pair of Khaki pants and a turtleneck, and as long as I was moving, I was warm. Today's hike took us across the saddle between Kibo and Mawenzi. There were no trees and no shrubs of any kind, just dirt and rocks. The scenic color for the day was brown with just a few small patches of grass here and there.

As the walk went on, I slowed down; I finally admitted to myself that I was having difficulty adapting to the altitude. As the group moved further ahead of me, I decided that my pace, from now on, would be more "pole, pole" (pronounced Pol-lee), or Swahili for slowly, slowly. I must learn to slow my pace so I don't burn myself out so soon; I'm really feeling the altitude. Even Hugh and Nancy said that it would be harder for me because I live so close to sea level. Finally, I reached the rest of the group at the base of Mawenzi. Altitude here is 14, 850 ft. Our hike to Kibo Hut tomorrow will bring us 700 feet higher than we are now.

We climbed up to the base of Mawenzi. It was about 50 feet higher, and I actually was climbing this time. John took a picture of us here. It was so windy at the base of Mawenzi that I put on my new windbreaker. It was here that I found some really neat pockets in the sleeves that I hadn't seen before; these could be useful during the summit climb. It also made me aware that I hadn't done a very good job of checking out my gear before I left the States.

After a brief stay and a quick lunch we had brought with us, we decided to head back to Horombo Hut. From here, I was able to see the top of Kilimanjaro. I took some photos; if they turn out, they could be my best pictures of the mountain.

The peak of Kilimanjaro. The final bid for the summit started at the base and went to the top near the left side near the snow line.

I refilled my canteen from a stream that flowed at the base of Mawenzi. The water was clear and cold, but I took care to purify it anyway. Going downhill was much easier than going up. We stopped to take photos of some black and white rocks called Zebra Rock. I forgot how Tom said it was formed. While we were resting I found some tracks near the path. Millard, one of the guides, said they were made from a leopard, but not to worry because they only feed at night. How reassuring, I thought.

When we reached Horombo Hut, Tom announced that we were all going to get a pan of hot water for washing; all we had to do was pick the order in which we were to get it. I made it a little easier by volunteering to go last. While I was awaiting my turn, I talked to Martin and told him about the hike to Mawenzi. He told me that Rose Anne and he rested today. Martin also said, "It will be good to wash. We must all be getting a little grimy by now." I wondered how we must smell.

While I was waiting to wash, I talked to some Austrians who came off the top of the mountain. One of the girls in the group was sitting at a table in the hall; she sat motionless for more than fifteen minutes. I walked to her and asked her if she was all right. All she could say in a tired voice was, "It was the worst thing I've ever done." (My best description of her would be that she looked two days dead.) According to some of the other Austrians, more than half of their group never made it to Gilman's Point

(18,760 feet). It was too hard for most of them, but some did make it to the top. I talked to one of the Austrians for a while. There was a very polite Frenchmen who was gracious enough to take a letter down the mountain for me and mail it. He would not even accept money for postage; this confirmed my belief that there are still good-hearted people in the world.

It is getting late, and I should try to get to sleep. (I've been drinking too much tea and the caffeine is affecting me.) I may have trouble sleeping tonight. Even Tom has gone to bed. He asks if I have writer's cramp yet from all the letter and journal writing I do. I don't have it yet and I don't mind writing; it helps to pass the time. Since there are no modern conveniences here of any sort, I lose myself in my journal and letters.

It is very quiet and outside it is as dark as can be. There should be a lot of stars out; if the clouds don't cover them tonight, I will go out to see them. After all, the flow-through process is calling. I will have to brave the dark one more time with flashlight in hand to walk the 300 feet to the so called "non-flush" facilities. If it is clear, I should also be able to see the lights of Moshi down below. I just realized that 40 hours from now the climax of this trip will be over and my moment of truth will have come and gone. I'm still thinking positive about the upcoming summit climb but I have some doubts.

Now I must blow out what is left of the candles and turn off the kerosene lamp. I'll relieve myself and go climb into my sleeping bag. At least I feel cleaner than I did earlier today, but I don't think that will help me sleep.

December 13, 1988 Kibo Hut Elevation: 15,920 feet

It is 12:30 p.m. I made the walk to Kibo Hut in 2 hours 58 minutes. I was the third in our group to arrive. I set out at a steady pace when I left Horombo Hut and stayed with it the whole time. But first let me tell you about last night.

Right after I finished writing, I left the hut to empty my bladder. I went outside in the dark of night. As far as I could tell, no one else was out in the entire complex. After doing my duty, I stopped to look at the lights of Moshi, down below. I turned off my headlamp to get a better view of the area below; the lights of the city were brilliant and there were just a few stars above shining through breaks in the clouds. All I could hear was the wind, and all I could feel was the darkness closing in on me. I turned my headlamp back on and was testing it to see how far the light would shine; suddenly, I could hear the sound of growling coming from behind me. If I hadn't already peed, I believe I would've then. I was alone in the dark with nothing. I didn't know what to do. I remembered Millard telling me that the leopards feed at night. It took all the courage I had to turn around and see what was growling. Whatever it was behind me was standing between my hut and me. As I turned around, the light from my headlamp showed me a dog standing about 20 feet away. I was glad that it wasn't a leopard, but the dog just stood there and kept growling at me. I slowly walked over to one side of it and back to the hut. As I opened the door, the dog walked away. I closed the door in relief; boy, how one's imagination can run. I climbed into my sleeping bag – my heart still pounding.

During breakfast I told everyone about the dog. Tom said, "He probably is a stray; they sometimes wander up here."

We left Horombo about nine this morning. Most of the group was still together when we reached the last water point; it was the last place to get water on the mountain, so from this point on all water has to be carried up. I filled my canteens from a small pipe in the ground and purified it as usual with iodine tablets. The porters were filling five-gallon water jugs, a cup at a time, from the slow running water; I was glad that I wasn't carrying one of those. Everyone in the group was trading flavored drink mixes with everyone else; it seems we were all getting tired of our personal selections. I also gave everyone in our group a Tootsie Pop, not just to share, but to help lighten my load. Then we broke up and headed out at our own pace to Kibo Hut. It was another peaceful walk; and though it didn't seem as steep as the walk to Mawenzi, the trek was six miles long.

Except for the very first part of the walk, the grounds were that of alpine desert: flat, barren and windy. I pulled out my new sunglasses that cut out one hundred percent of the sun's ultraviolet rays; I had been using regular sunglasses up to this point. I was walking on the same saddle that I had partially walked on yesterday. I saw no animal tracks of any kind and saw no birds. Somewhere along the way, I looked up and saw a high flying jet; it was the only one I saw. Again, the only noise I could hear was the wind and my footsteps. As I walked, I would kick up small amounts of sand and dust that was quickly blown away by the ever present wind. I thought of home a lot; maybe I was getting homesick, or perhaps I just didn't want to think about the climb to the summit.

I reached Kibo Hut just before noon. Instead of looking like the A-frame hut we had stayed in the previous two camps, it looked more like a stone stalag. It probably has to be built that way to withstand the strong winds that are always blowing through here. I sat down next to a rock in the sun, out of the wind, and ate my lunch. I also refilled my canteens from the cookhouse, which is now the only place to get water.

I'm nearly half-finished with my quota of water for today. I'm leaning against a boulder as I write this; it is warm and out of the wind. The air is fresh, but thinner. I'm only 700 feet higher than I was yesterday, but I can definitely feel the difference. Everything is done at a slower than normal pace, and the simplest of task can be draining. Even writing is difficult, and my penmanship is bad enough as it is. The group from Colorado is doing better than the rest of us because they have that 5,000-foot altitude advantage.

From here, I can see the trail that we walked in on. There are others from the group on it now and slowly approaching; they are spaced out and walking at their individual pace. I can't tell who they are because they are still too far away to see clearly. Behind me is the path we will take tomorrow. It leads to the scree field (Scree is loose rocks or gravel). If I feel like this when we start out tomorrow, I will have difficulties, to say the least.

It is later now. In the last few hours I've done very little physically, but a lot mentally. After getting my gear together, I took a walk over to a small outcropping of rock; I went there just to be alone and to do some soul searching. From the top of the rocks I could see all of Mt. Mawenzi in the distance. I can also see clouds below us, and I still can't get over the fact that I'm above the clouds. To make it even better, I have made it here all by myself. It is so peaceful, here; there is nothing but the cold wind.

We are all at Kibo Hut, but not many of the group are talking. One thing upset my short stay on the boulders: a pile of old, rusted cans. It was apparent that I was not the first person up here, nor would I be the last. It seems that no matter where you go or how isolated a spot you find, there will be those who destroy a place of beauty with their litter. It is hard to believe that even here, there is no escaping it. From the boulders, I can better see the scree field we will climb tomorrow; it has many switchbacks in it. Tomorrow's climb will bring us to the top of Kilimanjaro; it is only another 3,420 feet away. It is less than a mile in feet; mostly up a very steep hill.

I just looked over the last few pages I've written; it is easy to see that I've been jumping around quite a bit. I've not finished complete thoughts, and I'm hopping from topic to topic, but I've taken some time to regroup my thoughts. I'm not sure if there are a lot of things I want to say, or if I just keep putting them down to be written later. I'll try to get them written down before I forget them.

I'm sitting outside of Kibo Hut. It is a cold, damp, stone building; inside it is like walking around in a refrigerator at less than 35 degrees. The eight of us and Tom will be sleeping in one of the six large rooms that are filled with bunk beds; the porters have accommodations elsewhere in the camp. There is no stove in the room for heat. The only stove is in what we are calling the dining room; it has three long tables with benches. Dinner will be at seven; we're calling it our last supper! Through Les's binoculars, I can see Gilman's Point. It is at the top of the scree field and it looks to be covered with both snow and ice. We will rest when we reach it. We should also be able to see the top of Kilimanjaro from there. It will be an interesting climb. We will be close together when we go, not spaced apart like we were in the past. I will miss walking alone; there were advantages to that. It gave me time to think. I want to say that it (solitude) helped me answer some of my unanswered questions; I think there will be some changes in my life after this trip. I needed this getaway. I'm sure that it is possible, but it seems that you can't get too much more away from the regular way of life than this.

Since I've been in Africa, I've seen starvation, poverty, death and beauty like I've never seen before. (With the exception of the headache I have now, I can't say that I have had a bad life. I have my health, family, friends, money and common sense. I would say, what else is there? But I lack the most important of things: love. I have everything but someone to love and someone to love me back; someone willing to share her life with me, and mine with her.)

As the sun goes down, so goes the temperature. Only one lonely cloud remained in the sky, and the last rays of the sun were hitting it, and lighting it from behind. It was a majestic sight and it reaffirmed my belief in God; who else could make anything so beautiful? Then, I realized that I was standing in the shadow of Kilimanjaro. I thought to myself with a smile: isn't that the name of another book or something? It seemed poetic at the time. Knowing that I wouldn't be here a second night, I watched the sunset from the shadow of Kilimanjaro.

Dinner will be soon, and we've talked about going to bed right after; I'm not very hungry, nor is anyone else. The climb will begin at 1:30 a.m. so the scree field will still be frozen. Both anticipation and tension are high. Our group and our porters are the only ones here at Kibo Hut so we will be attempting the summit alone.

Dinner is over; we had our regular beef stew tonight without all the side dishes. No one was very hungry, which is common at higher altitudes. It is even difficult to keep drinking water, but at least I made my quota.

I'm now in my sleeping bag; in fact, we are all in bed. There is very little talking. Dinner was quiet also; the usual laughing and joking was missing.

John said, "Well, you know we're in for it when Les stops reading his bird book, and I stop eating." We all laughed, but it was true; from the very start of this trip, Les has always been looking something up in his bird book, and John has been more than capable of eating his fair share. Those things stopped once we reached Kibo; most of us had headaches or felt nauseous. Tom tells us what to expect tomorrow and what we are going to do. Nancy suggests that when the guides come to wake us in the morning that they do it with flashlights instead of kerosene lamps. She knows of someone who woke up to the smell of kerosene burning early in the morning; it made their group nauseated and caused them to vomit. Tom took Nancy's advice and instructed the guides to wake us without the kerosene lamps.

Before hopping into my sleeping bag and attempting to sleep before we leave for the summit, I check my gear one more time. I take everything out of my pack that I wouldn't need in order to make it lighter; all I will take will be my camera, down jacket, film, canteen and what I considered to be very important, my flag. I am the only person on the trip with a flag for the summit. Everything else will be non-essential and left behind; I will even leave this journal behind, even though it has been with me since the start of the trip.

(I wonder if anyone will read this if something happens to me. I wonder if my parents would read this and realize that I was having a wonderful time. If my life would end early, would they understand that I would rather go this way than in a fire back home?) It is so quiet here; the only noise is my pen scratching against the paper, sounding like the mouse I saw earlier, crawling along the dining room floor. I wonder what would make a mouse come all the way up here, but then again, I was asked the same thing before I left. Why? People said I should go someplace warm, lie on a beach and relax. I joked around with them before I left the States and answered, "Because it is there, and because I am doing it to raise money for MD." But, I haven't seriously answered the question now, as I'm on my way up the mountain: I am here to prove to myself that I can do it, and to do something that not everyone else can do. Just being in good physical shape won't cut it; I believe that it takes more .You have to be prepared mentally, as well as physically. As of this minute, I believe that I can finish this climb mentally – physically may be another story.

For me it will be rough. I know it; I feel it. I should have trained harder. This is no longer a climb for me; it is a quest. This is all I have right now, and I will go for it. I must get some sleep now; I'll turn off my headlamp and lay back like the others. I wonder what they are thinking; I wonder how many are praying or are even religious. I wonder if anyone has come closer to God along the way. I know I believe a little more. I should be sleeping, not writing; the guides with flashlights will be waking us in another four hours. Even if this is my last entry and someone reads this, he or she will know a little of how I've felt, what I did, saw, and learned. But I'm not done learning, yet.

Just one last observation to note: I saw a shooting star tonight. In fact, I saw many stars, with me higher up than Horombo Hut. Even the sky is clearer; I wonder what it will look like from the top.

December 14, 1988 Horombo Hut. Elevation: 12,500 feet

Much has happened and there is a lot to tell. It is almost 8 p.m. I'll write as best I can about the days behind us.

We were awakened, but not from a sound sleep. Most of us just lay in our sleeping bags waiting for time to pass. Millard, an assistant guide, knocked on the door at 12:30. Per Tom's request, no kerosene lamps were used. We jumped to alertness and quickly dressed into our warmest clothes. I wore long underwear, sweat pants, insulated socks, a turtleneck, a wool sweater, and my new bright red windbreaker; a heavy wool ski cap covered my head.

There was tea, coffee and biscuits that Tom had brought from Nairobi. I had some tea to warm me up. We watched the mouse that I had seen during dinner the night before, as it ran around the dining room. I think I had too much tea this last week, and I don't think my system is used to all the caffeine I'm taking in. We waited for the guides to finish what they were doing, before starting the last leg of our journey upward.

As we left Kibo Hut, I set my stopwatch. It was 1:25 a.m. The sky was brilliant with stars. In some places the sky was almost gray because of so many stars. I had seen a sky like this back in March of 1986, on a cruise ship off the coast of Venezuela, but this was more beautiful. What a great place to have a telescope. I gazed at the stars for a few minutes then looked down at the ground before us as we turned on our headlamps and started the climb.

There were eleven of us. Millard, who knew the route, was in the lead, followed by Les, John, myself, Tom, Nancy, Hugh, Blake and Martin. Joseph was the head guide and overseer of the expedition porters, and other assistant guides. Rose Anne was feeling too ill to climb, and with advice from all of us, and maybe even thoughts of Uncle Henry, she was persuaded to stay in the hut and rest. I felt terrible for her – to have come all this way and not make a try for the summit. This was to be the real highlight of the trip and it hurt to think that she would not be there with us. But in the long run, common sense must prevail.

Just as we reached the bottom of the scree field, the light from my headlamp strayed toward something shining off to the side. I took a look in that direction and the main beam from my light reflected off a cross that was mounted in the rocks. Soon, everyone had seen it.

It was a bit shocking; we couldn't help but stare at it. The cross was at the end of a mound of rocks, much like that of a grave. We learned later that the cross marked the spot where a Japanese climber had fallen to his death some years back. I then remembered that we had been told that we were going to pass by this place. It was the only such monument we passed. It was really an awakening. Was climbing a mountain worth dying for?

After an hour and a half of walking, I fell for the first time. Breathing was difficult and my lungs ached, but I still had no desire to turn back. Tom asked me if I was all right. I answered yes, but I was lying just a little bit. Fifteen minutes later, I fell again. I quickly fought my way back to my feet. It was obvious I couldn't keep up the same pace as Les and John. I fell behind Tom and took the climb one step at a time, watching my feet as I walked. Occasionally, I would look up into the sky. I saw several shooting stars and made wishes on every one of them. Funny, how I had never once wished to make it to the top of Kilimanjaro; that was something I was still determined to do on my own.

About two hours into the climb, we reached Hans Meyer's Cave. It was about halfway between Kibo Hut and Gilman's Point. It wasn't much of a cave, but it was a place to rest. Martin was the last of the group to make it to the cave; he didn't look good, but like me, he was determined. I drank some water from my canteen, which was the only canteen I had taken with me so I would not be weighted down. I learned two things here: the first was, even though the sun was not burning down upon us, I was still working up a sweat and I would need fluid replacement. The second thing I learned was that I should have bought an insulator for my plastic water bottle so the contents wouldn't freeze.

Tom remarked that none of us had vomited – yet.

He added, "At least somebody usually does by this point." Millard noted that he could not believe that we ate as much as we did at our last supper; higher altitude usually curbs the appetite. I thought we hardly touched our food last night. Some of us felt nauseous and had headaches, but not bad ones. I just couldn't breathe. I felt fine while I was sitting and resting, but ten minutes later, when we started again, I felt as though I was carrying twice my weight on my shoulders. Millard kept saying to us all,

"Pole, pole." I think he was really talking to Les. After that part of the climb, we called him the "Les Express." The guy seemed unstoppable and kept trying to pass Millard. It was evident that Les had trained well for the trip. I wished I had done the same.

I fell again before I reached Gilman's Point. Each time I looked up toward the top, I could see the light of my headlamp strike the ground ahead. The kerosene lantern that Millard carried ran out of fuel so Tom gave his light to Millard, and Tom walked close to me to benefit from my headlamp. The hike through the scree field seemed like an endless series of switchbacks going up the side of the mountain. I thought that I was going to fall again. I looked up. The light from my lamp did not rest upon the ground, but went straight on into space. The top of the ridge was just 20 yards away and seeing it gave me the inner strength I needed to push on. Just on the other side of the ridge would be Gilman's Point. Once there, we would get to rest; I needed it.

When we cleared the top of the ridge, the wind that had been blocked by the side of the mountain roared at us like so many lions. It was suddenly much colder, but we were at Gilman's Point. With the onset of the cold wind, it came time to pull out the rest of our extreme weather clothing. I had put on my wind pants, and put my down jacket on under my windbreaker. We rested and changed the batteries in our headlamps. I took a granola bar from the sleeve pocket of my slicker and ate it; the chocolate was sweet and stimulating. I washed it down with freezing water from my canteen. It was a good thing I hadn't brought my metal canteen with me; my lips would have stuck to it. The last thing I did before we started out was to retie my boots. I hadn't realized it earlier, but my laces were too tight and were cutting off the circulation to my feet. They were freezing, but felt much better. In my rush to get ready, I had tied them too tightly. After 10 to 15 minutes of a well-deserved rest, we started off toward the peak.

I decided to slow my pace; I was hurting badly and having a tough time catching my breath. I should have trained harder; not a little harder, but a lot harder. Just because firefighters are supposed to be in good shape, doesn't mean that I was in the best shape possible.

I fell behind Hugh and Nancy but eventually passed Hugh. There was no sign of Martin, Blake or Joseph. They must've fallen back so far that I couldn't see them. We climbed about 3,300 feet in elevation and what seemed like three miles in distance. We had one more mile to go and 700 feet in elevation. It was 4:30 a.m.

As soon as the group cleared the rocks of Gilman's Point, the wind cut through us. We talked about how long it seemed to take us to get into our cold weather gear. All movements, no matter how trivial, took greater effort. We walked single file. Slowly the gap between me and the rest of the group widened as they moved ahead. We were walking on the rim on the inside of Kibo, on a path about four feet wide. If one were to step off to the right, it would be a sure fall down a very steep hill and into the crater itself. It was possible to repel down into the crater, but not from this point. One would fall down it before they could climb down it; we didn't have the technical gear to climb down it, and I did not have the strength.

I fell again, and Millard helped me to my feet and asked if I wanted to turn back. Saving my breath by not talking, I shook my head, no. By this time most of the group was in front of me. There was still no sign of Martin, Blake and Joseph; they must have been moving at a pace much slower than mine. I hardly thought that possible, at this point. My pace was: step, take-a-breath, step, and take-a-breath. I felt I was going nowhere fast.

Then there were several large boulders that we had to climb over; they were about 30 feet high. It was also the hardest part of the climb. It was a place where you had to use your hands as well as your feet to climb. It was a much different type of climbing than we had been used to doing most of the trip. It gave us a chance to use a different set of muscles. I suppose that it wasn't really that hard; but in my present condition, it was difficult and strenuous. After the rocks, there was a small peak to walk around which took another 20 minutes. To my left, was an ice glacier some 60 or so yards away; I had never seen ice like that before.

By now my lungs were aching, but my stubbornness wasn't going to let me quit. I didn't want to let an inanimate object like a mountain beat me. But, I fell again, and again, each time making it more difficult to get up. Millard insisted that I rest, but I wanted to keep pushing on. It was on my 11th fall that I looked up and saw the peak, and a torn flag blowing from a pole almost 100 yards away. Then I saw Hugh sitting on a rock; he was hurting, but he'd had enough sense to sit down and rest. I asked him in a dry voice, "Where are the rest?" He pointed towards the flag. There they were, walking single file towards the peak; all but one that is. Nancy was walking back towards Hugh. She helped him to his feet and on towards the summit. She was doing much better than either of us. They were leaning on one another as they walked to the summit together. It was one of the more tender moments I had ever seen. I would've given anything to be able to take a picture of that, but I didn't have the strength to get out my camera. I just lay there on the ground watching them; that image will forever be with me. (How I hope to someday have someone who loves me like that.) I tried to get up and couldn't. I looked at the flag, and visions of Uncle Henry flashed into my head. Did he feel this way? Was I going to make the same mistake he did? Is this how the Austrian girl at Horombo

Hut felt? I honestly considered turning around. The quicker I went down, the sooner I would feel better.

I decided to rest a moment. I went to take a drink from my canteen, but by now most of the contents were frozen. I couldn't even pour it out to make it lighter, even if I wanted to; I never thought of just leaving it and picking it up on the way down. Risking stomach cramps, I grabbed a small handful of snow to get some moisture into my mouth. It was very cold, but refreshing. I gathered the rest of my strength and made it on to my feet. My lungs still hurt, but I took a step and another, and another. The closer I got to the flag, the stronger I became. I could see the others in the group hugging each other. They were there, and in a few minutes I would be there, too. I turned to look at Millard behind me, and smiled. He patted me on the back and said, "You will make it." And I did!

I couldn't believe it; I couldn't have been more happy or relieved. After hugging everyone from the guides to Tom, I didn't know what to do, so I sat down and cried. I felt a great sense of accomplishment. Nancy came over to me and put her arms around me: she was crying, too. Then, Hugh came over and put his arms around both of us, and we all fell over. It was one of my proudest moments; my goal was completed! I felt a sense of warmth come over me. I was at the top of Mt. Kilimanjaro, the peak they call Uhuru. It is Swahili, and it means freedom.

When I regained my composure, I stood and looked around. I checked my watch. It was 5:51 a.m. The climb took me 4 hours 21 minutes to reach the top. I grabbed my camera and took my first picture just as the sun was rising. It was beautiful! Tom then took pictures of my flag and I, to prove to the people back home that I had reached the summit.

Nick Comande and guide Tom Rippilino standing on the top of Kilimanjaro. December 14, 1988.

After looking at the condition of the flags that were already placed at the top, all torn and faded by the elements, I decided to take it back down with me and hang it with the others in the Kibo Hotel, in the city of Marangu. There it would last for years instead of just days.

I looked around to see what the others were doing. The guides were smoking (which I couldn't believe). I was still having difficulty breathing, and they were smoking! Hugh was off to the side vomiting; indeed, he was feeling miserable.

The plateau here is about a mile and a half across. I could see into its crater, and it too, was beautiful. I heard that some trips even go down into the crater; I would have to train much harder to do that. There were scattered patches of snow across the top, and there was even another large glacier wall on the other side of the plateau. After taking more pictures and still trying to get over the relief of making it to the top, I took out and signed *the book*. The book is kept in a box near the flagpole, which was placed here – who knows how long ago. Only the people who make it to the summit, or as I put it – dare venture to the top of Kilimanjaro – sign it. I signed the book, "I Nick Comande, 30, of Racine, WI., USA, climbed to the top of this mountain, 12-14-88, with a group of newfound friends, with a goal of raising money for the Muscular Dystrophy Association." I felt a dozen times stronger as I finished writing that line. For some reason I felt the weight of the world being lifted off my shoulders.

We were at the top for half an hour, before we began our descent. I would have liked to have stayed longer, but Les guessed that it had to be about -30 degrees (with the wind chill); I believe it was that cold. The water in my canteen was mostly frozen by now. We were all starting to feel the affects of the cold. I was sweating heavily before, but once I had stopped moving, the chill was starting to set in. It was time to get moving.

We finished watching the sunrise, then packed up our cameras and headed back. As we started to leave, I saw Blake and Joseph, the oldest of the guides, approaching us. We hugged as we passed; I was glad that Blake had made it. He said, "Martin made it to Gilman's Point and then went back." I felt bad for Martin; I felt that he had a great amount of determination and wished he could be here, but I'm sure he made the right decision.

I started to follow the others back down in the driving cold. If it wasn't for this, I would have stayed with Blake. As I walked down, I thought: "it took us 5 1/2 days to reach this place, only to spend a half an hour at the top." I stopped, turned and watched Blake as he set foot on the summit. He and Joseph were shaking hands; I wondered how he felt at that moment.

I have just taken a rest from writing. It is nearly 10:30 p.m. I'm tired, but I want to finish this while it is still fresh in my mind; also, I have to make a flow-through stop.

After leaving Blake and Joseph, I continued to follow the group. I was still walking slower than the others and managed to catch up with them at Gilman's Point. Here we found another pole stuck in the ground, and another tattered flag. At its base was another box with a book in it; we took turns signing it. I was glad to see Martin's signature there. I took out my canteen, and picked up a rock to chip a hole in the ice that had formed in it; I was really thirsty at this point. I also took my last Tootsie Pop from my sleeve and ate it. By this time the sun was shining brightly and it was time for sunglasses and sun block; no sense getting sunburned on the way down. By this time my heart rate had finally slowed back down. After a brief rest we started our descent down the scree field. We didn't go down it the same way we came up. Instead of using the cut back, we went straight down; it was steep, but doable. It was like running down a hill, but with one exception: we had to dig in our heels whenever we started to go too fast or were about to fall. We kicked up a lot of dust going down. We all ran or walked at our own pace, stopping to rest when we had the urge. The further down we went, the warmer it became; I stopped to take off some of my heavier layers. It was even getting easier to breath. As we individually reached Kibo Hut, one of the other guides met us with a thick orange drink. I'm not quite sure what it was, but it really hit the spot. It was something to help replenish our strength and replace the fluids we'd lost. When I made it into Kibo Hut I checked my watch; it read 8:37 a.m. The whole ordeal lasted 7 hours 12 minutes. It was a hell of a night. Martin and Rose Anne congratulated me on making it to the top, and I did the same to Martin for reaching Gilman's Point. I asked Rose Anne how she was feeling and she said she was better and looking forward to getting back to Horombo Hut.

John announced that he was going to head back there. I said, "Wait ten minutes and I'll go with you." It only took minutes to get my gear together and head out with John. We left the others there to rest and take their time. I wanted to get down to some thicker air. I was hoping it would ease the pounding of my head. Right before I left Kibo Hut, I turned to look up at the summit once more; I could see Blake coming down the scree field, and I was glad to see that he was on his way back.

I'm too tired to write anymore; I'll finish this tomorrow. It's almost 11:15 p.m., and it has been a really long day.

December 15, 1988 Kibo Hotel, City of Marangu Elevation: 5,000 feet

John and I had a pleasant down hill walk from Kibo to Horombo; we talked a great deal and it was the only time I really talked to anyone while trekking between huts. The descent was much quicker than the ascent. We made the trek in two hours – just half the time it took us to go up it. The only stop we made was at the last water point, two-thirds of the way down, to refill canteens. When we reached Horombo, we learned that we were going to be staying in one of the smaller huts this time; I shared one with John and Les, who followed shortly behind us. Our porters had left Kibo earlier in the day and already had our other gear down here. I unpacked my sleeping bag, stripped off my sweaty clothes and crawled in. By this time I was completely exhausted and felt awful, but not as bad as the poor Austrian girl I had spoken to several days earlier. It was a rough trek to the top and back today, but I'm glad I did it.

I slept heavily for four hours and woke up starving; I couldn't wait to eat. By now the rest of the group was back and we talked about how wonderful the climb had been. It was easy to say that now, now that the worst of it was over. Dinner was like a feast and everyone ate heartily again. I took a walk out to the lava flow, knowing that I would probably never be here again. I sat, and started to write the events of the past day. Later, I slept without difficulty and awoke with an insatiable appetite. I noticed that I had been losing a little weight, even though I had been eating well.

When I woke up each morning, the first thing I had always done was to look at Mt. Kili; to my surprise I saw that it had snowed on the mountain overnight. I was glad that we didn't have to climb it now; it would have become much more slippery. It looked like rain was coming and today's trek was to take us all the way back to the main gate where we started. I was packed and ready to go; Blake left right behind me. After a few minutes of walking, I stopped to take a last look at Horombo Hut with Mt. Kili in the background. It was hard to think that all of this was coming to an end; so much had happened in the last week. Blake caught up to me and we hiked down together.

We took our time going down the mountain, stopping to look at the different types of trees and plants. We even stopped to watch the clouds go up the mountain. It rained on us only slightly during our descent, and I was glad that it didn't rain hard; I really hate walking in the rain. Since we weren't exerting ourselves as much as we had on the way up, we didn't have to consume as much water as we had the previous week. The flow-through process was finally coming to an end; we no longer needed six quarts of water a day.

We saw some blue monkeys just above the Mandara Hut complex. We stopped here for lunch, before continuing the trek downward where the humidity picked up once we hit the rain forest. We finished the trek while getting only a little lost. Once we reached the main gate where we had started our hike, we were congratulated by some of the park rangers. Our bus was there waiting for us with some of the others from the trip; it brought us back to the Kibo Hotel, which by now did look like the Ritz-Carlton to us. Since Blake and I were sharing a room, we flipped a coin to see who would use the shower first; I won. It was great to take that long, hot shower, not to mention the other modern conveniences at the complex. It was great to be clean again – and no more drinking from a canteen! It was good to be back to civilization, but I was still a long way from home. It was a long hike today; we went from 12,500 feet down to 5,000 feet.

At 2 p.m. this afternoon, we (the whole group) got to watch Tom pay off the porters and guides. For his trouble, Joseph received $20 from the government, and $100 in tips. The assistant guides received $5 from the government, and $20 in tips. The porters received $3 from the government, and $10 in tips; all in American money. It will be worth a lot more on the black market. Joseph is considered to be economically well off in Tanzania. He owns a farm and is self-sufficient. He has traveled the 200 miles to the city of Arusha, the second largest city in Tanzania. Then, the porters began to sing a few songs about the mountain; Blake was the lucky one who had a video camera to record the event.

We were given certificates stating that we had made it to the top of Kilimanjaro, and Martin's certificate confirmed that he had made it to Gilman's Point.

We gave T-shirts and other items to our porters to show our appreciation; I had known about this practice before I left (thanks to Mountain Travel), so I packed extra shirts and other knick- knacks to give away. Tom told us that the total distance, from the bottom to the top and back, was roughly 70 miles – not a bad hike for someone on vacation. One final picture was taken of the entire group; needless to say, it was a proud moment.

December 15, 1988 Kibo Hotel 11:55 pm.

Dinner was at 7:00 this evening and all were present, clean, healthy and feeling much better. It was nice to have a regular sit-down dinner. I was elected to make a speech, and to give Tom the tips we collected for him before dinner. We ate, drank and shared thoughts of the climb. We also talked about what we liked and disliked about the climb. Nancy described it best: "It was surrealistic." We all agreed with the description. Tom told us that we were his "fastest" group on the final ascent to Kili, up 3,300 feet in three hours with another hour to Uhuru peak. I confessed that I should've trained harder than I did, and I didn't think I was going to make it to the top.

John said something that I found most interesting. He said, "Nick, for us the climb to the top was 19,340 feet high, but for you, it must have been like 29,000 feet because you had an entire city watching you." He was right, but I had never really looked at it that way. It was more than just a climb for me; it was a fundraiser. If I hadn't made it, the entire city of Racine would have known it. Had I been doing this on my own, for myself, no one would've known or even cared. But back home, people had made pledges; they were going to want to know about my progress. I wondered if this fact had been eating at me while I was on the climb, and I just didn't realize it.

When asked if I was going to hang my flag here in the hotel, I answered, "I will hang it here, providing that everyone here at the table sign it first." Everyone did sign it, and I proudly hung that bright yellow flag on the wall where flags from other countries were displayed for everyone to see. I had left a mark, and hopefully it is still hanging on the wall in the Kibo Hotel in the city of Marangu, Tanzania, Africa.

December 16, 1988 Nairobi Kenya

We left the mountain shortly after breakfast this morning to take our long drive back to Nairobi. Our bus pulled over so we could get out and look at the mountain one last time. It was going to be hard to leave here; it truly was a unique experience, and I will miss this place. Martin had taken one last picture of me with the mountain in the background. We boarded the bus, and as we pulled away I did my best to not look back. I feel I left the mountain a changed person and I learned many things here about people, about life, and myself. I'm not sure how to explain it; maybe it is something to be lived. It was a quiet ride to the Kenyan border; perhaps the others were taking the time to reflect on what we had succeeded in doing.

We said good-bye to Tom at the border between Kenya and Tanzania. He would not be coming with us, but would instead lead another group up the mountain. I believe he was planning to be back on top of Kilimanjaro on Christmas Day.

Upon our arrival into Nairobi, the group started to break up; we were staying in various hotels and had different departure times. I will miss my friends as we go our separate ways. Blake and I will be at the same hotel, and we will travel back together as far as New York.

I feel this journal coming to an end. It has been a real experience. Hopefully, I can top it someday, but that may not be for a while.

I arrived back in Racine after being in transit for just under 24 hours. I was glad that I came back when I did. I had thought about staying an extra day, but with Christmas coming, I decided not to. That decision saved my life. If I had flown back the next day, I would have been aboard Pan-Am Flight 103, the plane that exploded over Lockerbie, Scotland.

It was great to be back home, but isn't it always after any trip? My fundraiser was a success. I waited until just after Christmas to start collecting my pledges. This was more difficult than just getting the pledges the first time. I learned that people were willing to pledge money for an event, but to actually honor their commitment was another story, but I stayed persistent in my endeavor. Friends and family who had gathered sponsors took on their share by collecting, or at least attempting to collect, the pledges from their pledge sheets. This helped me a lot, but since I had collected 90 percent of the pledges, I had 90 percent of the collecting to do. It took a month and a half to finish, which included making a number of reminder phone calls and sending out a few letters. I was able to collect on 98 percent of the pledges. I thought this to be outstanding.

I had hoped to reach $2,000, but I actually raised $4,780. My friend James King and I drove up to the Muscular Dystrophy office in Milwaukee so I could hand over all the funds I'd raised for them. I had no planned speech when I arrived, but several times I wanted to say to Lynn Deedering, "Remember when you laughed at me?" But I didn't. It made me feel good to hand over all that money.

Lynn was thankful, and said she would be looking forward to helping me with a future fundraiser. James was never really given any credit for our climb. Sure, I did all the climbing, paid for the trip and raised most of the pledges, but had he not asked me to attend the MDA dinner that night, I would have never had the idea.

I have to admit that none of this would have ever taken place had it not been for James. I owe him many thanks for putting me on the uphill path. I feel that what we did was a good thing, and perhaps someday I may do it again.

Chapter Two
Mt. Aconcagua

(The adventure continues)

Six months after finishing the fundraising for Muscular Dystrophy and thinking about how much fun I'd had on the mountain, I decided to give it another shot. Something I'd learned so well on Kilimanjaro was the importance of training. If I were ever to do it again, I would have to be better prepared. But where would I go; which mountain would I climb? Once again, I consulted the book of Mountain Travel and paged through the sections on mountains until I found one that proved to be a challenge. It was called Aconcagua, meaning sentinel of stone; it lies on the border by Argentina and Chile. It is the highest of the Andes Mountains reaching 22,835 feet, and is the highest mountain outside of the Himalayas and in the Southern and Western hemispheres. The only thing I knew about the Andes – at the time – was that it ran the length of South America. A rugby team had crashed there back in the early 1970's; and they resorted to cannibalism to survive. Later, they became known as the famous Andes survivors.

A Swiss guide named Mathias Zurbriggen, first climbed Aconcagua in 1897. He led a British alpinist named Edmund Fitzgerald who became too sick to make the final ascent. The trail I would be taking – known as the normal route – is the same trail Fitzgerald took, but unlike Fitzgerald, I plan to summit.

Since I'd never dreamed of going to the Himalayas and had never even considered going to Everest, I decided that Aconcagua would fit the bill. It would be a much harder trip, though; this venture wouldn't have porters like my last one. It would require a lot more work; besides carrying all my own gear, I would have to carry community gear and supplies, also. Technically, it would be a more advanced climb because of the amounts of snow and ice; we would require crampons for walking, clothing for colder temperatures, and a lot more determination than I'd had on Kili.

Since the mountain was going to be so much tougher than my first one, I started training six months in advance. I'd trained for less than two months when I went to Kilimanjaro. Because I wanted to be more psyched up than I had been for Kili and didn't want to have to worry about anything other than the climb, I decided not to make this trip a fundraising event. I didn't want to have to do all the extra work that would be required before and after the climb. I decided that this mountain was going to be for me; I was going to climb it for myself.

In preparation for the climb, I spent countless hours on my bicycle and on a stair master with 7 ½ pound ankle weights attached. When I was comfortable with that, I wore a backpack and kept adding weights to it until I was up to 50 pounds. I figured I couldn't train for thin air, but I could train for endurance. In late January, I was off to South America.

January 30, 1990 Punta del Inca Hosteria Penitentes Elevation: 8,400 feet

It has been over a year since I kept a journal like this. I had once declared that I would never do what I was getting ready to do: climb another mountain. My last climb, which was also my first, was Kilimanjaro in Africa. Now, I'm north of the city of Mendoza in the country of Argentina, South America. I've been in the country for two days and in a hotel at 8,400 feet; it is our first stage of acclimatizing to the higher altitude.

I took a short walk, but I'll take a much longer one tomorrow with my pack. There are 11 paying clients on this trip from various walks of life. I'm the youngest at age 31, and Chuck from Canada is the oldest at 61; he has climbed this mountain three times from different routes and wants to try it again. Small peaks presently surround me as I sit in a valley; they keep me from seeing Aconcagua, since it is much further down the valley. It is warm and very windy; the sun is high in the sky and won't set until after 9:30 tonight. The days here are long and hot. (In Mendoza the temperature reached 106 degrees.) It is now 88 degrees, but the wind chill makes it cooler. At night the temperature drops into the 60's, which I feel is more refreshing.

As of now, I feel no side effects from the thinner air. We had some acclimatizing in Mendoza, which is at 2,000 feet. I'm up to 8,400 feet presently, which is 7,400 feet higher than my home in Racine. The object will be to acclimatize slowly to avoid pulmonary or cerebral edema. This is our main problem so far: we hear that there is little or no snow on parts of the mountain. This is important because we must melt snow for drinking water and cooking. The flow-through process, which I was so glad to end in Africa, is starting up again. To compensate for my body's loss of fluids while climbing, I'll be drinking six quarts of water a day.

I've stepped out into the night to see the moon and the stars. Because I'm so far south of the equator this time, the stars are not as familiar to me as they are back home; even the moon sits at a strange angle. This is the furthest south I've ever been. If I remember right, there will be a full moon on the night we are to try for the summit and a lunar eclipse the day before. It is only by chance that I will be in a place in the world where it can be seen.

There will be a practice hike tomorrow; I'll carry a pack. Hopefully, I'll remember what I learned on Kilimanjaro about hiking and keeping a good pace. I wrote some letters home and gave them to some climbers to mail for me; they were returning to Mendoza and would mail them from there. Out of their group of five, only two members made it to the top of Aconcagua. There will be 14 of us in this group. I'll be sharing a tent with Wes and Howard from San Diego; they have traveled together in the past. We've talked briefly in Mendoza; the three of us hope to take this mountain. If we are slow and sure, and stay well hydrated, I think we will do just that.

January 31, 1990 Hosteria Penetentes Elevation: 8,400 feet

I slept well last night, and today was a good day. We did the first real constructive thing since I've been in Argentina: we had a training climb today. It felt good to get out in the open air. I share a room with five other members of the group; I have the only top bunk. We are one big happy family here. I woke up at 9:00 this morning and had breakfast. Howard Zatkin and Wes Mudge (my future tent mates on the mountain), and Nasko, a Bulgarian chemical engineer from New York, and I set out on our own acclimatization climb. We walked and then climbed, scaling – in parts – up to 10,000 feet. We were up and back in 3 ½ hours. It felt good to stretch all the muscles that were so cramped up by the long plane rides. I only had 15 pounds in my backpack, but that will change tomorrow. I thought a lot about Africa while I climbed on the loose scree. Most of our climbing of Aconcagua will be this way. High temps have melted almost all the snow on the mountain and ice axes and crampons won't be necessary. Finding good water to drink will be difficult since there will be no snow to melt.

I'll get back to the climb. All that working out on the Stairmaster paid off; I felt strong, and I didn't feel the exertion I had felt at this altitude on Kilimanjaro. It was warm; I wore a baseball hat instead of the safari hat I wore in Africa, this was a mistake. The safari hat sheltered me from the sun a lot better than my baseball cap, and now I have minor sunburn on the back of my neck. I borrowed some cream from Howard to soothe the pain.

The four older climbers left earlier in the day; they were off to scale a peak higher than the one the four of us were on. They have been climbing all over the world, and have sort of separated themselves from the rest of us. The youngest of them, I believe, is 55. They move well for men of their age, and considering what we are about to do, we nicknamed them "The Over the Hill Gang."

I reached the summit of our peak first, followed by Wes, Nasko and Howard. Wes called the peak Mt. Wimp because it was not as high as the one the others had taken. Howard was babying his leg; he had pulled a hamstring. We looked around for a while before heading back to the Hosteria. It was really an experience to look over the valley; we were surrounded on all sides by towering peaks. I haven't accepted the reality that I'm actually here in the Andes Mountains; I never thought that I would make it. After Africa, I thought it would be a long time before I went away to such a far-off place. It goes to show how wrong I can be and how small the world is getting. When you least expect it – expect it.

Tomorrow we leave, and the group is starting to get anxious. My gear is packed and ready to go. After tonight there will be no more soft beds, and even though this place isn't the greatest, it will be like the Taj Mahal when we get back. It is midnight now; Sergio, our guide, is partying with a few of his friends. Latin American and ten percent Apache, Sergio is rumored to be one tough hombre. So far, he has climbed Aconcagua six times. He has climbed in other places over the world as well, including Everest, but he did not summit. Ricardo, who is our assistant guide, also has climbed in other parts of the world, and was the first Latin American to summit Everest. For this, he was congratulated by the president of Mexico and named athlete of the year. Augusto Ortega is the other assistant guide; he is shorter than I but very solid looking. According to Sergio, he can climb as well as Sergio, himself. They seem to be well experienced, high altitude guides.

February 1, 1999 Tent Camp in Horcones Valley Elevation: 11,000 feet

We're finally on our way. We hiked for 4 ½ hours today to get to, according to Dick Narwicki's altimeter, 11,000 feet. (Dick is a designer for Ford.) To get here, we all piled into a pickup truck at the Hosteria. Between human cargo and our packs, the truck was severely overloaded, and required two trips to get everyone and everything to our destination: The Horcones Valley. I couldn't remember when I had seen anything so beautiful. Looking down the center of the valley, I saw many rock formations with different shades of red and brown colors. We would be walking down the center of the valley towards base camp.

The sides of the valley seemed to reach thousands of feet on both sides of us; I felt like I was looking up at the Red Sea after it was parted. Standing at the end and rising above this seemingly never-ending valley was Cerro Aconcagua.

Mt. Aconcagua as seen from the Horcones Valley.

The view of it was immense, and we were still 22 miles away. I could see snow on the peaks, but nothing on the lower parts of the mountain. It will be a two-day hike through the valley to our base camp, and we will be surrounded by rock the entire time.

About an hour into our journey through the valley, we had to cross the Horcones River. Because of the lack of snow that had already melted and flowed away, the river wasn't very high or difficult to cross; it only came up to mid-thigh. The people around here call it the "chocolate waters" because that is what it looks like. I removed my hiking boots and crossed the 30-40 foot wide river in tennis shoes and then changed back, letting my tennis shoes hang from my pack to dry until I needed them again.

It is now 10:15 p.m.; we just finished a supper of freeze-dried food we brought along. The soup wasn't bad and neither was the other stuff we ate. I don't know what it was, but it had noodles and little pieces of meat; it was tasty. We also had a long loaf of bread from which we broke off pieces and passed around; dessert consisted of coffee or hot chocolate. During this time we talked about the mountain, and Sergio agreed with me; there had not been a great deal written about it. Most of what I had read came from Dick Bass's *Seven Summits*, which I read last September when I decided to climb another mountain. I wonder how many people went out after the famous Seven Summits after reading that book? I admit it: my interest was peaked.

We did dishes in the dirty waters of the Horcones River. We will all take turns at dishwashing; we are supposed to share the workload on this trip. It won't be like on Kilimanjaro where we had porters and cooks to bring us hot meals and carry our loads. The bulk of our gear was brought to this spot by Gauchos-led mules. (Gauchos are South American cowboys on horseback; they were friendly and even showed me the proper way to throw a Bo-Lo and how to use a whip.) They were to lead the mules all the way to base camp, and then return with them when it came time for us to leave the mountain. Any supplies needed above base camp will be carried…by us.

I'm in my tent now, which I'm sharing with Wes and Howard. The sun has gone down behind the wall of the valley and the temperature has dropped to 48 degrees. Between the three of us, we are generating so much body heat that it's still too warm to close the door of the tent. I suspect that the temp will drop further during the night. The other group members are in their tents. Dave and Sydney, Nasko and Dick, Paul and Chuck, and John and Cheryl are all sharing two-man tents; Sergio, Ricardo and Augusto are sharing the other three-man tent. According to Sergio, we are spread out over a small patch of land directly below a small peak called Cerro Almacen. We will leave here tomorrow morning by 8:00 a.m. and walk eight to nine hours to reach 14,000 feet and our base camp, Plaza de Mules. We will follow the Horcones River up the center of the valley.

I'm lying on my sleeping bag, finishing this daily log. The nail-beds around my fingers are already starting to dry and crack. At least I had my safari hat on today to help keep my neck out of the sun. I noticed that Howard was wearing a handkerchief tucked under his baseball hat to keep the sun off his neck. We must take care of ourselves; anything like sunburns, blisters, and diarrhea can cause problems for us, and this is only the first day. As for myself, I feel strong; those months of hard training will pay off, but the next ten days or so will tell for sure.

February 2, 1990 Base Camp Elevation: 13,800-14,000 feet

Today was a long day; wake up time was 6:30 a.m., and I was the first one out of the tent. I looked up into that beautiful sky above me; my old friend the Southern Cross was directly above me. I hadn't seen skies like this since Africa. I could hear the hiss of the white gas stoves, so I knew water was boiling. We'll use these stoves for cooking and melting snow higher up on the mountain, providing we can find any snow. Wes, Howard and I took our tent down, packed our gear, and were ready to eat by 7:30. At 8:30, the three Gauchos took our gear and started to load it onto the mules; they will drop it off at base camp and then head back out of the valley.

Between yesterday and today we covered about 25 miles total, and it was all down the center of the scenic Horcones Valley. We walked for about four hours before we stopped. Lunch consisted of day-old bread from yesterday (now two days old), salami, and a chocolate bar for dessert. We sat for an hour before continuing our trek. I should mention that we made two more river crossings before reaching base camp. Neither was difficult or exciting; we were just jumping from rock to rock. The air was windy, and sometimes chilly, as we walked in the shadows of the valley, but everyone was in very good spirits. We even sang. While we marched through the valley we sang "American Pie" and "Do Wa Diddy" and a variety of other songs from our past. But the singing continued only as long as the trek was flat and easy going; once the trail got steep, the singing stopped.

Base camp was only two hours away; it took me 2 ½ hours. One section of our trek was very steep. The Chilean Army had been leapfrogging us along the valley. Now I watched them hike up the trail with three mules following behind; they were making much better time than our group, but it still took them awhile to get up the trail. The mules kept stopping to rest, and so did I; not because I was that tired, but because they were blocking the path in front of me. Midway up the hill I noticed the carcasses of mules that had fallen from the trail. It was from this spot that I saw my first rockslide; it was a good 50 yards away, so I was not concerned about getting hit by loose scree or boulders.

On the last half of the steep trail up to base camp, I suddenly became exhausted and was again fighting for steps like I had on Kilimanjaro. Today, I carried a very heavy pack, and I had pain in my lower neck. I thought perhaps my pack wasn't adjusted properly and that was causing the pain. By the time I reached base camp the mules, which had brought up our gear, were already on their way back. Howard and Wes had beaten me up the hill and were putting the finishing touches on the tent; I felt bad that I had not gotten there in time to help. Howard suggested that I unroll my thermal rest and stretch out, but there were other things that needed to be done. The group was low on water, so Howard and Wes collected empty water bottles from everyone. Dave and I joined them, and the four of us went off to get water. Because there was no snow above us and no runoffs near us, we had to walk the 500 yards. This side trek was all up and down a number of small hills; plus, we still had to walk back with all the added weight. But soon we found a very large cave of ice with a stream flowing from it, and the water was extremely cold and clear; we filled our bottles. I planned to return the following day with a camera to get photographs.

Base camp was made up of at least 125 other people, including the 16 Chilean soldiers. I stopped by and chatted with them. They even asked me to stay for supper, but we had already eaten. Tonight's dinner was pumpkin soup with crackers and some kind of rice dish with cashews; dessert was again, and probably always will be, hot chocolate or coffee. I drank lots of hot chocolate; it not only helped keep me warm when the sun went down, but it helped me stay hydrated. I – along with everyone else – was back on five to six quarts of water a day. I purified everything I drank – just as I had in Africa. When I started to get a headache from all the hot chocolate I was drinking, I switched to hot water.

I think today will be the last day I'll be able to wear my safari hat; it had been very useful on the trek in, and I'm sure it will be useful on the way out, but it will be too windy to wear it while going up the hill. The sunburn I got a couple of days ago has cleared up, and I finally put my lucky St. Christopher's chain back around my neck. (I took it off so it wouldn't irritate the sunburn. I don't know why, but I feel like it's time to wear it again. Perhaps I'm feeling closer to God; I had felt this way on Kili in 1988.) I took a bit of a nap. It's been a long day and the temperature is dropping. The door to the tent is open; we didn't even close it last night and I don't know if we will tonight. It depends on how cold it gets. I'm wearing my long johns and I'm quite content here in my sleeping bag. It is 11:04 p.m. now, and I will be here for the next ten hours, at least. No one gets up until the sun reaches base camp and that won't be until 10:30 tomorrow morning; it feels very cold here until the sun warms you up. We will be spending a lot of time in our tents when we are not climbing. Once the sun goes down, it gets too cold to do anything else. Anyway, there is nothing else to do. I brought several books to read, and stationary for writing; between that and my journal, I should keep busy.

I looked out the door of the tent and into the night sky. We are camped about one mile west of Aconcagua. You can see the summit from here; it is only 10,000 feet above us. To the north are the Penitentes (ice fingers that reach into the sky.)

Penitentes or Ice fingers cut out of the Glacier by the wind. Found near Base Camp.

They were cut this way by the wind, and are well over 15 feet tall in some areas; you can walk up, and in between them. It is said that this is the only place in the world where the Penitentes exist. Also, we are next to the very same glacier that cut into the ground, shaping all these hills and valleys that we've climbed so far. Tomorrow is a rest day to help us acclimatize to the thinner air; it is important not to climb too high, too fast. Perhaps tomorrow I'll make it over to the Penitentes to snap some photos. I am tired, and I should sleep, so I will end this for now.

February 3, 1990 Base Camp Elevation: 13,800-14,000 feet

Another day is wrapping up here at base camp. There are less than 100 people in the camp, now; last week – it is said – was double that number. It was a long night for me; I did some considerable tossing and turning. It's hard to stay put when you're sharing a tent with two other people. I'm sleeping in a three-man, half-shell tent made by North Face; it's a good tent, and it really holds the heat well. Last night, we didn't even bother to close the door. The outside temperature was 32 degrees when we woke up this morning.

We were out of water this morning, so I volunteered to go get it; I wanted to take pictures of the glacier, anyway. The stream was only about 500 yards away. (As I carried the five gallons of water back to camp, it seemed longer) As I filled the bottles, I looked around; I was surrounded entirely by ice. Nearby was a boulder supported by ice; actually, it was more like a rock on top of a four-foot pedestal with all the ice melted away. I took the cold, clear water from the river that flowed right out of the glacier. As I walked back to camp, I could see the trail we would be taking the following day to ferry our loads to Camp I. We would be carrying some of our real cold weather gear, food, and white gas for the stoves – all things we'd need later. We would be climbing to 15,000 to 15,500 feet over steep terrain covered with scree.

Mt. Aconcagua. Note base camp in the lower right corner and climbers going up the trail to Camp one (not seen)

Since there is no snow, Sergio says we will need to bury our supplies or cover them with rocks; the day after, we will move the rest of the camp up to Camp I. A rule of thumb that I have learned from this type of leapfrogging up the mountain is to climb high, and sleep low. That's how this climb is going to be from now on; hopefully, I can pace myself better than I did on Kilimanjaro. The plan is to go slow and steady and make it there in three hours. The return trip to base camp, (Refugio, or refuge in Spanish, meaning the only place out of the wind) should take less than half of that time.

Today was a scheduled rest day to help us acclimatize; most of us rested, but there were those who took little exploration hikes. While I was getting water, some of the group hiked to a radiophone. Wes left a message with his wife, Jenny, and asked her to call my sister Sue and relay the message: "all is well." Tomorrow, for sure – if not tonight – I will write a letter to my parents and give it to someone going down the mountain; hopefully, it will get to my parents. The sun has just gone down behind the mountain, but it is still light outside; the temperature is dropping quickly.

February 4, 1990 Base Camp Elevation: 13,800 to 14,000 feet

I have time to kill before dinner, so I thought I would start jotting down today's events. I think we're having spaghetti again. I had another restless night. After writing, I read until 11:15 p.m., slept till 3:30 a.m., was up till 6:00 a.m., and then slept till 9:00 a.m. Breakfast was at 10:00. I had a lot of hot water, and hot chocolate, and a piece of that day-old bread which is now five days old, but it was good. I'm slowly loosing my appetite, but still drinking my five to six quarts of water a day. I know I'm well-hydrated because my urine is still clear; that's a good sign. Right now, I'm sitting on a rock outside my tent. Earlier, I went through my gear to make sure I removed everything I wouldn't need; each extra ounce or gram may matter a lot by the time we go for the summit.

Today the group took their cold weather gear and some of the community supplies up to Camp I, or Camp Canada, as it's called by some. I made the trip in 2 hours 50 minutes, which is not too bad of a time; I was third in our party to reach camp.

With the snow-covered peaks rising everywhere, I could see more of the Andes than I had ever seen before. I could hardly wait to get to the top of Aconcagua, and see as much as there was to see. It is said that if the air is clear enough, you can see the Pacific Ocean from the top; that's something I would like to see. We rested, ate some lunch, and then buried our gear under some rocks; these items would be safe until we returned the next day with the rest of our camp. While we were still at Camp I, some clouds rolled in and the temperature dropped. As we were about to leave, it started to snow. Wes, Howard and I took some pictures then headed back, having no clue as to what would soon cross our path on the return trip. Halfway down to base camp was the body of a climber who had not been so fortunate. This body wasn't like the one I had seen on Kilimanjaro – all wrapped up and being carried down by porters. This guy was uncovered and just laying out near some rocks. It was a somber moment for us. We discussed the situation briefly between ourselves, and figured that the people in charge of the base camp must know about him, (which they did) so we proceeded on our way. There was nothing we could do but leave him. Did I say it was a somber moment for us?

Clouds continued to roll in and out. I went down to the stream for water and took some soap with me to clean up; who knew when I'd get this chance again? It was great to wash, but the water was so very cold; there was ice along the sides of the stream, if that gives you any indication of how cold it was. It really woke me up, and it sure felt good to clean up.

When we come back down the mountain, I'll want to go back there and wash again.

I've gone through my gear and sorted it out, again, just to make sure all the non-essential items have been taken out. I'll leave my hiking boots here and start walking up in my double plastics [boots]. Today's climb felt good; it brought me up to about 16,000 feet. I had a bit of a headache, but that passed shortly after I took a few Tylenol once I'd made it back to base camp.

Here's a depressing sight: the body of the climber I mentioned earlier is being carried down by four of the base camp regulars. Some of the Chilean soldiers are going to meet them and help carry him down. Oh well, who wants to live forever? Time for dinner!

It is now later, but the same day. I was right; it was spaghetti – Mexican style with egg drop soup, and like all the rest of the meals I've had so far, it was good. Ricardo has been doing most of the cooking. After dinner, Sergio had a long talk with those of us just sitting around and oddly enough, it was on religion; not that it was odd to talk about religion, but having it come from Sergio just seemed a bit strange. It was an intense conversation – too much and way too long to get into it now – but it made me think. When I'm away from work, in places like this, I tend to think more about God. Perhaps that is why Sergio was on such a soapbox. He spends much more time in places like this than I do. I also started thinking about survival and self-preservation in places like this. Will I be able to beat the mountain, or will it best me? I feel that I can do it; in fact, I know that I can do it. My greatest enemy is, and will always be, the weather.

I feel great. Wes let me borrow his Walkman with selected bits of "Phantom of the Opera" on it; it's a great sound. Granted, I miss all music now, but this is holding a certain passion in my heart; how I've longed to see the play. I have tickets to see it in Chicago, but that is still several months away.

I should've brought a Walkman with me, like Wes and Howard's. I don't know if they realize how much more this will weigh higher up the mountain. I know they trained hard for this climb; they told me they had trained by running on the beach in their double plastic boots; that had to be a good workout. Nevertheless, I'm glad Wes has his Walkman. If I can't sleep later, I'll think about the music I've been listening to.

After dinner I shamed Paul into doing dishes; he hasn't done a thing for the community since we started out. The rest of the group was glad to see it, too. It is apparent that Paul doesn't like Sergio very much. During a dinner conversation before we left for Mendoza, Paul informed me that he had climbed with Sergio once before. According to Paul, Sergio, though a competent leader and guide, usually keeps the clients from reaching the summit. He said this has happened on two other climbs. (I'm not sure how to take this, so I'm keeping it to myself. I wasn't quite sure how to take Paul. During the last big dinner before we left Medoza. Paul held up a plate of french fries and said that in two weeks Wes, Howard and I would be fighting each other for the fries. It was a bit scary sounding, to say the least; and this guy was a doctor.)

Dave, Dick and I went down to get water at the place I now call Glacier Stream. The sun was behind the mountain, and the temperature was dropping faster than usual. (This time tomorrow we will be at Camp I; I wonder how cold it will be?) When we awoke this morning there was frost on the packs we'd left outside the tent the night before. Sergio said that the group is acclimatizing well, and tomorrow we are all looking forward to moving up to our next camp. If all goes well, we will summit in six days; hopefully, the weather will be good and we will all be in good health. The only medical problems so far are a couple of cases of diarrhea, jokingly referred to as "Aconcagua's Revenge." Spirits are high, and I'm suddenly experiencing a sense of déjà vu; this is the second time I've had it this trip. The first was at the Hosteria Penitentes before dinner one night, and now, I wonder if it will happen again. I must end this and finish a letter to my parents, so I can give it to someone to carry down the mountain and mail. (The letter never made it home.)

February 5, 1990 Camp I or Camp Canada Elevation: 16,000 feet

It is 25° F. and snowing. I woke up at 1:15 a.m. to take a walk and empty my bladder. The sky was overcast; I couldn't see the stars, so I laid back in my sleeping bag for another 2 ½ hours before I fell back to sleep. After I finished writing last night, I listened to Wes's "Phantom" tape some more; boy, how I enjoyed that! I must buy the tape when I get back home. After breakfast we packed up our gear, folded up the tent and set off for Camp I. The nicest thing about the three of us sharing the tent was that we simply divided it up and carried it out. Howard took the poles; I had the tent, and Wes had the fly. Today, my pack seemed much heavier than yesterday's; it took me an extra hour to get to Camp I. When I pushed myself, I had a hard time catching my breath; I hope this isn't a prelude of things to come.

The gathering clouds had started to settle. The weather was colder and windier during our climb today, and it started to snow. Wes, Howard and I put the tent together in the snow and then helped John and Cheryl with their tent; I had a headache the whole time. Sergio said he could feel electricity in his mustache, so all ice axes, ski poles, and crampons were moved a safe distance away from the tents – just in case. It was thundering and lightning; I'd never been so close to a storm cloud. I could hear thunder echo into the valley – the valley I could not see.

The snow was really falling and I couldn't see the nearest of peaks. I looked forward to climbing in the warmth of the sun. Perhaps the storm would only last for a few hours; just enough to give us snow to melt for water. Earlier we found a small trickle of water, not terribly far from Camp I, but it took forever to fill a one liter bottle.

As I write this, I've started to breathe easier now that I'm rested. My pulse rate is 102, but that will slow down. I have stopped exerting myself, and I've started taking Diamox per John's advice – 250 mg. twice a day – as well as Decodron, 1mg. twice a day. Taking these should help me acclimatize to the thinner air. I know I have to keep eating to keep my strength up for summit day. I just looked outside the tent; it is snowing even harder now. It's close to a white-out, and it is difficult to see the tent on the far side of the camp. We will be having dinner soon and I don't fancy getting dressed to go back out into the storm, but what else is there to do?

Later: While waiting for dinner I rested peacefully in my sleeping bag while the storm raged around us. I finished a book, which made me happy because now I can leave it behind; I won't have to carry its extra weight. Just as I closed the book, dinner was served – it's some kind of soup. Sergio brought it around to our tents so we wouldn't have to go out into the weather, but he accidentally spilled half of it. The main course – I believe – was beef stroganoff, or something close to that. I didn't eat much because I wasn't that hungry.

News Flash! It finally stopped snowing. I went outside to take some pictures of all the snow on the peaks of the mountains that surround us; this is how I had always pictured the Andes. Hopefully, the sun will come out tomorrow and warm up the area. Perhaps the little stream will be flowing much faster than before. I have 1 ¼ liters of water presently; this should get me through the night if I decide to drink. (I hate it when the flow-through process gets me up during the night.) It is now 9:57 p.m. and it is still light out; the higher up you go the longer it stays light. I took a short walk to the edge of the face that overlooks base camp; there was no snow there, but boy did we get it here.

Tomorrow's plan is to ferry supplies to Camp II at 17,400 feet and return to Camp I – climb high and sleep low; that's the motto.

February 6, 1990 Camp I or Camp Canada Elevation: 16,000 feet

The temperature is 20 ° F, and it's snowing – or should I say it's sleeting like a son of a bitch! I've been snowbound for the last 2 ½ hours, but before I explain why, I may as well start at the beginning. I slept on and off last night as high winds rocked the tent. Wes went out at 3:00 a.m. to relieve himself. I asked him what the sky was like. He said, "Its clear and the moon and stars are out." I was glad; we'd gotten enough snow in the last day. I tossed and turned for the next six hours until I was awakened by the sound of one of the Amazon stoves hissing as it boiled water for breakfast. Through an open gap by the tent's zippered door, I cold see blue sky. After dressing, I took some more pictures of the snow-covered Andes; the view was simply breathtaking, and I was right in the middle of them!

For breakfast I had two cups of hot chocolate and two cups of hot tea. I wasn't very hungry, but I did want the liquids in my system; you just can't get enough of them up here. The sun broke over the summit of Aconcagua at 10:10 a.m., and it started to warm up the area almost immediately. We packed up the gear that we would need to ferry up to Camp II and headed out. Almost as soon as we left camp, those same snow clouds – from the day before – returned.

I finished the trek to Camp II in a little over three hours, and had lunch which consisted of some salami, crackers and a handful of walnuts and peanuts. I finished my second quart of water and was now out. The clouds had rolled in and a gentle snow was falling. Howard, Sydney and I decided to head back to Camp I, leaving Dave, Nasko, Augusto, Ricardo and Wes behind. Sidney led the way – the wrong way. The only thing for us to do was to backtrack up the mountain and around the glacier, or we could take the short cut by going over the glacier. Since we didn't have crampons with us, crossing the glacier would be difficult. All I needed was to slip on the ice and break something. If I slid down it I'd go completely off the bluff. Neither way was appealing, but since there were so many rough spots in the glacier, it didn't appear so dangerous. Howard said he would follow. Sidney apologized for getting us into this mess and went back up the mountain. Howard encouraged me to lead because I was good at finding trails. (Last week when we climbed Mt. Wimp, Howard nicknamed me "Scout" for my ability to find trails. Wes called me Cisco, because it sounded more South American.)

So, Howard and I crossed the glacier. I soon fell into a sinkhole up to my waste, but I was able to free myself without difficulty. Howard avoided the area – wise move on his part – and blazed a new trail across; the rest of the trek back to camp was uneventful. It had started to snow much harder, and I was back in my tent with Wes and Howard by 4:30 p.m. Because of the cold temperatures and blowing snow, the stream we used to get our water was now frozen. Before we started using the stoves to melt water, I would fill my bottle with snow, drop in an iodine pill and some powdered Kool-Aid. I would put them in my sleeping bag to warm them up and melt the snow; I would be lucky to get half a liter of liquid. Wes and Howard each had a full quart. It was enough to get by, but not enough to stay as hydrated as we wanted to be.

Along with the intensity of the storm came the problem of boiling water, both for drinking and making dinner. Sergio was kind enough to bring dinner to our tents so we didn't have to go out into the storm. (If the weather keeps up like this, it could hamper the rest of the trip; I don't envy the thought of trekking through three feet of snow all the way up to the other camps or the summit.) My penmanship is awful at this point; I froze my hand filling my water bottles with more snow. It is more crowded in here as well; not only do we have three people in this tent, but we brought in some of our gear so it wouldn't get wet and freeze outside in the elements.

It is 10:19 p.m. The storm shows no signs of letting up; you can hear the wind howling and the beads of snow and ice bouncing off the tent. There is even occasional thunder. If the storm stops during the night and Sergio agrees, we'll move up to Camp II tomorrow. Wes, Howard and I will dress early; as soon as the sun hits the tents we will be packed up and ready to go. This will give us more time to reach Camp II in case bad weather follows. I know we needed snow at the beginning of the trip, but if this keeps up we'll have much more than we needed, and enough to make things difficult. If I can't make it up the mountain, that is one thing; if I can't make it up due to the weather, that's another. I finished the second of the three books I brought with me; I'll leave it here with the other items and pick them up on the way down.

Wes, Howard and I were talking about the snow; Wes feels that if we get two feet or more dumped on us, Sergio will scrub the climb. I don't know what he will do. If he puts it to a vote, I will vote to push on. I feel that I can climb this thing; I still feel strong and I don't want to fail this attempt because of the weather. At this point, I'm not sure I'll know when to quit; I don't think I'm foolish enough to die trying, like that poor soul they carried down the other day. We still don't know the story behind his death. I don't want to quit, and it hurts to think about going home a failure. This doesn't even take into account the money I spent to get here and the time I took training.

I started to wonder what would happen if we put the decision to a vote. Would a split decision splinter the group? Do we have the resources for that? I tried to think how the group would vote. I know that I would go; Dave would go. John & Cheryl were maybes; Howard and Wes – I couldn't tell. I don't even have a clue as to what the rest of the group would do. I believe I know what Paul would say: he would say that Sergio has found a way to keep us from going all the way to the summit. For now, we just have to wait and see; if worse comes to worse and the trip is called, I could at least say I tried. I could say that I'd seen the Andes, walked in them and photographed them. Either way, I would hate to be beaten by them. It sounds like I would take it personally; I know it's not right, but that is how it comes across to me.

I should try to sleep, but I'm not tired. Except for the trek, I've been laying in my bag either reading or writing. I'll try praying for good weather until I fall asleep; tomorrow may prove to be an interesting day.

February 7, 1990 Camp II or Camp Nido de Condor. Elevation: 17,500 feet

Present Temperature, 8° F. I didn't pray hard enough, and believe it or not, I did pray. There were high winds and snow flakes pelting the tent all night. When I looked out at 9:00 a.m. I saw that we had been hit by two more feet of snow, and it was 18° F., but at least the sun was out and there were no signs of any clouds. Sergio had long decided that we would move up to Camp II today, so I had wasted my time last night worrying about what would happen with the climb.

Breakfast consisted of hot water and whatever you wanted to put in it – be it powdered milk, cereal, hot chocolate, or coffee. I have two packets of hot apple cider, which I'm saving for tomorrow. I talked to a couple of guys from Canada who made camp right before the storm hit; they are on their way to the top as well. The rest of the group took some pictures of the snow covered peaks, as well as pictures of the group. Several of us had on all red-colored clothing, and we suddenly became known as the "tomato gang." Everyone wearing blue became known as the "blue cheese" gang. These were the only names we could think of, and I wondered if our subconscious minds were inspiring these thoughts of real food.

We dismantled the tent, but we didn't want to be the first ones to leave; we didn't want to break trail through two feet of new-fallen snow all the way to Camp II. We were the first to leave, however, and we did break the trail. I was second out of camp behind Wes, with Howard behind me. The snow was well over the tops of my double plastic boots. I felt noticeably weaker than I had yesterday. I marched behind Wes who is much taller than I; he had an easier time breaking the trail. It wasn't fair to Wes, but we were really moving along. I stayed behind him for an hour and a half before I suddenly lost all my strength. Howard passed me up and the two of them trekked up the path to Camp II. I slowed down considerably, and it took me four and a half hours to reach camp. Sergio, Ricardo and Augusto came by me next; they marched by me like I was standing still. At the rate they were going, they were sure to pass up Wes, who would be glad to have someone else break the trail for a while. I stopped periodically to rest along the way and tried to take a picture of the summit. During one such rest break, as I looked through the viewfinder of my camera, I saw a white wind coming my way. I snapped a fast picture, put my camera away and started back up the mountain. Then I realized that in my tired state I wasn't going to be able to outrun this thing, so I bided my time until it hit. Most of the whiteout – or whatever it had been – dissipated before it even got to me.

When I reached Camp II, Wes and Howard were going to start assembling the tent. (They couldn't very well do it without me because I was carrying parts of it.) They insisted that I rest for an hour; they had rested once they reached camp. I felt that it would be unfair to have them do it themselves, so I did my best to help; there were intermittent clouds in the area, and I thought the sooner the tent got up, the better off we would be should another storm hit. Once the tents were up, and the buried gear dug out of the snow, we broke for lunch. We ate cold cuts and crackers while our water for dinner boiled on the other side of the camp.

We napped for an hour, then we were called for supper; we had a rice soup and some other rice dish that tasted awful, and was – by far – the worst meal we'd had on the mountain, but at least I was still hydrated. (I was always glad to see that clear urine flowing from my body.)

As I write, it's getting colder outside; getting out of the sleeping bags could be tough tomorrow morning. I did take a short walk about 9:30 p.m. and took some pictures of the moon. There was a failed summit attempt today by some people we met as they were coming down the mountain. They said there was too much new snow and the winds were too strong to summit. I can't believe it; we've had snow every night since we left base camp. We're hoping for three days of sunshine and no more snow.

Tomorrow is a rest day; we will do nothing but get stronger, stay hydrated and relax. I finished the last of my books that I'd brought with me. I gave them to the Canadian guys to read. They were so grateful to have something to read; they didn't even care what the titles of the books were. Before I retired for the night, I took a last look around outside; the sky is clear, for the most part, but I've learned over the past week that it can change at the drop of a hat. The moon is getting full, and it is only two more days until the earth passes between the sun and the moon in a solar eclipse. It will be the first one I've seen outside of the United States; it will be decades before a solar eclipse occurs back in Wisconsin. It is by chance that I happen to be here for this one. Most of the clouds are below us now; I hope they stay there. If it is sunny tomorrow, I'll dry out some of my gear.

According to Sergio, the day we were to spend ferrying gear to Camp III will be canceled and we will spend an extra day acclimatizing here at Camp II. Then on the day after that, we will walk up to Camp III, spend the night and shoot for the summit; we will only be at really high altitudes for a short time. The hike to Camp III will give half of the group their first taste of air at 19,000 feet. I remember my fist time at this altitude on Kilimanjaro, and I remember how awful I had felt. Sergio said the attempt on the summit will depend on the weather, and we are at its mercy. Now it's time for rest. I replaced the batteries in Wes's Walkman, since I wore them down. I'll listen to "Phantom" before I fall asleep. I'm curled up in my sleeping bag now because it is cold; it will be tough getting out of it tomorrow.

February 8, 1990 Camp II or Nido de Condor. Elevation: 17,500 feet

It is a rest day and it is 1:55 p.m. The temperature is in the mid 30's and I'm taking this time to write. Last night was windy. We didn't get any more snow, but there was rain inside the tent. Because it was so cold, we zipped up the tent door all the way; condensation from our breathing and body heat formed on the roof of the tent. When enough moisture had built up, water droplets started to periodically fall down upon us.

Even though my sleeping bag was damp, I slept exceptionally well. I feel very fit, and the only thing I'm suffering from is minor sunburn to my cheeks and nose. I thought I had applied plenty of zinc oxide and sun block to my face. I had walked with my head down, away from the sun, but I didn't take into account the reflection of the sun's rays off the snow.

Since today is a rest day I plan on doing exactly that: rest. I felt hungry, and this is a good sign. I had breakfast and sized up the rest of the group. In my opinion, they are doing reasonably well with the exception of Paul. He appears to be dragging, and if I would be so blunt, a little senile. I spent the day listening to Wes's tapes and took a nap. I awoke feeling rested and completed my third quart of water for the day. I should have no difficulty finishing a few more quarts before I retire tonight.

It is now 3:20 p.m. The sun is high in the sky and I have just finished the usual lunch. I brushed my teeth. My face still hurts from the sunburn. I looked at it in the reflections of my mirrored glasses; I'm starting to look like death-warmed-over. A lot of skin is peeling from my forehead, and I haven't shaved in almost two weeks. I could use a shower.

Sergio says we leave at noon tomorrow for Camp III, also known as Camp Berlin (I don't know why). It will bring us up to 19,300 feet; that is just 40 feet lower than the summit of Kilimanjaro. Summit day will bring me to a new personal high in altitude.

According to our printed schedule, the hike to Camp III is a two-hour hike; however, it fails to mention how long it will take with a 65-pound pack on my back. Maybe the paths will be a little beaten down by then; the going might not be as slow as yesterday. The sun is very warm, but the winds can still chill you. Precautions must be taken to keep my sunburn from getting any worse.

The Chilean army has arrived and will be spending the night near our camp. They are going down the mountain with only three of their group of 16 ever making it to the summit, not a very good average for a company that is trained in hardships like this. I wonder where that puts our band of amateurs. I asked Sergio how many people climbed Aconcagua last year. His reply was, "Only God and they know for sure." He did tell me that 1,200 give or take, had applied for permits. He doesn't know how many actually made it to the top.

If all goes well we should be at Camp III tomorrow at this time. The eclipse is scheduled for 2:29 p.m., and I'll be on the trail. Again, I hope for good weather. There are some clouds out now and I'm starting to feel a change in the temperature as the clouds pass in front of the sun. The change is as quick as flipping a switch on and off. Last night, I lay in bed thinking about little conveniences that I miss: light switches, hot running water, warm beds, and anything besides freeze-dried foods. First thing each morning, I really miss some loud rock and roll and a newscast. We were trying to find out who won the Super Bowl before we left for the mountain, but were unable to do so. (I believe it was San Francisco over Denver). I even miss milk, and I'm not a big milk drinker, either; I don't think I took these things into account before I signed up for this expedition. Our time on Aconcagua is much longer than the time I spent on Kilimanjaro. It is slowly getting to the point where I will soon wish that this [climb] was over, but as I have said before: the worst is yet to come.

The clouds keep coming and going with just a hint of snow in the air. Jon and Mike, the two Canadians, have ferried their gear to our camp; they are storing it by our tent and have plans to take our site once we move out tomorrow. We shot photos of each other and said we would exchange them after we get back home. (I mailed mine, but I never heard back from Jon or Mike).

It is now 7:18 p.m. The sun is out for the most part, but the wind is picking up. As long as it doesn't snow, I don't care how cold it gets; I'm prepared for that. I went to fill up the water containers; I had to chip a hole in the ice of a pond near our camp. I flavored the freezing cold liquid with Kool-Aid, dropped in an iodine tablet and put it in my sleeping bag to warm it up. Drinking extremely cold fluids can cause severe stomach cramps, and the body uses even more energy warming itself. I've finished five quarts, so far, and I feel strong, but I wonder if it will be enough to get me to the summit?

It is 24° F. in the sun. Cheryl is feeling ill today, and John says it is definitely altitude sickness. Nasko, who is badly blistered on one side of his nose and has a touch of altitude sickness, is feeling much stronger since he started taking Decadron. Nasko carries a pair of one half gallon containers with him for his liquids. When he leaves for another camp, he will be carrying 8 ½ lbs. in liquids alone. I'm still using Howard's aloe vera gel to help my sunburn. David is fine; Chuck and Sidney are fine, but Paul is becoming very distant. (Personally, I think he isn't very coherent sometimes. Sergio knows of this and is watching him.) Howard and Wes have a mild case of "Aconcagua's Revenge," but are in very good spirits. Howard is looking forward to tomorrow; "one day at a time," as he puts it. I look at it as two more days and the worst is over. It would be bad if we were snowed in up there.

Just after dinner tonight, I walked up a small hill to photograph our campsite. Overlooking the other side of the hill is the valley we climbed yesterday and the day before that. I saw four people on the trail coming up; they had a ways to go. It reminded me of how I felt while coming to this camp. From here, you could even see into the Horcones Valley. There was no snow in the valley. I was amazed to think how 3,500 feet could make such a difference.

It is a whole new world here. Granted, it is colder, but the air is so much cleaner and fresher. My allergies don't bother me and I've had no bad side affects from the change of altitude. Being here has made me wonder how the first pioneers must have felt as they scouted out virgin territory, not knowing what they were getting themselves into. I have to face it; I'm only here because I've heard of this place through other sources. It is a challenging mountain that I think I can climb. What will I have to show for it when I'm finished with all of this? Just a large number of photos, or the ability to say, "Hell, I've climbed Aconcagua"? What's the point? Most people can't even pronounce the name of this mountain, and even fewer know where it is. What is the reason for doing it? Well, maybe my reason this time is to figure out what I didn't figure out while I was climbing Kilimanjaro. Things like, "What is the meaning of life" and "Why do people want to climb this mountain, or any other mountain for that matter"?

I haven't thought about those things or much of anything else. This climb is more strenuous than Kili, and most of my time is taken up thinking about the next step and how much further to camp. On Kilimanjaro my mind wandered so much more; it was a much more pleasant experience, and I don't think I appreciate the beauty here as much, either. By the time I get to camp, pitch my tent, store my gear, get water and finish all the other chores, sightseeing has lost its value. This vacation is pretty much like this: work first, and enjoy later, if weather, temperature and energy permits. Granted, this is not a normal vacation, and I'm not saying that I'm a rugged mountain man; but I feel that I'm a bit more so than the next person, and there are many, many more people who qualify as being more rugged than me. I hope to figure this all out in the next few days.

One last look outside the tent before going to sleep: the sun is out and the summit sits above us, tempting us to "come and get me." There is a slight haze around it; the peak is wearing it as a crown. It is almost like hearing the mountain say, "I'm the king around here." Even if I do get the chance to dethrone it, I'll leave this place, but it will still be there … on top.

February 9, 1990 Camp III or Camp Berlin Elevation: 19,300 feet

Temp 4° F. We made it, but we were lucky. The three-hour hike took me four hours, Wes made it in a shorter time, and Howard came in at 4:45. Our packs were a heavy 65 lbs. Even though I had trained hard for the weight, there was no way I could train for the altitude. My pace may have been slow, but it was steady. The climb up to camp was cloudy and there was light snow in the air. I was three-fourths of the way to Camp III when the whiteout hit. I couldn't even see the trail. There was no real place to fall back to and sit it out, so I just kept moving along in the track directly in front of me. There were seven members of the group scattered behind me at different parts of the trail. Through the blowing wind, I thought I heard someone calling for help, but from which direction, I didn't know. It could have been from someone coming down from the summit or coming up from down below. I hollered back a few times but there were no replies, so I continued on my way to Camp III.

When the whiteout finally ended, I could see Sergio coming from Camp III about 30 yards above me. The rest of the group made it up within the next three hours. I was exhausted, but feeling better than I had at this altitude on Kili. I helped Wes set up the tent, and as soon as Howard made it up, we all rested and eventually fell asleep. I had a pounding headache but took care of it with some Decadron. The cold is making it difficult to write. I have some silk gloves, but they don't keep out the cold. To continue, I must keep stopping to re-warm my hands.

I missed the eclipse. Because of poor weather conditions in the area I missed the event I was so looking forward to. What a coincidence – right time, right place, but bad weather. I hope this is the only disappointment I have this trip.

I took some pictures of the summit; it is only 4,000 feet away and it's looking so much closer now. There is a small shrine placed here in memory of climbers who have perished in the attempt. It makes me wonder if what I'm doing is really worth the risk of having an accident and possibly losing my life.

This campsite is much rockier than the others, and small boulders lie everywhere. Some are half covered in snow. There are also three small wooden domiciles here – one with no roof. The other two are barely high enough to sit up in. I'm sure they would help guard against the wind better than our tents. Our guides have commandeered one of these.

Supper tonight was some kind of soup, though I wasn't very hungry. Sergio announced that because of the weather conditions, we would not try for the summit tomorrow. It will mean spending an extra day here, doing nothing but waiting and trying to keep warm. The longest time I've ever stayed at this altitude was a half hour. Now, I'll be here for over 48 hours. In the long run it means an extra day until I can get a hot shower. I went to lie in my tent after dinner and had a great philosophical discussion of life, its worth, and its meaning with Howard and Wes. We talked of things like: "why people push the outside of the envelope", or "why they stay in the center of their box not daring to venture out." We also discussed "what age has to do with it", and "what really matters in life." Wes has a little notebook he carries with him, and each day he breaks the seal on a new page. The page contains a message, a note, and or a picture or an adage from his wife Jenny. Now that is what I think is special. I wish I had someone in my life like that. Those little things are what count. In fact, on top of the blackboard in Mr. O'Brien's history class – back at St. Catherine's – was a sign that read, "It is the little things in life that are infinitely more important." I always remembered that saying, and I always believed in it.

It is getting too cold to write now, so I'll finish this. I can still hear the winds blowing outside, but the clouds are gone. I can see the shape of the full moon through the yellow nylon of the tent. It must be very clear outside, but I'm too cold to go out and look. Why couldn't it have been this clear during the eclipse?

February 10, 1990 Camp III or Camp Berlin Elevation: 19,300 feet

Temp 18° F. Today was supposed to be the day we went to the summit, but because of the weather the last few days, it was not to be. Sergio says he is worried about avalanches at a place that we must go through; there's no way around. (Some people from another group were caught in an avalanche three days ago and were swept down 500 feet; they are lucky that was all that happened.) We are waiting an extra day so all the snow that has accumulated in the last few days will either settle or fall down the side of the mountain before we get to it.

I awoke at 9:00 a.m. this morning and was out of the tent by 10:00. I sat around and talked to John, Cheryl, Howard, Sidney and Dave until the water was boiling for breakfast. Breakfast was nothing to write about, so I'll stop discussing it here.

The mountains are beautiful to look at, and now that the skies are so clear you can see even more snow-covered peaks. Everywhere you look you can see the Andes. Sergio says it's a go for tomorrow. We leave at 7:30 a.m.; the sun will still be down and I'll feel cold like I've never felt it before. It will be a long day – nine hours up and four hours down, unless I feel exceptionally strong and can do it in less. A plus to tomorrow's climb is that our packs will weigh a fraction of what they did on the way up here. The only things I plan to bring with me are my ice ace, crampons, camera, down parka and water. It will be a great day and already I'm getting excited about reaching the summit. I know that when we return, I will be extremely tired after the climb and it will be so good to get into a sleeping bag and sleep the sleep of the dead.

5:45 p.m. (the same day) Where should I start? Today, I rested a while, had lunch (just soup but it really hit the spot) with the rest of the group. The weather was comfortable; there was no wind at all. I sat and talked with other members of the group and took pictures of our planned route to the top. There are clouds off to the north headed this way, and there is a ring around the sun which means wet weather is approaching. Up here there is no wet – as in rain – just snow and ice, which I hope will blow over. This mountain has had its share of snow for a while, and I remember writing last week that it didn't have enough.

As I sat in my tent during the day, I could occasionally look out the open door and see a blue sky. Periodically, I could see wisps of vapor floating by. It was the middle of the afternoon before I felt any trace of wind at all in the camp, but in less than an hour the entire camp was in a whiteout. With winds blowing and snow falling, I can't see the tent six feet away from us. I hope this ends soon; many of us are looking forward to tomorrow's summit. I don't know what Sergio would say, but I still want my chance. I'm drinking a lot of water to stay hydrated and I've only had one small headache all day. I feel acclimatized to this altitude and I'm looking forward to seeing what it is like near the 23,000-foot mark.

8:58 p.m. The snow is easing off a little but the winds are still blowing. I had a cupful of soup for dinner and some ten-day-old buns. Sergio says he isn't sure about tomorrow's climb, and he won't know until early tomorrow morning around 5:30 a.m. He also says this is strange weather and he has never seen four straight days of snow. If we do leave, it must be by 7:30 a.m. My gear is packed and ready.

Though I've always known this could happen, I never gave it much thought. If you traveled this far, spent this much money and trained for as long as I have, you would at least hope for a shot at the top. At least then you would be able to return home and say, "I tried." That's a lot better than saying, "The weather screwed us up." There is no other news, other than the fact that I haven't read a newspaper in two weeks, nor have I seen a television, talked to my family or worn clean clothes. I'd like to burn some of these.

It is 6° F. and dropping. How is my physical condition? I feel great. I've lost a little weight, my nail-beds are all broken with a little bleeding, and I still have minor sun burn to my face; my lips are all cracked. Other than that, I feel fine. The wind is really howling outside the tent right now; I'm glad it's securely fastened down. My clothing is stuffed down into the bottom of my sleeping bag so it will be warm when I put it on tomorrow, in case we go – no, not if, but when we go. It's getting too cold to write and tomorrow is going to be a long day, so I must get some sleep. The next entry is the one that counts.

February 11, 1990 Back at Base camp Elevation: 13,800-14,000 feet

8:13 p.m. Here it is, the moment of truth, but let's linger a bit. It was a bad night, it was long and very cold, and the wind howled louder than I've ever heard it before. It kept me up until 4:00 a.m. I knew the moon was out because I could see the light shining through the sides of the tent. I was buried inside my sleeping bag, head and all, which – once again – was wet from moisture building up on the tent walls. Wes thought he heard noises around 5:30 a.m., but I was tired from the long night and didn't hear a thing. At 7:00 a.m. I awoke to hear noises and stuck my head out into the wind to see what it was. I saw some of the group standing around one of the two wooden huts drinking coffee. I yelled, "Are we climbing today?" Dave answered, "Yes." I yelled back, "Why the hell didn't anyone call us?"

When 7:30 rolled around the rest of the group started to leave. Wes and I were still getting ready. Howard decided not to go. He was probably the sanest of us all at that particular point. I asked him twice if he was sure he wasn't going to go. He said that he was just too tired to go on. (Howard had experienced diarrhea on and off since base camp, and he was slowly being drained of his energy ever since.) When I was convinced that he was not going, I asked him if I could borrow his insulated water bottle, which he gladly gave me. Wes and I both rushed to get ready. It was a bad thing to do; adrenaline was racing, and already we were getting short of breath just from the mere thought of being left behind. There was no time for warm coffee, tea or anything to ward off the cold from the long night's chill. The only thing we had going for us was the fact that we had packed the night before.

I thought to myself: even if it is in the rush of the moment, at least we are on our way to the summit, or at least we are going to try. It was a cold morning, -11° F. on the tent's thermometer. This was without the wind chill. I put on the warmest clothing I had, knowing that when the sun came out I might be able to shed off a layer. I was ready; my heart was pounding from both the thinner air and the rush to get dressed. Wes told me to go ahead so I wouldn't lose sight of the rest of the group – the same group that had no reservations about leaving us behind. I said, "Fine," and I left. I wanted desperately to catch up to the others and not be a straggler, but I knew if I rushed – even with a light pack – I would wear myself out quickly. Because of the incline of the trail and the lack of air, I kept my pace of one step, and two breaths. Since I wasn't one of the slower climbers in the group, I thought perhaps I would just catch up. I also didn't want to lose track of Wes who would be following close behind. Wes is much faster than I am and didn't waste too much time catching up. A short time later, I turned back to check on him; I saw him sitting with his back to me. I was about 70 feet above him; I yelled to him over the wind, "What's wrong?" He said he was okay, so I kept climbing.

I looked back a minute later and saw Wes still just sitting there. I yelled again, "What's wrong?" Wes said that his fingers were cold. I yelled again over the wind, "Do you want me to come back?" He said no, that he'd be okay. So I kept moving up. I turned back a minute later to see what he was doing. Wes still hadn't moved. I yelled again to him, "Either come up or go back, or I'll come back to you." It was at this point on the mountain that getting to the top started to take second place to helping a friend, or a fellow climber, or anyone else that may have been in need. Again, Wes said that he was all right, but he was going back to camp. He stood up and did exactly that. Once I knew Wes would be okay, I turned and proceeded back up the trek. The rest of the group was out of sight around a bend, but I was still determined to catch up.

Unbeknownst to me, and after Wes and I had left camp, Howard – tired as he was – decided he still wanted to take a shot at the top. He dressed and left camp; one hundred feet or so up the trail, he ran into Wes coming down. They went back to camp together.

For me, the going was brutal; that is the only way I can describe it. I was still dressed to the hilt, but my hands were getting cold, and my feet were even colder. Great, I thought. I paid $240 for a pair of boots and they're not even keeping my feet warm. I kept moving and eventually caught sight of the rest of the group. Snow was still blowing everywhere, the wind-chill was phenomenal, and the sun was slowly starting to lift itself over the smaller peaks of the Andes, but I was closing in on the rest of the group. I had hoped my hands and feet would have warmed up by this time, but they hadn't. I thought back to Kilimanjaro and how cold my feet were, and then it hit me. In my rush to get dressed, I had once again laced my boots too tight; the laces were cutting off or slowing the circulation to my feet. This was another coincidence: two different summits in two different parts of the world. I was my own worst enemy! I had to take off my heavy gloves to loosen my laces. As soon as I took off my gloves, my hands quickly froze. It was nothing severe or permanent, but enough to make me extremely uncomfortable; all this could have been avoided if I had only been more careful.

As I was about to catch up to the group, I was still feeling strong – cold, but strong. I had no difficulties in breathing, and no sore muscles. I just had a desire to hit the summit, but as strong as I felt, something just didn't feel right. It didn't matter how strong I was – or anyone else in the party; Mother Nature was stronger. Soon, Sergio made it official. "Go back," he said. "Too cold, the snow is too high and the canaleta is too long in this cold." (He was referring to the traverse up to the canaleta which would take too long to climb with the snow as deep as it was; we would be done in by the cold.) So Sergio earned his pay that day by turning us around and heading us back towards Camp III.

The high point of this climb for me was just barely over 21,000 feet, and I was pissed. All the money, time and training had been for nothing. There would be no summit. The anger burned inside of me, but not nearly enough to keep me warm in light of the situation. Just as we started to turn back, I remembered the one thing I had to do before going back down the mountain. I pulled my flag from my pack; it was a large, red flag – 3x5 feet – neatly folded up in a zip-lock bag. It had my name, City and State, a very large emblem of my fire department and the name of the mountain; misspelled. But when I picked it up and learned of the mistake it was too late for me to do anything about it. I couldn't open it while wearing my over-mitts, so I took them off. Under the over-mitts I wore wool gloves, but the wind went right through the material. This is a mistake, I thought, and quickly replaced my over-mitts.

I couldn't hold the flag by myself, so I anchored one end to the ski pole I had been using as a walking stick. I held on to the other pole to keep from getting blown away. I knelt in the snow next to the flag and John took some pictures. With all the clothing I was wearing, you could barely tell it was me.

The highpoint of the Aconcagua climb. Approximately 21,000 feet.

John took several pictures with my Minolta camera. When I had pulled it from my pack and turned it on, my battery power read "low" – obviously due to the cold. If it could have, I'm sure it would've read "frozen." After John finished with the pictures, he gave me the thumbs up, and I quickly put my flag back in my pack. I returned the favor and snapped some pictures of John and Cheryl.

Ricardo and Augusto were waiting for us by an outcropping of rocks. They told us to warm up for a minute before proceeding. Cheryl asked me what my thermometer read; it read -13° F. Sergio guessed at the wind speed; which made it -80° F. with the wind chill. After a brief warming up period behind a large rock that served as a windbreak, Ricardo started yelling at us to keep moving. I reached down and grabbed a couple of rocks to bring back as souvenirs, and we continued our march downward. We pushed on. The sun rose higher into the sky; it was brighter, but certainly not warmer.

I came across a campsite built higher than our Camp III. There were three tents; it was sometimes hard to see them in the blowing snow. I had thought our camp was in a windy spot, but this site seemed worse. I don't know how I had missed seeing it on the way up; I must've had something more important on my mind, like catching up to the rest of the group.

I came around a bend and looked below me. In the distance was Camp III. Even as cold as it was, I still stopped to take a picture. Again, I dropped my pack to retrieve my camera. I thought, since this was the only time I would have this view of the camp, I had better take the shot. I was so cold. My feet were freezing; even my toes hurt. Suddenly, as I was packing away my camera, I caught a glimpse of something partially buried in the snow. It looked like part of a black and red jacket with a loose flap blowing in the wind. At least, I thought it looked like a jacket. But I really didn't care to look any closer; I didn't want to know if there was someone inside of it. Ricardo kept yelling at me to move along. Perhaps, he didn't want me to look any closer, either. I felt no compassion for the body in the snow – if, indeed, there was one; I didn't wonder about his age or nationality, nor did I wonder if I had met him at the Hosteria. The only thing on my mind at this point was reaching my nylon tent which stood blowing in the wind some 500 feet below me. Our goal of ascent had been quickly replaced with a goal of descent.

As we reached the shelter of larger rocks, the wind decreased and became less fierce, and our descending speed soon increased. I removed a couple of heat packs from the zipper pockets of the sleeves, opened them and slipped then into my mitts. They helped warm my fingers, but my toes were still freezing. When I was almost 100 feet from camp, I could see Wes and Howard at the door of the tent, both watching the group descend. I almost ran the last 300 horizontal feet back to camp.

I reached the tent and asked Wes if he was all right. Howard wanted to know what was going on. I asked Wes again, "Are you all right?" Wes answered, "I'm fine now, Cisco, but I think I nearly got frostbite." Howard asked me how I was doing. I replied, "My hands are warming up, but I can't feel my toes anymore." Wes and Howard grabbed me, pulled me into the tent and started to undo my boots. The wind was still blowing, but being inside the tent made a big difference. I pulled off my jacket, and the loose snow went flying around inside the tent. We had always tried to be careful about this in the past, but it didn't seem to matter now. Ricardo stopped by to see how I was doing. He knew my feet had been cold when we were on the mountain because I'd told him. Howard had just finished removing my boots, and Ricardo took off his own jacket. He told me to take off my socks. As I did so, I noticed deep impressions above my ankles, proof that I had laced up my over-boots too tight. Ricardo then grabbed my feet and placed them under his shirt. I could feel the warmth of his chest (which also felt quite hairy). Through his shirt, he massaged my feet to restore circulation. I hate to admit that this action surprised me, but it did. I would have never thought of doing it that way. (My plan was to open more heat packs, hold them against my feet or place them in my boots, but those things would not have worked as well.) As Ricardo rubbed my feet he began to share some of his tales on Everest.

I couldn't imagine what the weather might be like at another 10,000 feet. Wes explained his reason for returning to camp. In his rush to get ready earlier, he mistook Howard's balaclava for his own. As he climbed the mountain, his fingers got cold, like mine, and he couldn't breathe. Once he realized that it was the small hood that was affecting his breathing, he quickly removed his gloves and literally tore the balaclava from his head, but the wind immediately hit his fingers. He tried to warm them by putting them down his crotch. This still didn't warm his hands. As he sat deliberating on what he should to do, he heard my voice calling down to him from my spot higher up the mountain. That's when he decided to go back.

Once my feet began to feel better, I thanked Ricardo for what he had done to help me. I knew that if I were ever in a situation like this in the future, I would remember this trick. For now, I just wanted to climb into my sleeping bag and rest a bit, but that was not to be.

After a conversation with Sergio, Wes came back and stuck his head into the tent. "Hey Cisco," he said. "We're packing up and going back to base camp, so let's get off this f__king mountain." I put on my warmest socks and started to put things in order. Wes took some more pictures of me with my flag, and I took one of Howard throwing a Frisbee off a small hill next to our camp. Howard's goal was to throw it from the top of Aconcagua. It was great to see it sail through the air, but I still wished Howard could have thrown it from the summit. Within 45 minutes our gear was packed, our tent was down, and we were ready to go.

The three of us bade farewell to Camp Berlin and started down the snow-covered slopes. I felt strong and rejuvenated. My feet were warm, and as long as I wore my gloves, my hands would be fine. I felt that under these conditions, I could've taken the summit, but I've no way to prove it.

Wes, who is much taller than I, and has a much longer stride, came down to Camp II first. I met the Canadians, Jon and Mike, at our old campsite. They said, "Wes is off," meaning nature had called. I chatted with Jon and Mike while I packed up the gear that I had buried and left behind at this campsite. I filled them in on the last ten hours and how the trip from Camp III down to Camp II had only taken 40 minutes, tops. I thought I should be feeling stronger with the air getting thicker and the temperature rising, so I said good-bye to them and wished them good luck.

Howard and Wes had already left, and I could see them below me on the trail. I turned to look up at the summit, just to see how far I had climbed down; the entire summit was covered in clouds. Perhaps it had been a good thing that we hadn't pushed on; we could have possibly been caught in all that frozen mess.

At this point, I was walking in nine-inch deep snow. Travel was steady and I was still feeling strong. The sun came out from behind the clouds for longer periods of time. The temperature was warming, and instead of being cold, I was starting to sweat.

I caught up with Howard and Wes halfway between Camp II and Camp I. We rested and drank. I warned Howard that the tent poles were about to slide out of his pack. Then we moved on. With his long strides, Wes quickly left Howard and me behind. As we continued down, we started to shed our cold-weather clothing. Indeed, it was much warmer than it had been up at Camp III and above. Occasionally, I would stop and look behind me at the distance I had descended. The summit was still completely socked in. I was amazed at how quickly we could come down this beast when we didn't have to fight gravity. I could see the trails I had taken up the mountain; they were tough, but beautiful.

Wes was moving as though he had plans back at base camp. I was ten minutes behind him, but I couldn't keep up with him. I stopped to take off some of my heavier clothing, feeling happy that I had managed to get my pack, which was full and very heavy, back on. I had barely walked another 50 feet on a switchback before I lost my footing, tumbled once, and did a complete flip before the bulkiness of my pack stopped me from rolling any further. The only thing bruised was my ego. I had to slide my pack off before I could stand, but I did. I picked up that heavy pack and tugged it back on my tired, aching body. I didn't want to take the steeper trails and risk another fall. Instead, I took the trail Wes, Howard and I had taken the previous week – where we found the body of the unfortunate climber. It seemed like an easier route, but it turned out to be a big mistake.

I didn't realize it at the time, but the trail would take me out of the way and towards the Penitentes, much farther down and away from base camp. What should have taken just a short time to climb down – even with my full pack – actually took me an extra hour. I climbed out without knowing I'd made a wrong turn.

I made it back to base camp to find Wes's pack next to the spot where our tent had been, but there was no sign of Wes and no sign of Howard or his pack. He should've been there by this time. After all, I had been detained an extra hour just climbing back up to base camp, but I hadn't seen him on the trail. Sergio had been the first to arrive and was sitting with our supplies. I asked him if he knew of Wes's whereabouts. He explained that Wes had gone to make a phone call at the construction site of the new hotel.

I told Sergio of my side trip to the Penitentes and explained that Howard had been behind me and should've been here by now. I offered to go look for him, but Sergio said, "The rest of the group is still coming down the mountain, including Ricardo and Augusto. They will make sure Howard makes it back to camp." I took off my pack, finished the rest of my water and took off another layer of clothing. By now, the sun was gone behind the clouds. I kept looking up the trail for the other members of our party; twenty minutes later, I could see Howard on the trail through my telephoto lens.

Finally, Howard walked into camp and explained that not five minutes after I had left him, the tent poles, which I had warned him about earlier, fell out of his pack. With everything covered with ice, the poles slide every-which-way; it had taken him over an hour to recover all but two sets of poles.

(In a later conversation with Howard, in June of 1997, he confided to me that he had been totally drained by the time he got back to base camp that day, and that it had taken him such a long time to gather up the poles because he had been so tired).

As he finished telling me the story, I could see the rest of the group walking the last leg of the journey towards base camp. It had taken me nine days to climb to Camp III from base camp, and if I didn't include the hour I spent getting lost, it took me four hours to climb back down.

Wes was upset when he returned from the construction site. He had walked all that way to the hotel site, only to find it closed, and had been unable to make his call. None of us had taken into account the fact that it was Sunday. Without the daily reminders of newspaper, TV or radio it was difficult to keep track of the days. Some of us had kept journals, like Howard and I, and probably had a better concept of the days that had passed.

We were all back at camp except for Paul and Chuck. Paul was lucky to have Chuck as his tent mate. I learned that Paul had not been able to carry anything past Camp I. Chuck had been carrying most of Paul's things, as well as his own. I hadn't been aware of this last week when I said that Paul was losing it – mentally – and should not have been on this trip. When I get back and get the evaluation from Mountain Travel, I will have a few words to say about their screening process. Physicians should not be able to self-certify themselves as fit to undertake this type of ordeal. I'm surprised that Sergio let him go as high as he did. If Paul would've become unstable, either physically or mentally, we possibly would've scrubbed the trip regardless how good the weather might have been.

More bad news when John came back from the base camp main tent. Four days ago he had given medicine to a Peruvian man at Camp II and the man just died. John, who is a Neurologist, pronounced him dead and signed the death certificate. John had warned the man and his friends that he needed to go all the way down the mountain, but instead, they took him as far as base camp. The fools, they could've saved him! Didn't they know that when you're sick, it's time to leave? Common sense must always prevail in circumstances like this. I don't think anyone in the group wanted to reach the top more than I did, but I would have given up the summit in a minute to help anyone in our group.

After we had set up the tent for what we knew to be the last time, we sat down to a dinner of spaghetti and some freeze-dried soup. It tasted good after a long day like today. Everyone's appetite seemed to be back. I couldn't wait to finish dinner and get into my sleeping bag. I felt dirty and grimy, and I couldn't wait to take a shower, but I'd have to wait one more day. I looked up at the peak one more time before getting into the tent; it was still covered in clouds.

I'm in my sleeping bag now, listening to Wes's Bob Dylan tapes. Wes and Howard are fast asleep as is most of the camp. I should be too, but I feel I should write down as much as I can before I forget it. A look outside the window of the tent shows that it is dark and the clouds have rolled in for the night. I wish it was clear so I could see the stars like I did in Africa. I've only briefly seen the Southern Cross this trip – how discouraging.

A lot has happened since we started out; now it is almost over. I'm down to my last packet of hot chocolate and a granola bar. I'll save them for breakfast; it is better than the stuff Sergio serves us. This should last me until I can get out of the Horcornes Valley; at least it will be the last of the freeze-dried food. It will be a day of lasts: the last of the long hikes, the last night in a sleeping bag, the last of going to the john behind a rock.

Today was an eventful day. We missed the summit, traveled down nearly 6,000 feet, and saw an unfortunate and needless death. John checked Paul; he had a slight case of pulmonary edema. Chuck and Paul were the last ones into camp because Paul was moving so slow. His pack was empty; the rest of us had divided up his things among us and carried them down. We helped to pitch their tent and got them settled. Chuck is a very good and patient man for putting up with Paul; he probably deserves Sainthood. (I believe Chuck has an accounting firm in Canada.)

In a talk with Sergio, he said something which I found interesting – though I don't know how true it is. He said, "In my opinion, I feel that if weather conditions had been normal, only five of us (meaning clients, and excluding the guides) would have made the summit." He went on to say that (in his opinion) those making it would have been Wes, Howard, Chuck, Dave and me. I don't know how much stock to put into that. I tend to disagree, but what do I know? Obviously, Sergio didn't know that Howard was nearly wasted at Camp III, and Sydney, who has spent a great deal of time climbing, though sometimes slow, kept an excellent pace. I would have bet money that Sydney would have hit the summit. I also don't know why he discounted the others. As for myself, I was happy to hear that Sergio thought I would've made the summit; I felt that I could've made it, providing I had dressed properly, and had not laced my boots so tight.

I don't know if I plan to come back and try this again as Nasko plans to. I don't know what to think. I can't say I conquered this mountain just because I felt I could have, but I'm content with what I have accomplished today.

It is time to sleep; I have 22 miles ahead of me tomorrow, but at least it's all downhill.

February 13, 1990 Plaza Hotel, City of Mendoza Elevation: 2,000 feet

Due to circumstances beyond my control, I was unable to write yesterday. It was a very long day indeed. We arose late, almost 9:30 a.m., from a sleep richly deserved. The sky was bright blue with a few scattered clouds, and the sun would be shining on the camp within the hour. The summit – high above us – was still in a whiteout, and I realized I'd probably never see it again, or at least not on this trip. We ate breakfast and placed our tent in the sun to dry. As we started to pack up our gear, the same helicopter that had dropped off supplies at the new hotel landed near base camp; the body of the dead Peruvian was loaded on and flown out. It was a solemn and sobering moment for those who have not seen a lot of death.

Wes, Howard and I went for the water we would need for the long hike out. Sergio radioed for a truck to meet us at the same spot where we had been dropped off at the start of our trip, and he was having a mule sent to carry Paul out. (He is still sick, but once he gets off the mountain, he should be better in a day or two.) Our heavy gear will catch up with us later. When a few of us were ready, we were told to leave. So, at 12:15 p.m., our gear was packed, our tents were put away, and our canteens were filled. At that point Wes, Howard, Sidney, Chuck, Dave and I were off.

I left base camp with no regrets, and I felt satisfied with what I had done. After all, I was in much better shape, and I felt content with the fact that I could've made the summit had the weather been different. I looked at the mountain and thought to myself: if it hadn't been for an early winter, I would've beaten you. Once more I looked up at the cloud-covered peak high above me, turned, and proceeded to catch up with the rest of the group already moving down the trail.

The Red Sea effect of the Horcones Valley was still as breathtaking on the way out as it had been on the way in. We walked down its center; the walls reached up thousands of feet on both sides of us. Slowly but surely, the sky changed from blue to cloud-cover gray as the intermittent clouds joined together to blot out the sun. From our vantage point, it looked like the clouds had filled the valley and were pursuing us as we marched back to civilization. I wondered if the rest of our party, which was moving slower than us, had been caught in the rain.

We stopped several times to rest and refill our canteens. Sidney shared what was left of his gorp with us. Along the trail we discussed the climb, and aired our likes and dislikes. We commented on how fortunate Chuck had been. On the trip down, the airlines had lost Chuck's equipment, but as good fortune would have it, he was able to recover his own climbing gear that he'd left behind on an earlier climb. It was an extremely lucky break for Chuck.

By the time we reached the last river crossing, it was 6:00 p.m. This time the river was higher, wider, and moving much faster because of all the melting snow from the mountain. I was the last one to reach it due to a severe blister on my foot. When I crossed the river, it became very painful as small stones and grains of sand washed into the open wound; apparently, my tennis shoes weren't good enough to keep them out. On the other side of the river I cleaned the open sore the best I could, covered it, and put my hiking boots back on. There were only three more miles to hike out, but for me, it was slow going.

Once we reached the pickup point we dropped our packs. It was great to sit down after a long day of walking. It was 7:40 p.m. If Sergio's driver was on time, we would be able to sit and rest until then. It had taken us 7 hours 25 minutes to cover those 22 miles. I looked back down the valley towards the mountain. All I could see were clouds, and I knew that I would not be able to see the mountain again; but I didn't care. I felt victorious in a small way. No, it wasn't a summit, but it was a landmark for me – a new personal altitude record. I suddenly remembered a conversation Sergio and I had while waiting for the rest of the group to make their way down from Camp III. It was a discussion on what matters in life. Sergio has a semi-strange philosophy, and it is too long to write about or try to decipher; in short, I believe he is an existentialist, *but what does it matter*?

At 7:55 p.m. Sergio, Ricardo and Augusto showed up. They said the rest of the group was at least an hour behind them. The driver arrived and was so glad to see us that he hugged us all. He had heard of some of the mishaps on the mountain and was glad that we were not involved in them. I didn't write about them earlier because I used the time to document my trip, but now is as good a time as any to fill them in.

Three Austrians were camped near the 20,000-foot level of the mountain when they were hit by an avalanche. It was witnessed through a telescope at base camp; the witness said the tents were there one minute and gone the next. They are listed as missing, but presumed dead. In another situation three days ago, two Japanese climbers fell into a crevasse and froze; at least that is what Sergio tells us. No wonder this driver was glad to see us, and I was glad to see him so I wouldn't have to walk back to the Hosteria. He would take us back, and then return in an hour to pick up the rest of our group. There was no reason for all of us to wait for them.

I took one more look up the cloud-filled valley – at a place where Aconcagua would be if we could see it – but I was not to have a last view from here. I climbed into the truck with my friends and we left.

The ride to the Hosteria was very short in comparison to the long walk out. The staff was glad to see us also, not only because we had fun with them before we left for the mountain, but because we were big spenders. After dropping off our gear in our rooms, we went downstairs to eat. By this time we were starving; we wanted real, solid, tasteful food like steaks, potatoes and wine. While we ate, our main topic of discussion was the welfare of the others. It had gotten dark, and Sergio had sent the driver back to get them, but there had been no sign of them. It was almost 10:30 p.m. We volunteered to go look for them, but by that time, we were more than half in the bag. I'm sure that would've been interesting: five drunks out in the Horcones Valley acting as a search party! Sidney said, "If we got lost, who would be sent to search for us?"

The truck came back at 10:45. We were glad and grateful that – once again – we were all together. We all ran out to greet them, and carried their things to their rooms, then we ordered their dinner; once it was known that everyone was safe, the wine, beer and mineral water began to flow like it had never flowed before. We put a candle in Sidney's dessert to celebrate his birthday on the 9th, and we all sang Happy Birthday to him. One by one we took our showers; Dave was so anxious to get into the shower that he walked in with his clothes still on.

We sat in chairs, instead of on rocks, and we talked more about the climb. We talked about how sick and tired we were of freeze-dried food, but that's all you have when you're on the mountain, and it is so much easier to carry. Everyone had seconds on salads and fruits which were some of the things I really had missed.

One by one, members of the team went to bed. It had been a very long day, and my feet were still hurting. The big news while we were on the mountain was the inflation of the Austral Dollar; it went from 1800-to-1 U.S. Dollar, to 3000-to-1 U.S. Dollar. We'd had a good time that last night at the Hosteria, but now the trip was coming to a close.

At 6:30 a.m. this morning, we boarded a bus that brought us back to Mendoza and to the Plaza Hotel where the group first met over two weeks ago. Howard, Wes and I will be meeting John and Cheryl later this evening. It will be the last time that we will be together.

This brings me to the present. I'm sitting on the balcony of my hotel, I've just ordered my fourth mineral water as I sit here trying to catch up on my journal. I was just looking over the past couple of weeks.

What did I learn? Did I find the meaning of life? Would I do this again? These are all great questions, but what do I have for answers? Would I do this again – I probably would, but not on this mountain. I feel I could've beaten it, and I'm still content about that. What did I learn? I think I learned a lot; I learned that if Wes really had needed help on summit day, I would've scrapped the summit to do so. In fact, I would've stopped to help anyone on our climb – even Paul. I learned that it can get very cold up there near the top, and I learned that it is not what you're doing that makes things fun or important, but how you do it that counts.

Did I find the meaning of life? I want to say yes, but it may not be easy to explain. All of us have his or her own meaning to search for and find. I believe I may have found mine. To me, life is what you make it and how you live it. I believe that it all should be experienced and in every way. Do all there is to do – see all that there is to see – learn everything, and in all aspects become one with nature. This may sound strange to most people, but those with an open mind might agree. I feel that experiencing life in all conditions teaches us about ourselves; it reveals our inner strengths as well as our weaknesses. All the spare time I had on the mountain allowed me to think and do some soul searching; it was a chance to get in touch with myself. That is how I feel about it, not that it is going to make me a better person or anything, but perhaps it may give me a better outlook on life. That is what I have learned in the past weeks. To some, this may mean nothing, to others it may mean something; to me right now, it means everything, and that is what counts.

February 15, 1990 Somewhere over South America Elevation: 36,000 feet

I suppose I can say this trip is officially over. In the past few days I've traveled back to Buenos Aries and one-by-one said good-bye to the people I have been in such close proximity with for the past few weeks. I had that "all alone" feeling as I said good-bye to them. Howard and Wes were kind enough to pound on my hotel room door at five in the morning to say good-bye. They were off to visit other parts of Brazil. I had a great deal of fun with them and I couldn't have asked for better tent mates. I would welcome the chance to travel with them again.

I looked over some of these pages – just to pause and reflect on what I've done. All in all, it was a good time, even though we didn't summit. The people I met were great – most of them anyway.

We didn't have the family unity that I had felt on Kilimanjaro, but there was a certain closeness, and though it was deeper with certain people, I will and do miss them now.

Perhaps, someday we will even get together again. I'll land in Miami and surprise my parents who spend their winters in Naples, Florida, before I go back north to Wisconsin. They will be glad to see that I have made it back safely.

Chapter Three
Mt. Elbrus

September 1, 1991

My life has taken certain turns since I last made a journal entry. As I kept in touch with my friends from the Aconcagua climb, I had the idea to someday have a reunion for those of us who had become so close. The idea took seed, and in May of 1990, roughly three months after the Aconcagua climb, that is exactly what happened. Since most of the people attending were from the West Coast, Wes Mudge was kind enough to volunteer his house for the gathering Those who showed up at Wes's were: Howard (who had better show up since he lived only a few blocks from Wes), Sidney, John, Cheryl, Chuck and me. Everyone showed pictures and slides of the trip, and it was great to talk about different aspects of the climb. We talked about what we liked and didn't like about it. The idea that we should climb together again was even brought up, but what mountain would we try to conquer next? A number of suggestions were made, and as much fun as it would have been, we never did climb together again. During our discussions of possible destinations, Elbrus in the Soviet Union came up; after the reunion, I looked into it.

Mt. Elbrus, with an altitude of 18,510 feet, is located in the southern portion of the Soviet Union, just north of Turkey. I consulted my Mountain Travel wish book once again, and saw that they went to Elbrus, too. With over a year to train and prepare for the climb, I decided to make the climb more worthwhile by climbing it not only for myself, but for a charity as well. I instantly thought of the Muscular Dystrophy Association again, but since I had raised money for them once, why shouldn't I try to help another charity? I decided on the American Diabetes Association. Like MD, Diabetes is affecting a great number of people in the world, including my sister, Sue; my nephew, Ed; and my brother-in-law, Randy. Some of my friends and people I work with have the disease; so in the long run I would be helping friends and family as well.

I met with the Racine Chapter of the Diabetic Association, which was glad that I chose them and would be willing to work with me in raising pledges for their charity. They were much more receptive to the idea then the MDA had been when I first approached them. I explained that all funds raised would go directly to the charity, since I paid all expenses for the trip out of my own pocket. Counting airfare, visas, and Mountain Travel's bill, the whole trip would only cost me just over $5,000. The One Hour Moto-Photo of Brookfield, Wisconsin heard about what I was doing and donated film and developing cost for my photos. The ADA had pledge sheets printed, improving on the ones that I had used in the "Climb for Muscular Dystrophy."

The American Diabetes Association has a mountain to climb

American Diabetes Association.

Nick Comande, a firefighter from Racine, will be attempting to climb Mount Elbrus, the highest point i Europe, for the benefit of the American Diabetes Association. You can share in his adventure by pledging money for every 100 feet he successfully climbs.

Mount Elbrus is 18,510 feet tall and is part of the Caucasus range in southwestern Russia. Cománde will begin his ascent on September 15, 1991 and plans to reach the top by September 24.

By pledging 5¢ for every 100 feet Nick climbs, your contribution would be $9.25. If you pledge 10¢ per 100 feet, your contribution would be $18.51. It i also possible to make a flat donation to the ADA in recognition of Nick's efforts.

Wish Nick luck and pledge what you can!

American Diabetes Association
Racine Chapter
P.O. Box 1883
Racine, WI 53401
(800) 776-7118

Mount Elbrus — 18,510 foot climb, the highest point in Europe

Pledge/foot:	**.01¢**	**.05¢**	**.10¢**	**.25¢**	**.50¢**	**$1.00**
Total Pledge:	**$1.85**	**$9.25**	**$18.50**	**$46.27**	**$92.55**	**$185.10**

	Name (please print)	Address	Phone	Pledge per 100 ft.	Flat Donation	Total Pledge
1.						
2.						
3.						
4.						
5.						
6.						
7.						
8.						
9.						
10.						
11.						
12.						
13.						
14.						

I spent the two months before the climb raising pledges. If I wasn't training or working, I was going door-to-door of area businesses, and I placed my pledge sheets in all the fire houses. People once again pledged their dimes and nickels for each 100 feet I would climb. I felt I could raise

$10,000 with the Racine Chapter of the ADA helping me, so I set that as my goal. I would not be gathering pledges alone; this time, the ADA members would be out there with me.

Even my friend Howard and Wes made pledges to my cause and wished me the best of luck. Two weeks before the climb, I learned that there would be only one other member in the climbing party other than the guides; his name was Dan Weidner. It was to be a small group: Dan, the guides, and me, but I was sure it would be fun all the same. Five days before I was to leave the U.S. for the Soviet Union, war broke out.

I learned that it wasn't so much a war as a coup. As soon as I learned what was going on I notified Mountain Travel, and asked them if the trip would be canceled or not. They were not sure and needed a few days to see what had happened. Even with the shootings and small riots, the State Department did not put a ban on traveling to the USSR. I was to fly into Moscow, where all the disturbances were happening.

I was really looking forward to this trip, but I didn't want to jump into something that I couldn't get myself out of. It would be very bad if the climb were canceled because of the coup. Deep down, I felt bad for the ADA; they had given me a lot of PR, raised pledges, and given me moral support. This would all be for nothing; without a climb, there would be no fundraiser.

Just as quickly as the coup had started, it ended. The Soviet Union would be no more, and communist rule would be coming to an end. I left for Moscow on schedule.

September 18, 1991 Soviet Union Dacha

It's been roughly 17 months since I've had the honor of writing in a journal like this; I feel that it is long, long overdue. I'm having a hard time believing that I'm in the USSR. I remember how I grew up being so afraid of it: how frightening the Red Scare had been. How could I have been so wrong? Why was my social upbringing and education so misleading? Why was I led astray?

I've been in the Soviet Union for two days already, and I've learned so much. I've made new friends. I'm having a great time, and I'm about to go on another challenge named Elbrus. I left Moscow at 10:00 this morning. I won't get a chance to see any of it until I return.

I was greeted right outside the baggage area of the airport in Moscow. A tall, thin young man stood holding a sign with my name on it. I approached him and told him that I was Nick Comande. He shook my hand, and in very good English, but with an unmistakable Russian accent, said to me, "Welcome to Russia, I am Sasha, your guide." Sasha, whose real name is Alexander Morev, made me feel right at home. He took me to a car where the other half of the climbing party waited. I was introduced to Dan Weidner, a man 55-years-of-age or so; he welcomed me. He was a history teacher from Livingston, New Jersey. I apologized for my plane coming in an hour-and-a-half later than his, causing him to have to wait. We drove past Red Square, and I hoped to have a chance to walk through it before I had to return to the States.

As I rode through the city of a foreign country to my hotel, I once again saw a different way of living. Moscow, being a large city in itself, is different. I saw different makes of automobiles; architecture that is hundreds, if not thousands of years old; people selling items out of the back of trucks; and people filling up their autos from the back of tanker trucks instead of filling stations. Another sight I was not used to seeing was the Russian military; they were everywhere.

We were taken to the Hotel Ukraine, a very old and tall looking building; we checked in. Directly in front of the hotel and across the river (I didn't know the name of the river), was the equivalent of the White House in the United States. A large, white, impressive looking building that would later suit my needs.

After checking in, Sasha took Dan and me to a nearby restaurant where we met Katrina Harshan – Kat for short; her husband is the owner of Soviet Travels. It was through them that Mountain Travel booked this climb. Sasha briefed Dan and me about what we would be doing once we left Moscow and traveled south to Mt. Elbrus. Dinner was an experience for me; I shared my first bottle of vodka with my new friends and even tried caviar. I suppose it tastes good, but it tasted even better once I started the second bottle of vodka. With dinner completed, we walked back to the Hotel Ukraine for some greatly needed rest; I was feeling signs of jet lag, so I unpacked only what I needed for the night. The room had a TV tuned to CNN, so I could keep tabs on what was going on at home. I saw a couple of cockroaches in the room; that made me feel a little uneasy. I wasn't used to that back home, but I wasn't at home now, was I?

Sleep didn't come easy. I was wide awake by 5:00 a.m. and decided to take a short walk across what I later learned is the Moscow River to the Russian White House; I had something special to do there. A friend of mine, Barb Cooper, wife of fellow firefighter Mike Cooper, offered a $100 donation to the ADA, if I would bring back a picture of myself wearing jeans in front of a famous landmark. For most people this would be a simple thing to do, but for me it was difficult. I'm not very fond of denim and I hadn't worn it since 1974. Barb, who knows of my dislike for jeans, could not pass up the chance to get me into a pair; and she knew I wouldn't pass up the chance to make $100 for the ADA.

I had bought a pair of jeans back in the States, so I put them on early that morning and with the help of a local jogger had my picture taken in front of the Russian White House. I promptly returned to my room, removed that rough, blue material that was already making my legs sweat and break out, and repacked them. It is the only time I've worn them, to this day. The rest of the day was to be spent sightseeing and relaxing from the flight. I had not seen a great deal of Russia, except for what had been in the news. CNN had been covering the story of the coup just days before I left, and here I was driving past those same gold spires on the tops of cathedrals which had been standing for hundreds of years. I even had the opportunity to walk through the famous Red Square.

Earlier in the day I met Svetlana Morev, the wife of my guide Sasha. She was with her friend Helen Orzenaja, who also worked as a translator and guide for Soviet Travels while in the city of Moscow. Both women spoke very good English and gave Dan and me tours around Red Square, the Kremlin, the beautiful St. Basil's and other historical sights. For lunch and dinner we ate at restaurants with the most wonderful handcrafted artwork, murals, and paintings I had ever seen in an eating establishment. I felt as if I was eating in a museum. Strolling musicians went from table to table playing music native to their country.

When asked what we wanted to do that evening, I asked to go back to Red Square; I had become quite taken by the place, including the thousands of square feet of brick which had been marched upon by countless Russian troops over the decades. I was even in time to see the Russian version of the changing of the guard at Lenin's Tomb. Sasha and Svetlana went back to their home and left Dan and me in the custody of Helen and Katrina. It seems that Katrina has relatives in Wisconsin and has even visited my home state.

Sasha and Nikolai arrived at 8:00 a.m. on the 18th and took Dan and me to the airport for our flight to Mineral'nye Vody.

After a two-hour flight from Moscow to Mineral'nye Vody, and a two-hour bus ride, we stopped for lunch in the city of Pretegoersk. The hotel had a dining room large enough to hold several hundred people. Sasha told us we were special; we went in and sat at a table set for four. We had countless servants at our beck and call. Meals were good, but I had to learn how to say, "No sour cream," in Russian; it was put on everything. As we finished eating and were getting ready to leave, one of the hotel staff rang a bell, and several hundred people entered the dining room to eat.

I asked Sasha why we hadn't eaten with the others and he replied with a smile, "You get much better service this way."

Our bus ride to our final destination took another hour-and-a-half, with a few stops along the way. The first was at a mineral spring. We walked through a large cave, and there at the end was a large natural pool filled with milky, green-colored water. Several people were swimming in it, while others were bottling the water to take home with them.

We also picked up a woman by the name of Ludmila, who was to be part of our personal staff at the "dacha" where we would be staying. Our last stop was at a roadside market where many fruits and vegetables were bought for our stay.

Our bus driver, Freedrou, who hit *only* every other bump, drove us down the winding road of the Baksan Valley until we reached our final day's destination: a place known as " Dacha Usengi." This is located in the Baksan Valley, north of Turkey, between the Black Sea and the Caspian Sea, in the Georgian area of the Soviet Union. The dacha is a former KGB rest home and a very nice place indeed. Sasha, who had friends or family in high places, was allowed to use this for Soviet Travel's clients. I asked him if many important Russian leaders stayed here. He ran off a list of names; none were familiar to me. He wasn't sure if Gorbachev – the Russian man of the hour – had stayed here.

At the end of the Baskan Valley, out of sight from here, are the twin peaks of Mt. Elbrus. One peak is 18,510 feet, and the other is 18,450 feet. When the time comes, our goal is the western peak – or the higher one.

We are doing a number of acclimatization hikes in preparation for the climbs. Sasha and our assistant guide Nikolai Savine (Kola as we called him) took Dan and me on a short two-hour hike to limber us up for the longer ones. For a man in his late 50's, Dan stayed right with us. Just because you get a few years on you, doesn't mean that you can't climb. I learned this from the "Over-the-Hill Gang" on Aconcagua.

In our two short hours of climbing, I saw a raging river, a high altitude pasture with grazing sheep and steers, and the ridge that separates Russia and Georgia which is located at the end of the "Usengi Valley." We may get the chance to climb it if all goes well and we summit Elbrus on the first attempt. It felt good to walk on a trail I knew nothing about; it was something new and exciting, but I was glad it was a short hike. I was still suffering the effects of jet lag. This surprises me; I very seldom suffer from jet lag, and I usually have no trouble sleeping on a plane. In my excitement of traveling to Russia, though, I had not slept; instead I read an entire book. Because we were late starting our climb, we had to rush to see everything before it became too dark; we had not come prepared for darkness.

The area was beautiful; tall trees lined both sides of the river, and there were no city sounds or racing traffic – just fresh air, peace and quiet. Though we made it back safely before dark, we had to hurry, and in so doing, a blister started to form on my right heel. After a wonderful dinner of steak and vegetables I retired early to catch up in my journal and my sleep; and a welcome sleep it was.

September 19, 1991 Dacha

I feel that I should clarify some of yesterday's points. The bus ride brought us into the Baksan Valley or "Bucksan Valley" as Sasha calls it, because we had to pay a lot of bucks to get here. Actually, Baksan Valley means Sparkling Valley, and it truly is. While enroute by bus we traveled along many sparkling, crystal-clear streams which flowed into a river. We made several stops along the way to the dacha; one was to pick up some of the staff that would be taking care of things at the dacha, and the other was at a roadside market where we purchased fruits and vegetables. I tried to sleep on the bus; I couldn't, but when I finally went to bed last night, I fell to sleep almost immediately.

I awoke at 5:05 a.m. – much earlier than I wanted. I had breakfast, which consisted of cucumbers, tomatoes, a curd-like pancake, bread and jam, scrambled eggs and tea, and to top it off, a Pepsi. The soda here is very sweet, so we always cut it with water. Each meal comes with slices of cold ham, salami and cheese. There is plenty to eat so I will not starve. I brought a bottle of *Lawry's Seasoning Salt* with me; I was told the food could be bland. I shared it with my Russian guides who thought it was remarkable.

The first of our real training hikes started after breakfast. We took our bus to the Shelda Valley (Shelda means strawberry.) We hiked for an hour to an altitude of 8,000 feet and a spot called the "Smile of Shelda." That part of the valley is shaped like a smile and faces Mt. Shelda. Sasha stated that his first group of the season took two hours to get here; his second group, an hour and forty-five minutes. I hope I can summit in less time than his other groups. We reached the Smile of Shelda, which Sasha also called Miami Beach because of the small area of sand next to the river that flows by. The river is a typical glacier river – very cold, clear and very drinkable, just like the waters from Aconcagua. There are many rocks ranging in size from the minuscule to two stories high.

We rested here for half an hour and talked of the summit; we compared stories and our different lifestyles. Sasha was very open and honest when talking about his homeland, the difficulties he has in living here, and how he doesn't let things get him down. He was very knowledgeable of the American way of life, and loved to ask questions about the way I live.

Sasha also told me of Mt. Elbrus. He said the weather can get bad in the afternoon, so it is best to be on our way down by then; he would not commit us to taking the west, or the higher summit. Though it is only 20 meters higher, he said the climb is much steeper. I told him that I wanted to take the west summit and told him about my fundraising climb. Every foot higher I climb will mean more revenue for the ADA. I pulled out my red and white flag that I hoped to hold while on the summit of Elbrus and showed it to Sasha. I told him that he could help me hold it, have his photo taken with me, and show that he had helped with my cause for the ADA.

The trails today were not difficult; it was as if I were walking in the woods of northern Wisconsin, except here the rivers rage 120 feet below me, and I'm surrounded by mountain peaks. Wisconsin has nothing like this. It felt as though we were removed from civilization, but we weren't. Just an hour on foot would bring me to a well-traveled road or some type of resort, many of which doubled as ski resorts in the winter months. Even the road sounds were drowned out and could not be heard over the roar of the river. I tried something different this time. For the first time in my short climbing career, I brought a Walkman with me. Instead of being one with nature, cut off from any form of convenience, I was boogying in the Baksan with Madonna. I felt that listening to music quickened my pace. I'm afraid that listening to music while climbing will distract me from being closer to nature, and I may not do all the soul searching I did on my two previous mountains.

After the morning's hike and lunch back at the dacha, Sasha, Svetlana, Dan and I took another hike down a trail that led to a mineral spring. I had never seen one before, and I thought it would be interesting. Along the way, Sasha and Svetlana picked mushrooms of various sizes – some as large as saucers. Never before have I seen such mushrooms. During this one hike I learned more than I ever had about mushrooms – which ones were good to eat, which ones were poisonous, etc. Sasha even told me about all the different ways to prepare them. I told him that I personally didn't care for them, but would be willing to try them tomorrow. Sasha agreed to prepare them especially for me.

It took us 40 minutes to reach the spring, and it was well worth the walk. I couldn't believe it; People were sitting around a shallow cement wall, as water bubbled up from the very center of the stone and gravel. We filled our canteens and drank. I could taste the high levels of minerals in the water, and surprisingly, it seemed carbonated. Mixing it with powdered drink mix made it taste almost like soda, but with a hefty mineral aftertaste. The locals make daily visits; they believe drinking the water makes them healthier, allowing them to live longer.

We stayed and drank for a while longer before returning to the dacha. More mushrooms were picked along the way, and then I saw something on the other side of the valley that I had missed earlier: a waterfall – a 600-foot high waterfall. It was a beautiful site. At the base was a small river that ran down the middle of a quaint village of 20 or so houses – all with goats and sheep grazing in their yards. It was another way of life that I had never seen before.

We walked back to our modern dacha with marble floors, electricity, and even a rather large viewing room, as it was called. This room held 30 to 40 seats. A small television was at the front of the room. Behind the television was an enormous tapestry some eight feet high and 20 feet wide; it was all handmade. Sasha flipped a switch in another room, and the tapestry rolled up to reveal a giant movie screen. It was here, Sasha told me, that KGB members would watch illegal western propaganda films – or rather – American-made movies.

Dinner started off like any other meal with plenty of vegetables; the main course was stuffed- peppers, and Pigs in a Blanket. I was "Sayut," (full, in Russian) before I left the table. Sasha took us downstairs to a billiards table (this one was very different from the game of pool I had learned in my younger days), a 10 x 10 ft swimming pool, a sitting room and a sauna. This truly was a great place to be. An iron fence enclosed the entire compound which included a garage that held another four or five vehicles. During our stay at the dacha, we had our own bus driver, cook, and waitress. If we needed anything, all we had to do was ask. It was by far the most luxurious start of a climb I had ever experienced.

September 20, 1991 Dacha

Today was not the best of days. I awoke to find it very cloudy outside, and the room was quite cool. This place has not seen heat since I've been here, and the marble floors keep that coolness with them; but I will be fine.

Today's plan is to take a chair ride up Mt. Cheget, then hike from 9,000 feet up to 11,000 feet. Not only will this help us acclimatize, but it will also give us our first view of Elbrus – a moment I have been waiting for.

Because of the poor weather, the chairlift was not working, so Sasha changed our plans. He took us to the base of Elbrus instead, where we took a tram part-way up the rocky slopes. We then hiked to the top where we found a chairlift that works during ski season. We hiked up to 11,500 feet without packs, so the going was easy. I could finally say that I had climbed part of the mountain, but the real test is still days away. It was cold and even snowing a bit during our hike; we weren't prepared for this kind of weather. The only thing that made it tolerable was listening to music from my Walkman. Today, it was nice to listen, but tomorrow my pack will be heavy, and I may just leave it behind. I want the peace and solitude of the mountain to be with me again, and I think I would be a fool to bring the Walkman along.

Dan tried climbing with ski poles for the first time today; he liked them and will use them in the future. I had a headache when we reached 11,500 feet, but I believe it was from the cup of coffee I drank before we started out rather than the altitude. The coffee had been strong and very bad, but I drank it for the warmth. I usually don't drink coffee.

It was good to get back to the dacha for a warm meal and a relaxing evening. Dan and I lost at billiards – again. I retired early.

September 21, 1991 Priutt Refuge Elevation: 13,860 feet

According to my thermometer it is 40° degrees here at Priutt Refuge; this place could be a lot worse. I have a table to eat dinner on and a bed to sleep in. It was cloudy and rainy all the way to the mountain's base, so I could not see the summit of Elbrus. When it became colder, the rain did not stop, it only changed to snow. My pack weighed all of 60 lbs and the two-hour hike was not all that bad, but I had hoped the weather would change.

The first part of the hike was easy. We took two trams up the first part of the mountain and then rode the ski lift that wasn't operating the day before. The ground was wet and muddy. In places the rocks were slippery, and it was raining. When we crossed the 12,000-foot mark on the trail, the rain turned into snow. At least, the snow would fall off our clothing, whereas the rainwater would seep in.

I could see our goal for today vaguely in the distance; it looked like a very large, silver-colored mobile home some three stories tall with small square windows scattered across its surface. Its corners were rounded. There were electric lines running on poles up to the Refuge, but since they were broken in several areas, I was quite certain they were not working. Behind Priutt Refuge another mile up in elevation were the twin peaks of Elbrus – the highest point in Europe.

Priutt refuge and seen from above. Photo taken while returning from an acclimatization hike on Mt. Elbrus.

Near the entrance to the Refuge were scattered machine parts, rusted cans and an old discarded snowmobile that someone had been working on for the past five months. Off to the side was a small, stone building, which was the only facility, and next to that was a larger collapsed stone building that I later learned had been a shower room – until it was bombed by the Germans in WW II; it was never rebuilt.

I was greeted at the door by Olga, a husky, blond Russian woman who's English was not the greatest, but what she lacked in communication, she made up for with enthusiasm. Olga did what she could to make our stay comfortable.

The Refuge is three stories high. I have my own room, and I have my gear spread out on an empty bunk across from mine, drying for tomorrow's climb. The wind and snow blew the entire day, and I still can hear it howling on the other side of the wall. I had a small headache when we started out and I still have it; I napped for an hour before a dinner of chicken, instant potatoes, grapes, bread and cheese. Sasha pulled out a guitar. Not only did he play well, but he sang both Russian and American songs. We listened to Sasha for an hour before Kola came into the room. He said it was clear outside and we could see the eastern peak of Elbrus. I grabbed my headlamp to see my way through the dark corridors and stairways, and made my way down to the Refuge's first level entrance.

Outside, as I looked up at the mountain and the dark sky filled with stars; there lay the snow-covered, Eastern Peak of Elbrus surrounded by stars. How long I had waited to see it, but it wasn't to last. In less than three minutes, the bad weather had covered it up, and moments later it began to snow on us. We returned to the shelter of the Refuge. There was no heat, and the only warmth came from the cook stoves which we used to melt snow into drinking and cooking water. Staying at Priutt was like living in a refrigerator with the door closed and the light off; that's my best description of this place.

Sasha sang some more songs, and Dan hummed along. I went to lie down; my headache was back. I had brought my Walkman with me, so I listened to some music to relax.

September 22, 1991 Priutt Refuge Elevation: 13,860 feet

Today is Sunday, but it doesn't feel like one – it feels more like hell. What started out as a semi-decent morning sure did change. At 10:30 a.m., Sasha, Kola, Dan and I started out on a practice acclimatization hike so we could get some altitude and a chance to walk with crampons. It had been a while since I had done that. Svetlana, who has climbed Elbrus before, wasn't feeling well so she didn't go with us.

It was windy and very, very cold – my thermometer read 5° F. – so I was wearing most of my cold weather clothing. After an hour-and-a-half of climbing upward we took a break. I did quite well walking in crampons again; I only fell once and that was on the way down.

The wind never let up and the snow just kept blowing; visibility was so poor that it was difficult to see more than 30 feet in any direction. There was not much point in going on. We still had to go back, and even that would be difficult; our trail was being filled in with snow as quick as we broke it. I was cold, but my feet were warm, and unlike Aconcagua and Kilimanjaro, my boots weren't laced so tight that they cut off my circulation. I'm on my third mountain, and I have finally learned how to lace up my boots.

Suddenly, the wind stopped blowing, and patches of blue sky appeared above us. I was hoping the bad weather was finally passing. The thought of losing another summit to bad weather made me feel terrible. This time there was the pressure of a fundraiser behind me as well. Last time – on Aconcagua – it didn't matter if I reached the summit or not. This time everyone would know. The press releases and radio spots to help obtain pledges were much more extensive than my Kilimanjaro climb, and the thought of going home a failure was beginning to weigh heavily on my mind. In the very short time I've been climbing I've made one summit and lost another; this was to be my tiebreaker. But I haven't lost it yet, all I need is 15 hours of good weather to summit and get down.

We had gone far enough for the day – even though we couldn't see the refuge through the blowing snow. Both Sasha and Kola knew where they were, but it was difficult to find the trail markers. Kola, Sasha and I spread out from each other to search for the markers; Dan stayed close to Sasha. Kola quickly found one of the markers and we were on our way.

Oops! One of my crampons caught the other while I was taking a step, and I somersaulted into a knee-deep pile of snow. The trail going up had been mostly covered with ice; now – coming down – it was covered with snow. Tomorrow's summit attempt would be more difficult if we had to posthole through all this snow. Why are the mountain gods against me?

The weather has shown no signs of letting up, and the few patches of clear sky have been covered by clouds – again. Svetlana is ill; Sasha says its altitude sickness. I'd hate to see the trip get called because the help got sick. It only goes to show that the mountains play no favorites.

The only good thing that has come out of today's climb is the fact that I felt good while climbing. I felt strong, and I was able to go forward up the mountain even though it was slow going. I had been warm – maybe too warm – but I didn't want to stop to take off a layer of clothing in the wind. We climbed up to 16,000 feet, only 2,510 vertical feet from the top, plus ten hours to do it. (I don't know how far in horizontal feet).

Coming back down the mountain towards Priutt Refuge, my thermometer got so iced up that I couldn't read it; my ski poles were the same way. I couldn't adjust them for the downward slope, but I made it.

Dan was cold; he told me so. He couldn't wait to get back into his sleeping bag to warm himself up; he stayed there for hours. I hopped around from room to room, had lunch with Nikolai and Sasha, and even ran outside to snap pictures of the summits when the clouds momentarily cleared away. We will plan on trying for the summit tomorrow, just in case the weather is good. If not, we will wait one more day, but that will be our last chance. So what do we do – wait for a good day or chance it tomorrow? We will only have one shot, and the strength for only one attempt. If we wait the extra day, we will at least be better acclimatized.

4:53 p.m. Feeling nauseated; it is either caused by altitude sickness setting in or the last cup of extremely strong tea acting on my stomach.

6:30 p.m. Clouds are setting in; even if we summit in this mess we wouldn't see much. As of now the plan is to rise at 2:00 a.m. and check the weather; if it's good, we go. But, I have at least one last adventure for me tonight: a trip to the outdoor facilities.

September 23, 1991 Priutt Refuge Elevation: 13,860 feet

To make a long story short, I didn't summit, but then again nobody else did, either. I awoke from a sound sleep, hot. I had gone to sleep wearing too much clothing, and now I was sweating. I stripped down to my underwear and made myself more comfortable. I lay in my sleeping bag, unable to sleep because of the wind, howling like a hurricane. The anticipation of possibly trying for the summit had also kept me awake. I knew we wouldn't go.

At 2:00 a.m. I heard Sasha get up and check the weather; at 2:30 a.m. I heard two other climbers who had come to the refuge leave for the summit. Why would they try it in this weather? They came back after four hours; they had been stopped by high winds and blowing snow.

I tried to sleep, but all I managed to do was get a few winks. At 7:00 a.m. Sasha woke us and told us breakfast would be at 8:00; we would try hiking upward again. He warned us that it was windy – very windy – but clear outside. Sasha pulled me aside and said, "I make no promises, but bring your flag, just in case."

His words were like a little sparkle of heat; they warmed my heart. We dressed and left the refuge at 8:30 a.m. We surpassed the high from yesterday, but the going was still slow. There was still too much snow and it slowed us down, greatly. What should've taken us two hours took us more than three.

I knew already that we would not summit. I wasn't cold, and I didn't overdress like I had the day before. Instead, I was warm and comfortable and I climbed like an animal. I walked behind Sasha and kept bumping into him; I placed my boots in the same holes he had made with his. I thought to myself: each step will take me another foot closer to the summit. Many such steps would be needed, but I believed I had them in me. After four hours of climbing we still had a long way to go. Sasha said, "This is what top look likes if we were to make it there." I knew damned well we weren't going to make it there, at least not this day. We were just below the saddle and above the Rocks of Pasthukov's

We decided to take some photos and then go back. At least we would have something to show for today's climb.

The high point of the 1st Elbrus Climb. Forced to turn back due to extremely high winds and deep snow.

Sasha said, “If we are determined, we can try one more time at 2:30 tomorrow morning.” We will leave everything behind except for what we really need – no ropes or harnesses – just what we really need: a canteen of water each, some granola bars, my small pocket camera, our warm clothing, and most importantly, my flag. If there is no wind, and a lot of this snow blows away before the wind dies down, we will run up the side of this mountain.

It may have been wishful thinking on his part, but it was all we had. We made it up to 17,100 feet before going back down. I was disappointed, but the climb was not over yet. Sasha said to me, "If it wasn't for the weather, you would've summited by now." I had heard that once before and I'm not sure I believed it then. We still had one more shot at the top, and in that basket I would put all my eggs.

It is 7:00 p.m. – much too cold to write. Last summit attempt is in seven hours.

September 24, 1991

Now, to pick up where I left off; dinner was at 6:00 last night – earlier than usual; bedtime would be at 7:00 p.m., and we would rise at 2:00 a.m. to get ready for our summit attempt. Dan has already said that he was not going to go with us. I was glad because he could be a little slow. I was thinking only of myself now and the ADA; it wasn't right or proper, but that is where I stood. .

Sasha said that I was a good fast climber, and that I should go alone with Nikolai. I thought: great, it will be Nick and Nikolai on the mountain, while Sasha took Dan and Svetlana down the mountain. After all, there was no point in them staying any longer than they had to.

After dinner, Sasha played more Russian folk songs on his guitar. Together we did *On Top of Old Smoky*. We talked and compared our homelands; I learned a great deal more about Russia and the Russian way of life. Before long it was time for bed. I knew I would need my rest; I was having a hard time getting warm. Even the thought of getting into a cold sleeping bag gave me the chills.

I ran into three members of a 14-member party: two girls and a guy. They were English; and they were spending the night at the refuge. Their faces were blistered and cracked from the long hikes they had taken in the Caucasus. They asked me how the weather had been, and I answered, "Cold and windy." The gentleman with them asked if it was true that there was no central heat or electricity. I replied, "It is true; not only does the refuge not have central heat, it never has, and the electricity was knocked out by a storm last week." I didn't mean to be rude, so I asked them about their ventures, and then I excused myself and went off to bed.

I lay in my sleeping bag, trying to get it warm. From the floor above me, I could hear Sasha sing his Russian ballads about well known Russian mountain climbers. I was surprised at how much of the language I was retaining. Even the words and phrases I'd learned by tape were coming back to me. Somewhere along the way I fell asleep.

I awoke at 12:10 a.m. to hear the wind on the mountain howling louder than I had ever heard before. I prayed for a break in the wind, and when I looked through the frost on my window, I could see the moon shining; it was a full moon. Two days earlier, I had learned a little about Russian folklore; it said a full moon means a change in the weather. Well, at this point, the weather couldn't change fast enough for me. I knew it was only wind, but it would be a cold, strong wind – something I didn't need. I could see the trails of snow (more commonly known as snow flags) at the top of the Western Peak, and this peak had a really big flag being blown off.

At 2:00 a.m. Sasha came into my room; I was already awake. He said in his quiet Russian voice, "The sky is very, very clear, but it is also very windy. I guess the winds to be over 30 KPH." The temperature was at 5° F. when I went to bed, so with the wind chill, it would be -55° F. or better. Sasha said, "It is far too windy to move now; if you want to wait two or three hours you can try with Kola." The decision would be mine. It was too windy to try now. I was an amateur on the mountain, and I knew it, but I wasn't thinking just about me; I was thinking of the ADA. For every hundred feet I *didn't* climb, the pledges and donations would come up minus that amount; I owed it to them to try. I had spent $5,000 of my own money to get here and countless hours raising pledges for the ADA; I couldn't let it all go to waste. There was still a chance that the winds would die.

This day would be my last chance to summit. I didn't ask Sasha if I could spend an extra day. Based on previous discussions, I knew his answer would be no, and I knew why – we were out of supplies. I approached Kola in the room where we were to eat, and asked him if he would mind trying for the summit. He answered in his very broken English, "Why not? I like to walk." So that was that – there would be one final push to the top.

Kola and I put on our crampons in the little alcove just inside the doorway of the refuge; there were many holes in the floor from the crampons of previous climbers. We left the shelter of the refuge and entered into the blowing snows of Elbrus. We weren't sixty feet from the refuge before I started to feel the wind going through me. I thought I would be warm as long as I kept moving, but moving anywhere was going to be tough. Not only were we fighting the wind, but the snow – more than knee-deep in places. We were making no progress as the sun began to rise, shedding its light upon the mountain; now we could see the snow, blowing and drifting, all the way up to the saddle, where the two peaks go their separate ways.

The sun had turned the peaks to gold. I looked upon their beauty and forgot all about the summit; I knew it was lost. I didn't take a picture; I knew, deep down, that a picture would not capture this moment; this was a sunrise to remember!

Kola and I looked at each other, knowing that we weren't going anywhere but back to the refuge. Yes, we could have plodded through the snow, maybe even summited, but it would've taken us too long, and it would not have been the safe thing to do. It wasn't worth making it to the top, only to find out that we couldn't make it back. Climbing is about accomplishing something, not dying or losing body parts in the process.

Still, I was depressed about not being able to summit, partly because I felt like I hadn't accomplished what I had set out to do. I was going back home, and I would have to tell the ADA that I didn't summit for them. I have to live with the fact – at least I tried.

With the summit out of reach but not out of view, we decided to pack up and head down the mountain and back to the dacha. Olga cut her finger while making our last breakfast here; I retrieved my first-aid kit and astounded her with its contents. Pruitt didn't have a first-aid kit according to Olga, so I gave her everything I had in mine.

By 11:00 a.m. we were packed. I put on my crampons for the very last time, and the five of us – Sasha, Kola, Svetlana, Dan and myself – walked out into the wind and blowing snow and started down the hill. I stayed behind the rest of the group and kept turning around to look at the mountain. I hurt with each step that took me farther away from the mountain; I was doing exactly the opposite of what I wanted to do. All the way down the mountain, I tried to convince myself that it hadn't been the mountain that had beat me, but Mother Nature herself.

After half-an-hour of walking, we reached the chairlift; both the lift and the trams were working so going down was a breeze. We were back in the dacha by 1:00 p.m. and were greeted and congratulated (for what I don't know). I was in a hot shower by 1:05 p.m. Lunch was served at 2:00 p.m.; it was great to eat real food off real plates.

Sveta is feeling much better now, but she felt better as soon as she came off the mountain. She informed us that the staff was cooking Shish ka bob at 5:00 and we were invited. It was a great party with my new Russian friends. We literally broke bread together, ate, drank vodka and cognac like it was water; I even helped cook. By 9:00 that evening, after vomiting and being somewhat wasted, I collapsed on my bed where I slept until awakened the following morning.

September 25, 1991 Dacha

Today was not a very good day as we rode a chairlift part way up Mt. Cheget, and from there hiked up even higher. In the winter this is a great place to go skiing – so Sasha says, but today there was no snow and no wind. What we did have was a great view of Elbrus: the two snow- covered peaks basking in the sun with no wind to disturb them.

Mt. Elbrus as seen from Cheget 2 days after climbing off the mountain. The left or West peak is 60 feet higher.

If only we could've stayed one more day; I would've been approaching the summit now. That is behind me, but I found it difficult to enjoy the other surroundings. Opposite me was Mt. Donguz-orun; Soviet Travels runs tours along part of this traverse. Photographs were taken (Russians do not say pictures) of Elbrus. I was trying to put my defeat behind me – look at this in a positive way – and enjoy the rest of my trip.

But then it occurred to me; what if there was a way to climb the summit in a day? Kola and I formulated a plan: what if we left the dacha by 5:30 a.m. and made it to the trams by 6:00? We could ride them up to the chairlift, and take that to where the snow tractor waits to bring the refuge managers to and from the refuge; the tractor could take us to the Rocks of Pasthukov's, where we would begin our climb! Kola said I would have to pay all the operators to be at their posts early. It would cost me all together 2,000 Rubles or $75 – well worth it if we could do it.

Sasha was less than thrilled with the idea. He said that I would have to be back before 6:00 a.m. the following morning to take the bus back to Mineral' Nye Vody. Kola said we would take only what we needed. Unfortunately, there are several big "ifs" to the plan. This could only be done if the tram operators showed up on time; if the chair lift operator showed up on time; if the tractor driver was there on time and the biggest "if" of all: if the weather cooperated. Everything would depend on that; it was a slim chance, but it was a chance.

September 26, 1991 Dacha

The spirit was more than willing, the flesh was strong, but Mother Nature was not cooperating. The weather on the peaks was very bad and the winds were strong so we did not even attempt a final summit bid. I honestly can say that I exhausted all hopes and avenues of summiting Elbrus.

Sveta looked at me and said she knew what I was thinking, but I knew that it would be okay.

I must be content with what I did, and the ADA must be content with what I will have raised. I will tally up the pledge sheets when I get back and pro rate them to the corresponding number of feet. The highest point of any of my climbs on Elbrus was 17,000 feet, according to Sasha, so I will use that as my figure.

After breakfast in the dacha's spacious dining room, Sasha and Kola led Dan and me along a river for a view of another beautiful waterfall. We continued on for another two hours along a different river until we came to a very secluded spot, where we sat and had lunch. Sasha said that it usually takes three hours to hike to this place. He called me a "real animal." I believe this to be a tribute to a climber, but I had been told the same thing on Aconcagua, as well. I wondered if this was something guides tell all their clients who don't summit, just to make them feel better. Strangely, I had been praised on the last two mountains that I didn't summit.

I looked at Dan; he looked tired to me, but he didn't want to admit to it. We talked of our homelands and disposed of myths that each of us had about the other. I asked Sasha if it was true that his people were not told of America's landing on the moon. He said, "It was in our paper Pravda, but it was a small article on page four."

We enjoyed the solitude of the area for an hour, listening to the river running next to us. Before leaving I built my only cairn, which was the only thing I left behind in the Soviet Union. I wondered how long it would be until it falls or is knocked over. In the back of my mind I could still hear myself saying that I want to summit. This one was lost, but where would the next one be? I thought of flying back to Moscow the next day and calling home to let the city know how the climbed had turned out. Perhaps it would be in and out of the papers before my return. Otherwise, I would just grin and bear the outcome.

The walk out of the valley will be my last for a while because I don't know when – or if – I will climb here again. Sasha and I talked about August of next year. Staring over the raging river next to me, I looked at him and said, "We'll see what happens."

I filled my water bottles from the cool, clean waters of the river, knowing full well that it would be the last time this trip. We walked out of the valley eating raspberries off the bushes along the way.

Our final dinner at the dacha was late and full of mental confusion for me. Though I felt I was going home a failure, my time in the valley had been wonderful. I had made new friends, seen new sights and learned that the Red Scare wasn't so scary after all. Dinner was as good as always. The napkins, which had always been folded differently for each meal, were the same as our first meal, standing straight up and out of the tops of our glasses.

After dinner I asked Sasha if it would be all right for me to go into the kitchen to thank the cook for all she had done. Sasha said, "It would be a fine thing for you to do." He walked me into the kitchen, and there, seated around a very small table, was the entire staff of the dacha. There must have been nine people at a table meant to comfortably accommodate four; all-the-while, the five of us had been seated at one of the two tables in the dinning room that would comfortably seat eight. The staff was so impressed that I was asked to squeeze in at their little table and have seconds, or thirds, or anything else I wanted. I was made to feel so welcome, that Sasha left me there while he left to play billiards. Neither the staff nor I knew enough of each other's language to carry on a conversation, but we had the most fun trying.

I did my best to thank everyone for all they had done. I ate more than I needed to, and excused myself so Sasha could beat me in one last game of billiards. I'm sure there are many other things that I should write about tonight, but it is almost midnight. We will arise at 5:00 a.m. to depart at 6:00. I am tired, and I will try to remember them tomorrow.

September 27, 1991 Back in Moscow

I awoke at 5:00 a.m. and had breakfast at 5:30. I had packed everything the night before. The sun was slowly rising and I felt bad because I would be away from all this beauty by afternoon. No more peaceful hikes or crystal streams, just the smell of diesel in the air and all the accompanying sounds of mass transit. I knew it would end, but the end seemed to come so quickly. We left at 6:00 with our driver, Freedrou, who took us to the airport. Once we return to Moscow, I only will have another 24 hours before I depart.

Dan and I checked our tickets. He leaves tomorrow morning at 6.00 a.m. Our plans are to visit Arbot Street (a place to buy souvenirs.) For me, it's a last visit to Red Square.

We made a fuel stop at the same hotel we lunched at in Pretagorsk. We said our good-byes to our server, Ludmila, and our outstanding cook from the dacha. From here we could see Elbrus; it was the first time Sasha had ever seen it from the road and never with this much snow on it this early in the year.

It was hard to say good-bye in either American or Russian; I opted with the Russian phrase: "Dasvidannay" – till we meet again. I have the feeling that I may be back here in a couple of years.

Through the haze we could see the twin, snow-covered peaks, top to bottom, far in the distance. It looked like a fine day to summit for someone, but it sure wasn't going to be me. Sasha said that it was too early in the year for this much wind and snow.

Dan and I arrived at the airport and were placed in the VIP lounge. Because we were visiting Americans we were treated to whatever we wanted by the staff. I didn't even pay for my own postcards. Ten minutes before our flight was to take off, an airport official came to get us. She escorted us past all the waiting lines, through security and out to an empty bus large enough to hold a hundred people. From there we were driven out to the runway where our plane was waiting.

The flight on Aeroflot was uneventful and Katrina and Helen greeted us upon our arrival in Moscow. Because we were down to the last hours of our stay, Sasha and Svetlana took our bags to our hotel while Katrina and Helen took Dan and me souvenir shopping on Arbot Street where American money was definitely in demand over the ruble. Locals, knowing we were tourists, tried to buy anything and everything we had on us, from my used cassette tapes to my shoes and backpack. Helen acted as translator and helped me buy some things I wanted to take back home.

We were then taken to the Hotel Peking where Dan and I shared a room – not that we would be spending much time in it. Dan had to leave by 4:00 a.m. to catch his flight and mine was several hours later.

Next we were taken to a high point in Moscow at a Russian University at the end of the roadway. This look-out point was very long, and many people came here to look out over the city of Moscow. I saw artisans selling their wares and several bridal parties having their photographs taken.

Nikolai, our driver while in Moscow, drove us to a Hungarian-type restaurant, but the food was Georgian all the way. It was here that we met up with Sasha and Svetlana. In the next room there was a wedding reception going on, and our small party had a room of identical size. In our group there was Sasha and Svetlana, Nikolai, Helen, Katrina, Dan and myself. There were many bottles of wine opened that night, but only because there was only one bottle of Vodka. Everyone made a toast, but the one Kola made stood out. He said in his broken English, "Because our group is so small, we are not tour guides and clients … we are closer than that … we are friends."

It was a touching moment. Dan asked the guides to sign a wine bottle for him, and I had the climbers of the group sign my journal. With each course of our meal, a new toast was made – another local custom I had learned. My toast was fast and off the cuff, but nevertheless it was poetic. I said:

I've leaned many things
And made new friends;
But I'm sorry to say
It's nearing the end.

But there will be a time
When we gather like this,
When I come back here
To re-climb Mt. Elbrus

It received a cheer, and made Svetlana cry. After dinner she confided to me, "Out of all the clients we've had, I will miss you the most." It was a nice thing for her to say, and Sveta's voice was always so soft and sweet. It was a grand time for everyone. Nikolai and Kola were the only two who did not speak English, so everything was translated for them so no one would be left out. The only time Russian was spoken was when I would try to speak it, and then we would all laugh.

Dinner ended near 10:00 p.m., and good-byes were said all around. It was a very sad event. Sasha drove Helen, Katrina, Dan and me back to Red Square so we could walk through it one last time. He waited for us on the other end of the square near St. Basil's where a teenager had landed his plane several years back.

Both Dan and I wished we had more time to spend in Russia to travel a bit. We caught the last Changing of the Guard at Lenin's Tomb that evening and walked to where Sasha was waiting. Dan was ready to go back to the hotel; he was tired. I didn't want to leave, so Katrina and Helen said they would walk me back to the hotel while Sasha drove Dan back.

I quickly agreed to the idea; it would give me another chance to walk Red Square and see some more of Russia by night. For some reason, walking Red Square was my favorite thing to do in Moscow; this place was so big and prestigious.

Helen, Katrina and I walked all the way from the square to the hotel; it wasn't a long walk. I didn't want to go back to the room, I wanted to paint the town "red," but at 11:00 p.m., everything started to close down.

As we walked in the cool night air to the Peking Hotel, Katrina, Helen and I made more comparisons to our country. Katrina had been to the States on several occasions, but Helen had only been as far as Germany.

At the doors of my hotel, I said good-bye to both Helen and Katrina, and thanked them for their hospitality and kindness. Helen and I agreed to be pen pals or "pen friends" as they say in Russia.

I stopped at a phone booth to make a couple of quick phone calls back to the states. Their phone booth took my Visa card. Twenty-six minutes – and $460 later – my family and friends back home knew that I was safe; they also learned the outcome of my climb.

I tried to be quiet entering the room so as not to wake up Dan; he had his alarm set for 3:30 a.m. Sasha was to pick him up at 4:00. That morning, Dan and I exchanged ideas for next year. He said, "Nick, you're a heck of a guy, and I'd go anywhere with you." I thought it was a nice thing for him to say. With that he left, and I went back to sleep with a 6:00 a.m. wake up call.

September 28, 1991 On British Airways flying home.

I awoke an hour before my wake up call. I was showered and packed by 5:30 a.m. Sasha was not coming to get me until 8:30, so I went for a walk in the cool, damp air. It was my last "red" morning, as I called it. Even though the skies were gray, I was still blue with depression about missing the summit. There were a number of people on the streets – many walkers and joggers getting their daily exercise before going to work. How similar this is to life back home; and to think that I was taught to be afraid of these people and their way of life.

Sasha met me just as I was walking back into my hotel; we had breakfast in its commissary. It was the first time I had ever eaten hotdogs for breakfast. Though it is common in Russia, I don't think I could do it regularly.

With bags in tow we left the hotel and met Nikolai, our driver from yesterday. He was with Kat and Helen. Kat had other things to do today and would be unable to tour with me this morning, but she would never forgive herself if she did not say good-bye, and she had crossed town just for this. I made a joke about her not having enough pull with the company to take the day off. She laughed and said she would talk to her husband (the owner of Soviet Travels) about it.

Sasha, Nikolia, Helen and I went to do a little sightseeing before I had to leave. As a treat, Sasha took me to the oldest fire station in Moscow; it was well over a hundred years old and reminded me of my own Station 5 before it had been remodeled. Sasha showed his tourist guide card to one of the members of the station and they let us enter. Apparently, this guide card of Sasha's is very influential; as he told me it opens many doors, but it is very difficult to get.

Since the fire service in Moscow is run by the military, I was not allowed to take photos. But I was shown everything, and was allowed to ask anything I wanted. I noted some of the differences in the living conditions of the station. There were no frills in this station – the mattresses on the beds were almost non-existent, all the plates on the table were chipped, and the station was in dire need of painting.

Similarly, the fire engines stood ready with their doors open, and the fire gear of each man lay beside it ready for action. Useless piles of paperwork stood waste high in the office, and everyone looked busy training.

It was well worth the visit, and I thanked Sasha for taking himself out of his way to make me feel at home. We did some last minute souvenir shopping before taking a slow ride to the airport. Svetlana met Sasha, Helen and I at the airport. We had a long lunch while we recapped the highlights of the trip, and talked about the possibility of someday coming back.

We walked up to the security gate and Sasha stopped and said, "This is the end of the border for us." I said, "W-h-a-t?" Sasha replied, "We can go no further; we will say goodbye here." I was shocked; I thought there would be more time for me to say the things I wanted to say, but there wasn't.

Sveta already had tears in her eyes. Again she said, "Out of all the rest … I will miss you most." She then gave me a pin from Sasha's collection; translated into English it read: "Fireman of Excellence." Sasha gave me a big hug. A handshake wouldn't do, he said. Helen also hugged me, and I told her I would write so she could learn more American words and some slang. I was still in shock about having to split up so quickly. I said, "Thank you!" and turned to leave. My last glimpse of my three comrades was of them walking through the door of the terminal. Suddenly, I felt alienated in a strange place without them, but that was all right; that is how I entered this country, and that is how I will leave it.

Memories of this trip will linger for a long time. While I failed to reach the summit, I succeeded in making new friends, traveling to a country that was once taboo, and learning that it isn't. I jumped into the red tide, and saw that it was also blue and white. What is the only difference between Russia's way of life and our own? They are striving to catch up to ours. I will miss my friends, but it is okay; they will miss me, and that is what friendship is all about.

As I sit on this crowded plane, I think of the openness of Red Square, my new friends that I will miss, and all the work that I will have waiting for me when I return home. Pledge sheets must be collected and tallied, letters must be sent out, and a final report must be made to the ADA. I wonder how much money I raised for them, and how much I lost by not reaching the summit? I'll find out soon enough.

The flight attendant just brought me a second glass of orange juice, something I missed very much during my stay in the Soviet Union. It's funny how some things are taken for granted and unappreciated until they are gone. Perhaps this trip taught me a little more than I thought.

October 1991 Racine, Wisconsin

I returned from Russia to find that my fundraising capabilities had fared better than I had on the mountain. After I collected the pledge sheets I had distributed, and the Racine Chapter of the American Diabetes Association brought in their pitiful few, we had managed to raise $8,755. I brought in over $5,000 of that total with the rest divided amongst the other seven or eight board members. I have to say that the other members of the board did not share the same sense of enthusiasm as I did when it came to raising pledges. Think how much money might have been collected if they had collected as many pledges.

Here I had spent all my money to pay for the climb, train for it, go out and get signatures on pledge sheets. I had collected most of the money for the ADA, and they in return, had not shared the same conviction. It was disheartening, and I felt let down, but on the bright side it was far better than what I had done for the Muscular Dystrophy Association. This time, I raised almost $4,000 more.

Because so many more pledges were collected, it took that much longer to collect the money. Everyone on the ADA board would be in charge of collecting the money from those they had signed up. Since I had signed seventy percent of the pledges, it would take me the longest time to collect all the funds. It was a good feeling to finally be finished with that job, and it was a good feeling knowing I had once again helped a Charity; it gave more purpose to my climb. I could look back and say, “No, I didn’t summit, but the ADA is much closer to their own summit.” This mountain was not the highest I have climbed, but it was a new all-time high for me in fundraising.

Chapter Four
Mt. McKinley

(The dream of Denali, or was it really a nightmare)

Once I had finished collecting for the American Diabetes Association, it was time to set my sights on something else. I still had the climbing bug, and the bite only seemed to get worse after rereading *Seven Summits* by Bass. I wanted another mountain; one I would have to work for. Elbrus was great, but it was a posh trip compared to Aconcagua. What I needed was an expedition. So I looked at the famous Seven Summits. The highest peak on the seven continents of the world.

I didn't want to go back to Aconcagua, so I looked into the other famous seven summits. I'd done Kilimanjaro, and Aconcagua just didn't feel right at this time. Elbrus was slated for August of this year, and Kosciusko in Australia, which is only 7,316 feet high, wouldn't be enough of a challenge; it would take me longer to fly there than to climb it. Vinson (in the Antarctic) was too expensive, and Everest was *way* too expensive. I also didn't have the two months time it would take to go climb it, nor did I have the skill or ability, yet.

This left only one of the seven: Mt. McKinley. McKinley is located in Alaska and is the highest peak on the North American continent at 20,320 feet high. Mt. McKinley (or Denali, as it is called by the natives) was first climbed in 1913. I checked with Mountain Travel to see if they still ran climbing trips to the area. I learned that, not only did they have trips to McKinley, but they now were called Mountain Travel-Sobek. They sent me the necessary paperwork and trip itineraries in November of 1991. After reading the information, I decided this would be my next trip.

Because McKinley's location is so far north, and is colder for longer periods of time, this climb possibly could be very brutal, should the weather be unforgiving. The trip itinerary explained the numerous possibilities of delays and hardships, but its description of the climb made it sound as though my chances of reaching the summit of McKinley were much better, even with weather delays, than with Aconcagua.

The itinerary also stated that this trip was dangerous; you had to be prepared, both physically and mentally, to climb it. Preparation couldn't have been stressed more. The people of Mountain Travel-Sobek wanted you to know, for certain, that you wanted to climb this mountain. Simply being in top shape would not be enough; you had to be of sound mind. (This should be the case on any mountain.) Since I wasn't climbing McKinley for a charity, I wouldn't have the added pressures of making it to the top; I would just have to focus on the climb and not worry about what would happen if I didn't summit.

Even if I were to summit McKinley, it would not be a new altitude record for me (I had been higher on Aconcagua), but it would be a challenging and respectful climb to add to my meager list of achievements. I sent in my check and climbing resume to Mountain Travel-Sobek and was accepted to go to Mt. McKinley in May of 1991.

The one good thing about this trip – expense-wise – was that it was the closest to home. I was spending only hundreds of dollars to get there instead of thousands. The money I saved in air-fare was put towards upgrading my climbing equipment; after all, this was going to be a cold mountain to climb. I met the rest of the members of the group in Anchorage at a place called Hillcrest. All nine clients were to stay at this bed and breakfast with an exorbitant number of bedrooms; we would share the three bathrooms. It was crowded, but nothing we couldn't live with, and once we were on the mountain, we would be much closer. The members of the group were from various parts of the U.S, except for one man named Hank, who was from Holland.

There was one woman on the trip; her name was Susan Babcock. The previous month she had been on a cruise to the Antarctic looking for unnamed peaks to climb, and she wanted to look at the penguins. By chance, a couple of friends of mine, Wes and Howard from San Diego (my Aconcagua tent mates) had also been on the boat. Susan has done some extensive traveling in the last year, and by now, has probably been to three of the four corners of the world.

Rodrigo Mujica, our trip leader, wasted no time getting down to business. He had us take out all our climbing gear so he could check it out and make sure it was satisfactory. Rodrigo, who has climbed McKinley before, is well aware of all that could happen up there; he told us what we could leave behind and what we should replace before we go.

There was a sporting shop, specializing in climbing gear, within walking distance of Hillcrest where many of us purchased lengths of rope for tying in our sleds, caribiners and other extras Rodrigo said we would need; I had spent another $100 before leaving the shop.

After the gear check was completed, we were free to have dinner. Though it was getting late in the evening, the sun was still high in the sky; it would not get dark until 11:00 p.m. For dinner I joined three other members of the group: Harrison Price, an attorney from Texas, Neal Swann a facial plastic surgeon from California, and Bob Elias from California. Bob, who likes to be called Elias, was planning a trip to climb Everest. The McKinley trip was just for practice. We walked the cool streets of Anchorage to a restaurant recommended to us by Rodrigo. During dinner, we discussed past climbs and talked about the mountains we didn't climb.

We stopped off for a nightcap at Anchorage's famous Chilkoot Charlie's bar. I didn't stay long because I wanted to get back and make sure I would be set for tomorrow; I felt a little tired, like I had a cold coming on.

May 10, 1992 (Mothers' Day) Base Camp Kahiltna Glacier Elevation: 7,200 feet

I awoke this morning knowing that this would be the last time I would be sleeping in a bed for a while. By late this afternoon, we will all be on the mountain. We gathered for a group photo in front of the B&B to kill the time while we waited for our bus to pick us up. It was also during this time that I learned that even though I had signed on to this trip with Mountain Travel-Sobek, the guides of another company would be taking us up the mountain.

At 11:00 a.m. a small, white school bus picked us up for our journey to Talkeetna. It had five rows of seats but the last 2 ½ were filled with our climbing gear. Our guide, Rodrigo, took his personal vehicle. We made one stop for lunch along the way and I bought a newspaper, the *Anchorage Daily News*. The headline read, "Planes collide near McKinley." Apparently, two small aircraft – on tours around Denali – clipped each other's wings. Both aircraft sustained minor damage and both made it back to Talkeetna safely.

The planes were of the same size as the ones we would fly in on. After reaching the airport in Talkeetna, we dropped off our gear in front of Doug Geeting Aviation and walked a short distant to the Talkeetna Ranger

Station. Talkeetna is not very large at all; it looks like it is right out of *Northern Exposure*, but it's considerably smaller. In the rangers' station, we all gathered to sign in and let the rangers know that our group was going up the mountain. We also watched a video about the mountain that explained common hazards and told us how to avoid accidents while we were there.

The video had been made in several different languages, including Korean. According to a park ranger, the Koreans are the most careless. I thought to myself, why would anyone want to do anything careless on a mountain? There is already a certain risk, why add to it?

We all walked back to the airport and proceeded to put on our cold weather gear. From here we would fly to our base camp at Kahiltna Glacier. Because the planes were small, we could only be flown in three people at a time. While waiting my turn, I made a fast phone call home to wish my mom a happy Mother's Day; later I took photos of one of the planes involved in yesterday's incident over the mountain. I was on the last plane with Lionel, Harrison and John Alexander.

Our plane was deep red in color, and equipped with skis for landing in snow and wheels for landing on runways. The door pulled off, which made getting in and out much easier, and our gear was stowed in a cargo area that rested below the cockpit of the plane.

Just before we were to board the plane, John told us that he had decided not to go. He had been talking to Lionel for the past half-hour and, for whatever reasons, he preferred to stay behind. John had been to Denali once before and didn't summit. It was unfortunate that he wasn't going with us, but he wished us luck. With that, we boarded the plane and left on a 30- minute flight to Denali base camp.

The flight was smooth, but it opened my eyes. In the distance – surrounded by numerous peaks of various sizes – towered Denali; its rugged peaks reached into the sky like jagged knives all covered in snow. Some were covered with so much snow that I couldn't see any rock below them, and I wondered how we were going to land a plane in the middle of that.

As we closed in on Denali, the peaks of the smaller mountains were increasingly closer to the plane. The pilot pointed out the location where the two planes had collided yesterday. We made a sharp turn around one of the peaks, when suddenly, there before us lay base camp.

In the middle of a wide valley, in a sea of white snow, were tracks where previous planes had landed and taken off. Small dark shapes could be seen milling around; these were the other climbers in our group, and those of other parties, on their way to climb the mountain. All totaled, there were up to 50 people in base camp. I could see a trail leading off towards, and around, one of the smaller peaks. I guessed this to be the trail out to Camp I. Outside of the base camp there were no marks in the snow except holes from the crevasses. The rest of the area was pristine.

The pilot landed smoothly on the runway of snow. It was my first such landing and I was thrilled and excited to be back on a mountain. We collected our gear, found Rodirgo and started building base camp; it was high above the other campsites, and looking over them. By the time we flew in, half of the tents were all ready set up and a kitchen area was cut into a snowdrift. I learned that I would be sharing a tent with Chris, the other assistant guide, and Hank, the gentleman from Holland. Hank spoke English very well; we would have no difficulty communicating.

As I looked out over the Kahiltna base camp, I saw a number of bamboo poles with flags tied to the top of them. They were mostly six-feet-high and they marked the spot in the snow where other climbers had buried supplies until they returned from the upper camps. At the bottom of the base camp, not far from the make-shift runway was a red and white tent where the camp manager lived. This is where the short wave radio was kept and communication made with the ranger station back at Talkeetna.

Tonight's dinner was spaghetti; it was good and I was hungry. I was glad we weren't starting on the freeze-dried stuff yet. Next, we all shared tales about our past adventures. Susan told me more about her trip to Antarctica, and Hank told us about Kasurbraum. Elias was thrilled at his upcoming trip to Everest and probably was the most enthusiastic of us all.

There were some low-lying clouds around the peaks of Forraker and Hunter so you couldn't see their peaks, and from where we were in the valley, we couldn't see the peak of Denali, either.

I was not feeling my best, so I retired to my tent. I found it difficult to write so I made short the day's entry in the journal.

I was glad to be back on a mountain, but physically, I just wasn't feeling my best.

May 11, 1992 Base Camp, Kahiltna Glacier Elevation: 7,200 feet

The conditions in the tent are cramped; it makes it difficult to write. This three-man tent is not as large as the one I shared with Wes and Howard on Aconcagua. The quarters are very close and there is no free room. If one person in the tent moves, the other two occupants will know. I slept well last night – nice and warm in my sleeping bag with only one pee break during the night. Hank woke me only once to stop my snoring. I woke up refreshed, but I was coughing quite a bit.

After breakfast we learned how to rope up properly and tie sleds into them so we can haul our first cache to Camp I. It should've been a great hike through the snow on this perfect looking day, but it was not to be.

As we prepared to leave camp with our first haul, we were stopped by the camp managers. The worst storm in ten years was heading our way. On Rodrigo's orders, we stopped what we were doing and started to build windbreaks around the tents. Using a lightweight aluminum saw, we took turns cutting out blocks of snow, and carried them to a spot where a wall would be built. Eventually, all the tents would be surrounded, and the wall would prevent the wind from blowing directly onto the tents, making them that much warmer inside.

The wall was as high as the roof of the tent and would last us throughout the storm. Since the storm was supposed to last until Friday and it was only Monday, we would be cooped up for the next few days. The thought of delays depressed me; they would really cut down the chances for a slow acclimatizing climb to the summit.

At noon the sky was still clear blue with the storm coming in from the west over the Bering Sea. I finally stopped thinking about myself and started thinking about the people at camps between 14 and 17,000 feet; I wondered if they knew the storm was coming?

Once the camp was secure, Rodrigo showed us how to use ropes in rescue and made us practice with belays and ice ax arrest. He wanted to make sure we knew how to do it and made us understand why we were doing the things we did. To date it was the most formal training I've had on a mountain for rescue of any kind, and it suddenly gave much credit to those who have already climbed this mountain.

It started to snow about 2:00 p.m. The winds have not yet arrived, but there is plenty of time for that. The camp is well protected and Roger, Neal and Elias started work on a large snow cave. They said it would be warmer and more comfortable than their tent, which I firmly believe.

A lot still can happen on this trip; we have just begun. Just because one day is lost doesn't mean that all will be. I've had bad weather on mountains before and I'm hoping that I'm not weathered out of another. No one has ruled out the summit. While I'm in the tent tonight I will try to write some postcards, but they will be brief. The group here is okay, but there were never any formal introductions made. Right from the start, I felt like this trip was rushed; we were rushed to have our gear checked, rushed to go buy supplies, rushed to get here, and now that we're here, were not going anywhere.

I'm still coughing quite a bit and I hope it passes soon. Since I don't feel much like writing, I will end this entry now.

May 12, 1992 Base Camp, Kahiltna Glacier Elevation: 7,200 feet

More than three feet of snow fell during the night. With visibility down to 70 feet, no one is going anywhere. Last night, I was warm in the tent; in fact, I was too warm. I woke up during the night and was sweating profusely. I stripped down to my shorts and lay in my sleeping bag listening to the occasional avalanche.

The sound of them started with a sharp break or crack and was followed by a rumbling that sounded more like a jet flying overhead than tons of snow falling down the side of a nearby mountainside.

At 8:00 a.m. I climbed out of the tent to see if I could see the other side of the valley. I cleared the snow off the top of the tents while Rodrigo heated water for breakfast. Neal was visiting a Korean camp, which was on the hill below us; one of their parties fell some 900 feet down a slope above Camp I. He has a large hematoma to the head and is unconscious. Neal doesn't think he will make it if he can't get him to a hospital relatively soon. There is no chance of the weather breaking for several days, so even a helicopter can't fly in to pick up the injured man. There isn't much I can do here except sit, wait for dinner, and hope the best for those injured and stranded above us at higher camps.

There is talk of making another snow cave or igloo. Three members of the party slept in it last night and said it was warm and much roomier than the tents. Why should we have to stay crowded up in tents when we don't have to? If we are going to be stuck here for a few more days, why not be comfortable?

After breakfast, Chris and I took a walk to the other camps. No one is to leave camp alone – just in case you step upon a hidden crevasse. We felt our way down to the airstrip and dug out the landing markers; if a plane were to come in, the airstrip would be visible from above.

We then visited the latrine at base camp. Right out in the open, over a pit at the end of the airstrip, is a large wooden box with a lid that lifts up. It serves as a toilet. Here you can sit and watch the planes take off and land as you're busy doing your duty. The next person in line stands a couple of hundred feet away to give the user some privacy.

To help pass the time, Chris and I spoke to several members from other camps. When we returned to camp, I dug out my backpack and sled so they would not be too deeply buried when the time came to use them.

8:38 p.m. The temperature is 20° F, the wind has picked up and the latest weather report says there are two more fronts coming in. The snow on the path from the tents to the latrine is nearly four-feet deep; they have to be walked periodically to keep them clear. We take turns cleaning the snow off the tops of our tents every hour so it doesn't build up and collapse them. There is no sign of a break in the clouds and it now has been snowing for the last 30 hours. When it's falling heavily you can't even see the other side of the valley and everything is covered in white.

I met some French people from Quebec: five guys and a girl who are climbing the same route. (The normal route) The snow is so deep that one of the guys was doing what looked like the butterfly stroke. It's that deep. The snowflakes are smaller, but very consistent.

The Korean is in his tent, alive but unconscious. We learned that he had been the fourth member of their team to repel down the rope when it broke. We also heard they were trying to establish a new technical route to the top of Denali.

On a personal note, I'm a bit disappointed. I know it's early in the trip, but I don't like to just sit here. Rodrigo said, "We still have plenty of time to summit." I hope so. He also said that he had never seen this much snow at base camp before. I'm coughing a lot yet, and I've had several cold sweats throughout the day.

Dinner was a specialty of Rodrigo's – tortillas; I ate them but I wasn't very hungry. I've done so little while I've been here. (Short of clearing snow off the tents.) On my other trips, I at least had a couple of practice hikes by this time. I spoke to Bob Elias during dinner, his trip to Everest leaves this August 15th. He will be climbing with 11 or twelve other people including Sergio-Fitch Watkins, my guide from Aconcagua. Elias is anxious to get moving, and – in my opinion – is the most enthusiastic

I should mention that there is more room in the tent tonight. Chris, the assistant guide, moved into Eric's tent with him because the others were sleeping in the snow cave. It spread everyone out a bit, but we'll all be back together when we move up to our next camp. Because of the extra room, it is much easier to write. I was able to spend some time talking to

Hank who is from Holland; he works at some kind of print shop and has scaled some of the higher peaks of the Himalayas. He is a much more accomplished climber than I.

The only good news for today is that we will try a small carry tomorrow if there is a break in the weather, or perhaps we'll move the entire camp in one day – to make up for the lost time. Either way, I'll feel like I'm getting something done. The wind is picking up and it is getting cold in the tent. I'm going to brush my teeth now and try to get some sleep.

May 13, 1992 Base Camp, Kahiltna Glacier Elevation: 7,200 feet

I was awakened by the sound of a helicopter at 6:15 this morning; the sound of the rotors cutting through the wind sounded extremely close to our camp, but in reality it was landing 300 feet away between the runway and the other tents at base camp. With these images running through my head I suddenly realized it was clear outside. I wanted to stick my camera out the door of the tent to take a picture, but I knew that the walls around the tent were too high to see over without getting out of the tent all together.

Not only did I not feel like getting dressed, I didn't even feel like getting up. I was coughing and running a low-grade fever; I was not feeling at all well. I lay in my sleeping bag listening to the muffled voices of the other campers and waited to hear the helicopter take off. Within a matter of minutes of landing, it did just that.

I could tell by the brightness on the other side of the nylon tent that it was very clear outside and the sun was shining. I lay in my sleeping bag and stayed there until breakfast at 9:00 when I slowly pulled on my clothes and managed to drag myself out of the tent. The sun was bright and the reflection off the snow made the area a comfortable temperature, but it was still a sunburn hazard to exposed skin.

I looked over the entire base camp area; all the markers – laid by climbers already on the mountain above us – were completely buried with snow. I remembered that some of the markers were over six feet tall; now there was no sign of them. It would be difficult to find your own cache if you didn't know exactly where it was. The area was a sea of unbroken white, except for a few trails between some of the camps and the giant circle caused by the wind of the landing helicopter. The snow-covered valley was all virgin.

By chance, I had my camera with me when the first plane from Talkeetna arrived. The runway markers were still buried under several feet of snow, but that didn't stop the pilot from coming in. As soon as the skis hit the ground, the plane cut into the snow like someone diving into the water, and it didn't stop sinking until the top of the snow had reached the fuselage. Plumes of snow were blown up by the wake of the propeller until the plane gradually came to a stop. A second plane came in minutes later and the same thing happened. The snow will have to be packed down on the runway before anything will be able to fly out.

After breakfast we went out to drop off a load of supplies at our first camp. We were divided up into teams of three and tied to a rope; I was second behind Lionel, and Eric was tied in behind me. Not only would this be the first time I'd walked tied into a group of people, but it was also the first time I'd walked with snowshoes. Because of all the freshly fallen snow, they would be needed.

The weather was beautiful, and like Aconcagua we walked along a valley with peaks towering over us on both sides.

In the valley in route to Camp 1. Freshly fallen snow covered the peaks covering crevasses and causing avalanches in the surrounding areas.

The differences were that we were roped together in case someone fell into a crevasse; the color was not brown, but white, with new layers of pristine snow as far as the eye could see. There was the occasional avalanche. I had never seen one in person before, and I found it truly amazing how tons of snow would suddenly decide to let go its grasp from the side of a mountain and tumble down.

The different teams took turns leading the way and breaking trail; we did this to share the work of stomping in the deep snow with our snowshoes. I thought once we got moving, I would feel better, but I didn't. Halfway to Camp I, I realized I was sick. I couldn't stop coughing, and I couldn't catch my breath. The weight of my pack, which wasn't really that heavy, was draining me completely. Lionel kept telling me to keep up with him so he wouldn't drag me on the rope.

I believe that Lionel, who was much taller than I, didn't realize that it took three of my steps to his two. By the time we reached Camp I, we quickly buried our gear and headed back to base camp.

On break while on a supply drop to Camp one.

I was exhausted and spitting small amounts of blood – probably from my throat being so raw from all the coughing I was doing. I knew it wasn't pulmonary edema; I was way too low for that, or so I thought.

We made it back to base camp in record time. I was struggling to keep up with Lionel and I could tell from the tone of his voice that I was getting on his nerves a little. By the time I reached base camp, I realized that this trip was over for me. I was sick and I didn't think things would get better as I went higher. I will see how I feel in the morning and then make a decision. The worst that can happen is that I go down and get better and lose the $3,500 I have invested in this trip. If I continue, I'm then a hazard to the other members of the climb. I don't think it would be right for me to take that chance and ruin their excursion. I spoke to Rodrigo about my health and shared my thoughts about not going up with the rest of the group tomorrow. He told me, "Wait and see how you feel in the morning before making a decision." I just took a couple of Ibuprofen, and I'll go to sleep. It hurts to write now, and it is too depressing.

May 14, 1992 Base Camp, Kahiltna Glacier Elevation: 7,200 feet

Last night I had a difficult time sleeping. Hank, on the other hand, slept soundly and did not have to wake me to stop my snoring. I was still coughing and my ribs were hurting. My throat was raw and I was still running a fever. I would tell Rodrigo when I saw him that I would not be going up with him and the others. As much as I wanted to summit, it would not be a wise decision. From the start of my first mountain I always said, "Common sense dictates all." I didn't want to get sicker, and I surely didn't want to ruin the trip for anyone else by getting incapacitated higher up.

When the call for breakfast came I climbed out of my tent with the others. I wasn't hungry and I didn't feel very well from the lack of sleep. I told Rodrigo that I was planning to go down today, instead of going up – the direction that brought me here in the first place. Rodrigo said that it would be for the best. If I became sicker higher up the mountain, it would only make things more difficult.

I felt bad for not being able to continue, but deep down I knew it was the right move. As camp was being packed up for the move upward, I said good-bye to the others in my group. I gave my thermos bottle to Hank because his was leaking; no reason to take mine down if someone else needed it. I also gave him my extra socks (he had forgotten his) and I gave my water bottle insulator to Chris because he didn't have one. Even if I wasn't going to the top, I could, at least, make it a little easier for those who were going.

I said my good-byes to the rest of the group. When I told Eric that I was going down, he told Rodrigo that he was going to go down, too. Eric confided in me later in the day that he really didn't want to climb Denali and that he hadn't even paid for the trip; some family member had paid for it.

The rest of the group packed up the camp, and supplies were buried here for their return. Eric and I waited for the planes to come and drop off other climbers. We would then board them for the return trip. As I waited, I continued to cough and spit up little drops of red into the snow next to me.

With the sun shining, the plane ride out was just as beautiful as the one coming in, but clouds in the distance would end that soon. Just after takeoff I could see the rest of the group spreading out along the trail headed to Camp I; they looked like little black dots all in a row, marching on a vast sea of white. I silently wished them good luck.

We landed back in Talkeetna and retrieved the gear we had stored at the airport. My gear was in a bag with Harrison's. I left him a Granola bar in his pocket in case he needed a snack after his long journey up the mountain. Eric and I left the airport and stopped at the ranger station to let them know we were off the mountain. Once we learned that we wouldn't be able to return to Anchorage until tomorrow, we booked a room for the night at the Historic Fairview Inn. I bought a newspaper to find out what had happened in the rest of the world during my short stay on the mountain. It said that the Korean man, who had been flown off by helicopter yesterday morning, would make a complete recovery, and – adding insult to injury – a record number of people summited Mt. Everest in a single day as the temperature on top reached 32° F.

The day in Talkeetna was long. I have never been one to sit in a bar drinking for no reason, and even though I was off the mountain, I still didn't feel well. There was not much to see, and the upcoming Miner's Day Celebration was still two days away. I really didn't feel like staying around for it. As quaint and rustic as the little hamlet was, it wasn't for me.

The following day, the same bus driver who had brought us here came and picked us up in a station wagon; there was no need for the bus with only two people. He brought us back to Anchorage but was nice enough to make a quick stop so I could see the mountain one last time. There was no missing this mountain. As the wind blew snow from its peak, it stood tall through the clouds.

I left Anchorage the following day and flew home to Wisconsin. I had bronchitis, and inside of two weeks I was feeling like my old self.

I eventually heard how the rest of the members had made out on the mountain. Susan Babcock had a bad ear infection and came down early as well, but I give her much credit. She faired better than I did. Neil Swann made it as far as the summit ridge, and the rest of the group walked upon the summit. According to Harrison Price, the weather on the summit was good, and Roger even made a phone call with his satellite phone. I give a great deal of credit to all of those in the party who made it. It has always been said that Denali is a tough mountain to climb, and they did it with bad weather against them. A lot of snow had fallen and new trails had to be broken. I can only say, "I wish I could've been with them."

Chapter Five
Mt. Elbrus

(Revisited)

With Denali's failure behind me, it was time to get my mind set on a more positive note. Since February of 1992, I was in fax contact with my past Russian guide, Sasha, back in Moscow. Sending faxes was not as easy as it is today. Since I didn't own a fax machine, I resorted to sending them through a local Econoprint. Cindy and Kerri – I'm sure – were tired of constantly trying to send them for me. They resorted to setting their fax machine to send my faxes in the wee hours of the morning. This was the only time they could get them to go through.

Sasha said he could save me some money for my climb if I went directly through him instead of using Mountain Travel-Sobek as a go between. It dropped the cost of the trip over $600; since I had already lost over $3,500 with the McKinley trip, it was nice to save some money. I had no formal backers to help me with the cost on any of my climbs, and these trips were expensive.

Sasha said it would be great to have me back in Russia; he even invited me to stay with him at his house until my visa expired, if I would like. We faxed back and forth for several months and decided to climb Elbrus earlier in the year than our last climb; we would try to beat any bad weather. He also informed me that we would be climbing the mountain alone. I thought this would make for a wonderful trip; it might not be as much fun because I wouldn't be meeting new people, but I would certainly be among old friends, and that is what mattered.

Since Elbrus, I always had the feeling that I had let the American Diabetes Association down. It was not a technically difficult mountain to climb, and it was one I should have summited. I approached the Racine Chapter of the ADA and informed them that I was going back to Russia and would like to raise money for them once again. The people at the ADA were thrilled at the prospect; once again it would cost them hardly anything financially, and I was paying the expenses. The only real cost to the ADA was the printing of the pledge sheets, and I believe they were donated. I was told at the meeting a month before I left, "We'll get the pledges, you just get your ass up the mountain." It seemed like a fair proposition.

What I did ask of the ADA was that they get out and help me get pledges this time. Last year, I did 90 percent of the footwork raising pledges and most of the collecting. I wanted help, and I wanted to raise more money than I had the year before. Again, my target goal was $10,000, which was only $245 more than I had raised last year. To help with the pledges, I did radio shows, and newspaper interviews. The pledge sheets from the last climb were changed from the previous ones I used. It had my photo taken at the high point of my first Elbrus climb put onto it and it was listed as the 2nd Annual climb. I wasn't sure if I liked that or not. It had that double meaning. To me deep inside it said that I was climbing for the ADA again, as well as I failed it before, so now I have to go do it again.

The American Diabetes Association has a mountain to climb

American Diabetes Association.

2nd Annual

Nick Comande, a firefighter from Racine, will be attempting to climb Mount Elbrus, the highest point in Europe, for the benefit of the American Diabetes Association. You can share in his adventure by pledging money for every 100 feet he successfully climbs.

Mount Elbrus is 18,510 feet tall and is part of the Caucasus range in southwestern Russia. Comande will begin his ascent on August 29.

By pledging 5¢ for every 100 feet Nick climbs, your contribution would be $9.25. If you pledge 10¢ per 100 feet, your contribution would be $18.51. It is also possible to make a flat donation to the ADA in recognition of Nick's efforts.

Wish Nick luck and pledge what you can!
American Diabetes Association
Racine Chapter
P.O. Box 1883
Racine, WI 53401
(800) 776-7118

Mount Elbrus — 18,510 foot climb, the highest point in Europe

Pledge/foot:	.01¢	.05¢	.10¢	.25¢	.50¢	$1.00
Total Pledge:	$1.85	$9.25	$18.50	$46.27	$92.55	$185.10

	Name (please print)	Address	Zip Code	Pledge per 100 ft.	Flat Donation	Total Pledge
1.						
2.						
3.						
4.						
5.						
6.						
7.						
8.						
9.						
10.						
11.						
12.						
13.						

Well I hung my pledge sheets in businesses, and gave them to family and friends; I never left home without one. Even my fellow fire fighters made donations. I did my best to raise more in pledges than the previous year, and I tried to convince myself that the Racine Chapter of the ADA would do the same.

I wouldn't need any new equipment for this trip; the One Hour Moto-Photo in Brookfield, Wisconsin agreed to donate film again, and I wouldn't have to have a new flag made – just modified.

So, with clear lungs and a bright outlook, I went back to Russia.

August 31, 1992 Dacha Elevation: 6,000 feet

I left the United States for the country formerly known as the Soviet Union, but which is known today as Russia. I flew to Frankfurt and then on to Moscow. I didn't sleep much because the flight was a little bumpy. My plane departed late both times, but the pilots made up the time in the air. I stepped off the plane and broke into a sweat; the temperature was in the mid 80's. Last year it had only been in the mid 40's.

I walked out of customs to find my old friend and guide Sasha, and my friend Helen, who took me on the local tours; it was good to see them again. Sasha drove me to his mother's house where I would be spending the night while she was away on holiday. I met Sasha's wife, Svetlana, as well; she would not be going with us to Elbrus this time. We took a brief drive around the city and Sasha asked where I wanted to go. I immediately replied, "Red Square." The three of us walked through Red Square and took some photos of me with my flag in front of St. Basil's where we watched the changing of the guard. It was here that Sasha informed me that I would not be his only client; three other people would join us for our climb of Elbrus. While I was slightly disappointed in this, I welcomed the opportunity to meet the other members of the group.

After Red Square, we took a ride to the point that looked out over the city. The view was just like last year. There were many people, including several bridal parties, artist and musicians, but it was so much warmer. The other big change from my last trip was the exchange rate. Last year it was 200 Rubles-to-$1, and now it was over 900-to-$1.

When it was time for dinner, Sasha and I went to a large restaurant where we met Katrina Harshan, one of my translators and guide in Moscow from my first trip. It was good to see her and she expressed gratitude that I was using her company (Soviet Travel) on my second climb of Elbrus. She was with other clients, so we chatted only briefly. I was then introduced to the other members of the climbing party. First there was Robert Anderson, from New Zealand; he was off to climb the Seven Summits unassisted in any way, except financially. He was fortunate enough to have the backing of several large companies. There was Joe Blackburn, from Connecticut, who will be photographing all the climbs. Sandy Wylie, a friend of theirs from England, will be tagging along. The meeting was brief; we would have time to talk tomorrow as we travel south to Mineral' Nye Vody.

We left early this morning for the airport and waited five hours for our flight. Here I met the last member of the group; his name is Mike, and he'll be our assistant guide. We all sat at a table for awhile, sharing stories of our past climbs. I told of my trip here last year. I shared the ups and downs and noted any information that might have been useful to Robert and his party.

When we departed, we were bussed straight out to the plane; the others passengers had to walk out. Aeroflot Airlines did not have the same quality service as its American counterparts, but it did get us there – even though one of the tires on the plane was completely bald. The flight was hot, and I was bothered by several flies. Had it not been for the flies, I'm sure I would have slept the whole way.

Upon our arrival to Mineral' Nye Vody, another old friend from the last trip, Boris (my bus driver from last year) welcomed me; he remembered me and hugged me. This time he had a helper, Freidour. We boarded the bus which had been delayed slightly by the other member's copious amounts of baggage.

The drive to the dacha was five hours long; this included lunch at 5:00 p.m. (the same place as my last trip) and a stop at the mineral pool. You could see the twin peaks of Elbrus some eighty kilometers in the distance. They stood alone in a cloudless sky as a crescent moon looked down on them. Sasha said, "This is a good sign." I felt success in the air.

By the time we reached the dacha, it was dark; the only lights shining in the Baksan Valley were those of the houses. There were no street lights, so there was not as much to see from the bus. I wondered if anything had changed in the last year.

The dacha looks the same. We were given rooms upstairs, but we will share them. I'm back in the same room and bed as last year. It has a great view of the west side of the valley from the bathroom window; it's something to look at while you do your duty. Robert and Sandy are in the room Dan occupied last year. Lyuba is back as our faithful waitress. She also remembered me and welcomed me back.

I'm tired and I still have jet lag so I'll end this for now. It feels good to be back among familiar surroundings, and I'm looking forward to tomorrow's hike.

September 1, 1992 Dacha Elevation: 6,000 feet

Today was a good day. I awoke from an undisturbed sleep and breathed in the clean air. I noticed right away that my Diomox is working; my fingers are tingling and my bladder is full. I decided to cut my dosage in half, so I'm taking only half a pill in the morning and the other half at night. Breakfast followed shortly and consisted of vegetables and tea.

I couldn't help but notice that between Robert, Joe and Sandy, I was the third wheel. They spoke amongst themselves, and at times acted as though I wasn't there. Before we went out hiking I stopped in Robert's room – where everyone had gathered – and explained to them that I originally had signed aboard this trip in February. Just because the three of them had been together for the past three months didn't mean that I should be left out of whatever was going on; after all, this climb was just as important to me as it was to them. Robert assured me that we were all in this together. While I appreciated his reassuring words, there would be many times when I would still be made to feel like an afterthought.

We took our first hike today, back to Childa (pronounced Shilda, meaning strawberry) Valley. I brought a Walkman this time, and boogied in the Baksan like last year. It felt good to work up a sweat on these minor hills. I should have been in a little better shape, but there wasn't much else I could do at this point.

It took us just over 1 ½ hours to reach the flat rocky area at the end of Childa Valley; already, people were there. Sasha said, "This has become a popular place this last year because it is the closest thing to a beach in the area." There were perhaps 20 people of varying ages – mostly women and children. Some of the locals asked to take pictures of us and we took pictures of them. Joe asked me for some of my Tootsie Pops (which I had an ample supply of) to give to the kids in exchange for taking their photos. We rested and skipped stones into the icy waters of the Childa River while Robert climbed some rocks. This time, the water was too murky to drink, but we found an outlet from which we could fill our water bottles with clear water. Nothing beats the taste of cold, mountain run-off water. The sun was hot and shining directly behind Childa itself, making it difficult to take a good photo, but we made do and took one anyway. It was nice to feel like part of a team again.

We said "so-long" to the locals and hiked back to the road where our bus was waiting. By 2:30 we were having lunch; it seems like all we do here is eat. This afternoon, instead of hiking up to the Usengi Valley like last year, we opted to go rock climbing instead. Robert had a rope and I had my harness, so I belayed him, leaving Joe free to take pictures. The wall was less than 65 feet high and Robert climbed it without much difficulty. I managed to get halfway up before falling. It wasn't too bad since I'd done so very little of this in the past, and I didn't have the right shoes. It was something different and it was fun. My only regret was that I didn't get into the Usengi Valley to photograph that great waterfall that I had seen last year. Joe doesn't realize what a photo opportunity he missed.

When we returned to the dacha, the sauna was ready; it felt great, and it had been much too long since I had enjoyed one. Robert, Joe and I hopped between that and the pool just outside the sauna door. Here we told war stories about different mountains we had been on and even preserved some of the conversation on Robert's video camera. (I would've liked to have had a copy of it.)

We baked in the sauna until dinner when we again feasted on Georgian delights. Sasha then discussed with us the options of climbing Elbrus. Recently, the second cable car up the mountain had fallen off its cable; several people had been injured, and a couple had been killed. This meant that we would have to walk much farther up the mountain carrying all our supplies that much higher. Robert and Joe have a lot of camera equipment to bring with them – too much for us to carry in one trip, and renting a helicopter will cost over $1,000. The more economical and practical way will be for Robert and Joe to hire some porters to help carry their equipment. Sasha will check on that tomorrow.

I was able to view some of the footage Joe caught on video. He and Robert hope to put together some type of mini-series. Maybe I'll even get to be in it, although I doubt it. Robert has been very helpful in explaining some of the ins-and-outs of raising funds; I hope that I will be able to put them to good use next year. If all goes well I might be able to get to Antarctica and climb Mt. Vinson.

I'm in bed now; the same one as last year. I'm hoping to fair much better than I did last year. Clouds started to roll in later this evening, but they weren't reticulate, which is a good sign. Time will only tell how the weather will change, and fortunately we still have plenty of that. It is time to turn in; tomorrow will be another active day.

September 2, 1992 Dacha Elevation: 6,000 feet

I awoke at 7:45 and showered quietly so as not to awaken Joe, my roommate here in the dacha. Joe is a professional photographer. I went outside, sat on the porch, and smelled the fresh air of the forest; I could hear water running in a nearby river. It was just like last year – same people (guides and staff), same smells, same food and same room. The only thing I wanted different was the climb's outcome.

After breakfast we went to view Donguz-Orun (Russian for big nose), a 4,468-meter peak, and the highest peak other than Elbrus in the Caucasus. Our personal bus driver brought us to the base of Mt. Cheget, where we rode a chairlift up its side. It belonged to a resort that was closed for now, but soon would be opening when the snows began to fall in the valley. (This resort – like others around here – was seasonal and used mainly as a ski resort in the late fall and winter.) We rode the chairlift up to a lookout spot with a restaurant and bar much like the ones we have in Lake Tahoe. There are many posters of people skiing. People come here during the off-season to view the mountain and its surrounding region. I remember the area well; it was from here that I got my very first glimpse of Elbrus.

The weather was good and there were only a few clouds. Through my telephoto lens, I could see people coming down from the summit. How I hoped to have that same experience. After photographing Elbrus, we hiked over to the other side of Cheget; from there we would view Donguz-Orun and the small lake that lay before it.

As we walked along a dirt path, we encountered sheep grazing in the high altitude pasture before the snows come. Farming is very big in the valley and keeps many of the old locals self-sufficient. By the time we reached the lake, I had met some people from Great Britain. Their guide was going swimming, but the lake had filled with melted ice and snow off the mountain range; it was near freezing, so we all declined his offer to join him.

We sat looking at different things as Sasha pointed them out. He told us how many people had died trying to climb the side of Donguz-Orun (the side facing us); it was a place of many avalanches. I can't remember if he said anyone had ever successfully scaled that face.

As we took our break and the clouds started to roll in, there was one small avalanche on Donguz-Orun. Well, so much for good weather, I thought to myself. Since the chairlift operator decided to go home early to beat the bad weather, we were forced to walk down the side of Cheget. I tried to make time to stay ahead of the approaching storm, and was rained on only lightly. Our ever-faithful bus driver, Boris, was waiting for us in the parking lot, and talking with other locals who had set up the area like a flea market to sell their goods. When we were ready to leave, he returned us to the dacha, and the storm hit just a short time later. It thundered, as though the mountain gods were warning us to stay away – not that we would've listened.

Unlike my previous climbs, we would sauna and swim at six o'clock; then dinner would follow. We finalized plans for the next day's activities which would bring us partway up the mountain to Priutt Hut (the place where I spent so many cold nights last year). We started packing at 10:00 p.m., and it is now 1:40 a.m. I'm writing this while Joe finishes his packing. I must get to sleep; there is a lot to do later today.

September 3, 1992 Priutt Hut Elevation: 12,652 feet

I awoke before my alarm; it was 7:50 a.m. I took a hot bath, not knowing when I would be able to do so again. Breakfast was at 8:30, but I wasn't really hungry with all the excitement of starting the climb. Two locals – very muscular in build – joined the party to help carry Joe and Robert's extra equipment. Everyone was wished "farewell" and "good luck" by the members of the staff as we left the comforts of the dacha for the harshness of the mountain. I said goodbye to our little home-away-from-home, at least for awhile, and boarded the bus with the rest of the group. (At this point, I wanted to refer to our group as a team, but I still didn't feel a part of one.)

Boris dropped us off at the base of the first tram at 9:30. The ticket clerk for the tram finally showed up an hour later; *he* obviously didn't have a mountain to climb that day. Taking the tram up this part of the mountain would cut a day off the climb. I watched the summit of Elbrus come into view as the tram gained altitude along its cable. Once we reached the top of this, we would have to start walking.

As I stopped to look at the two wall plaques where we disembarked, the tram station was familiar to me. One memorial was a remembrance to a fallen climber, and the other was to honor the man who had served as head of their rescue service in the area; he had died on the mountain. This time I snapped a photo of them, and proceeded with the others up the side of Elbrus.

The dirt colored trail was wide and looked well traveled; the green of the valley now lay behind me, but it would be a welcomed sight upon my return. We walked at our own pace to the snow line that was still more than a thousand feet above us, but it was getting increasingly closer with each step we took. Normally, we would have taken a second tram up this part of the mountain, but because it fell off its cable a couple of weeks ago, it hasn't been in use. I could see it resting on the ground still several hundreds of feet above me. (Sasha has no idea when it might be repaired.)

It felt good to get under way; this was the part of the trip I'd been waiting for. I made several stops to rest along the way; one was at the level of the fallen tram, laying some 200 feet below the tram station. Nearly a third of its walls were missing, and impact marks showed where it had struck the ground. I tried not to think of it as being crowded with people – people carrying ski poles and whatever else – as it plummeted down the side of the mountain.

We rested for a while at the vacant tram station; it took me one hour, 42 minutes to cover the distance the tram could cover in less than seven minutes. The next part of the walk would be from the top of the tram station to the top of the chairlift. Sasha explained that the chairlift operators, on their way to work, would ride up to this spot on the second tram, but since it was not working, there was no need for the run. No one, neither operators nor sightseers, would walk this distance up and down every day; only those willing to climb Elbrus would be up here right now.

Last year, Sasha had instructed Dan and me to climb up to the top of the chairlift to help us acclimatize. Now, a year later, I was climbing – once again – to the chairlift when the temperature started to drop. The ground was much wetter in places as a result of melting snow. The higher I climbed, the more peaks and mountain ranges I could see in the area. My pack was heavy and I was beginning to feel the weight, all the while wishing I had my Walkman along to distract me.

It took me 51 minutes to cover the distance of the chairlift, and the whole time I kept looking up at the summit, watching the clouds far in the distance, hoping they would stay there. Along the top of the chairlift, nine red and white trailer-sized cylinders laid side by side. Rescue personnel would live here during the skiing season. They also had a snow cat to bring people to and from Priutt Hut, some 2,000 feet above us.

At the snow line there was a definite drop in temperature. We gathered as a group, and Sasha had the driver of the snow cat bring us up to Priutt Hut. I tried to take a picture of Robert, but he asked me not to. I supposed it would not be good if anyone saw him riding a snow cat on an unassisted climb up Elbrus, but taking the snow cat saved us at least an hour and a half of walking on our own.

Sasha kept an eye on the weather; he said it did not look favorable, but I remembered my climb up to Priutt last year in a snowstorm. I knew the conditions were more favorable this time around.

Once we reached the refuge, we unloaded our packs from the snow cat and ventured into the refuge. I was surprised to see that the electricity was working. There were no other people here that I could see other than the hut manager and an Austrian named Daniel. We were given rooms in which to rest and store our gear. Sasha told us that the weather looked bad. A front was moving in, so instead of taking a day to acclimatize we would shoot for the summit tomorrow. For me, the going might be slow, but that would be better than not going at all

We had a quick dinner and then we were off to bed; we will wake at two a.m. and be on our way by three. My gear is laid out and ready to go and I hope to get six hours of deep sleep before we leave. It will be great to get this knocked off in a short period of time. I had not thought much of the fundraiser in the past few days and it was nice not to have any added pressure. I feel content and confident about reaching the summit; I only wish I had the extra day to acclimatize – I could use it.

September 4, 1992 Priutt Hut Elevation: 12,652 feet

My alarm woke me at 2 a.m. and I looked out the window of my room as I reached for my watch. Through it, I could see a brilliant array of stars; I knew then that the sky was clear. Sasha knocked on my door to see if I was awake. I answered him, and he said in a quiet Russian voice, as if trying not to wake anyone, "Breakfast in 10 minutes." I had a small headache and took a few Tylenol and my Diamox. For all intents and purposes I was ready to make a push for the top, but thought to myself again that I could be in better shape; of course it is much too late to be thinking about that now. I checked my jacket pocket one last time to make sure I had my flag with me and then went to join the others.

For me, breakfast consisted only of tea. I was not really hungry, and that probably was due more to the excitement of finishing something I'd started almost a year ago, rather than from altitude. Today was my day to help the ADA; I didn't want to let them down like I had last year.

Sasha informed us that the snow cat was outside, and for three dollars, the driver – the same guy who had brought us here – would take us up to the Rocks of Pastukhov. Since I had climbed to that part of Elbrus on my own twice before on my first trip, I didn't mind the ride. With my cold weather gear on and crampons secured, I joined the others in the back of the snow cat for the ride up Elbrus.

We climbed out of the snow cat. The "group" originally consisting of Sasha and me had grown to a good size. Besides us there were Robert, Joe, Sandy, Mike our assistant guide, and Olga our cook and hut manager from last year. Not with our group, but also going up was the Austrian, Daniel, a surveyor working in Russia. He was here on holiday and was climbing

Elbrus for no apparent reason. It only goes to show there is no real reason why people do this silly sport of climbing mountains.

The sky was fantastic. Both peaks of Elbrus were outlined in the stars, and the Milky Way created a band of white so thick with stars you'd think you could walk across it; it was truly a magnificent day to climb. The snow cat turned around and left us on our own. There was no moon to cast reflected light onto the smooth, white slopes of Elbrus, so we used head lamps to illuminate our way; as the sound of the snow cat got farther away, we started up the side of Elbrus.

As usual, I started out pacing myself too fast. I could feel the adrenaline pumping through my body and all I could think about was reaching the summit, not the East, but the West summit. It is only 65 feet higher and a half hour longer to climb, but it is the top of Europe. It would also add another 65 feet to the pledges of the fundraiser. This time, I was going to pull this one off for the ADA. With my crampons digging into the ice, I pushed onward to the top.

I looked behind me from time to time to watch the sunrise. An orange sky lit up the eastern part of the Caucasus. The only clouds in the sky were far in the distance and posed no problem for us; there was little or no wind to impede us, either. It was truly a great day to climb.

By the time I reached the saddle between the East and West peaks, I had slowed down considerably; the entire group was in front of me with the exception of Joe and Sasha. I was feeling a little tired, and I could feel a blister starting on my foot. My head was pounding and I had the urge to urinate, but I couldn't. We rested at the saddle at a dilapidated, old shack – something you would need to crouch in to sit. In the shack we placed items we would not need for now – things like extra water, down jackets and other warmer clothing that we wouldn't need on such a nice day, but were brought with just in case.

Sasha went ahead and secured a rope with an ice screw at the steepest part of the climb that was roughly 100 feet high. We really didn't need it, but Sasha, being the conscientious guide that he was, placed it there for safety purposes.

With crampons digging into the ice, I started my ascent up the steepest part of the climb. My footing could have been a bit more solid in one spot – I slipped and slid down the side of the hill several feet; fortunately, only my pride was hurt. Until now, I had never really climbed anything steep with crampons. Also, I had learned the importance of zippers on pockets; in the few feet I had fallen, I lost both my small water bottle and my sun block. They slid on the ice back down to the bottom of the hill – where I would get them on the way back down. Both will be needed later.

I made it the rest of the way up without incident. There was still no wind and the sun was warm, but I never thought of looking at my thermometer. I took off my jacket to keep myself from overheating and I was slowing down even more; finally, Joe passed me up. I was moving – ever so slowly and ever so upward, steadily. Feeling deep down that I would reach the top, I felt happy and excited that I would not go back home a failure; I would be able to collect the full amount of my pledges, but I still was not there – no sense counting chickens before they've hatched.

As I climbed higher, I could see more and more of the Caucasus; I had never seen what was on the other side of Elbrus before this; last year the sky had been overcast.

Then, there came a time when there were no more ridges, no more ravines; at last, I could see the summit, and as much as I hate to admit it, I shed a tear. I can't explain how good I felt, but my goal was in sight.

Sasha and Joe were already there; the rest had started down, each congratulating me on my way up. They knew I would make it and in turn I congratulated them. Ten minutes later, I was on the top of Europe! With this accomplishment, I shed a few more tears of joy.

Joe and Sasha congratulated me. I looked at my watch; it was 12:45 p.m. I started to pull out my camera to photograph the event, when suddenly, I was consumed with a feeling I'd experienced only once before in my life. I can't explain the sense of overwhelming joy that came over me, nor can I explain the sense of happiness and accomplishment I felt. I stood up and looked around at all that was below me, took out my flag, and had my picture taken with it.

Nick Comande on the top of Mt. Elbrus, the West peak. September 4, 1992.

The weather was still holding, and the sun was shining brightly upon us. I still couldn't believe I was here; I had finally reached a summit for the ADA. I had accomplished a second summit for myself, and hopefully it would bring in a lot of donations.

We started to collect our gear for the walk back. I picked up some rocks to take back as a souvenir. Sasha and Joe started down, following in the footprints we'd all made on the way up. I stayed behind, and for a brief few minutes, I stood – alone and higher than anyone else in all of Europe.

I left the summit at 1:15 p.m., dreading the thought of walking on a blister for the four hours it would take to get back to Priutt.

I picked up the water bottle and sun block I had dropped on my way up the trail, and the extra liter of water I had left at the shack on the saddle. I was very thirsty and drank greedily while saving half a liter for the rest of the hike down. I tried to urinate, but I was unable. Sasha said, "It is time to go, we must get back before the afternoon winds come," but they were already here – nothing bad – but there was a change in the temperature; my thermometer read 0° F.

With the rest of the gear packed up, Sasha, Mike and I left the saddle; the others were already on their way back to Priutt. They didn't need a guide; all they had to do was follow the footsteps we had made on the way up. The only part of the climb we needed to worry about was that steep area, and we'd had no mishaps. It was a good climb, seven people reached the top of Elbrus and there were no injuries.

Because of my blister I walked very slowly; I had no choice. By the time I made it off the saddle, the rest of the group was spread out above and below the Rocks of Pastukhov. The sun was still high in the sky, and though I was moving slowly, I was confident that I would make it back before dark. Sasha, who was some 300 feet in front of me, kept urging me on. By the time I made it to the Rocks of Pastukhov, I told him to go on. I could see Pruitt and knew the way back; I didn't mind walking alone. In fact, I rather enjoyed it; I had the whole side of Elbrus to myself.

The ice that was frozen when we started was now thawed under the heat of the sun. The ice would no longer support my weight, and I kept breaking through it, slowing my pace even more. When I was 45 minutes from the refuge, Mike met me with half a liter of tea – which I was very glad to have since I had finished the last of my water on the traverse. He accompanied me the rest of the way back to the refuge.

Robert was waiting at the door with his video camera; it was 6:45 p.m. I was back; I was safe; and most importantly, I had reached the top of Elbrus. It took me 17 hours 45 minutes from the time we left this morning until my return. My time, from the start of my climb yesterday to the summit, was 25 hours 45 minutes. Everyone else made it in less time, but they've been acclimatized from climbing most of this year.

I walked into the ready room of Priutt; Robert accompanied me and we talked while I removed my crampons and gaiters. He commended me on my accomplishment. I thanked him, but I said it was no big deal. I said, "Look how quickly you did it." He explained that he does this all the time, and that he trains for climbing the year round; if he was trying to make me feel better – he did.

After dropping the rest of my gear in my room I joined the rest of the group in the dining room to see if there was any dinner left. The dining room was on the lower floor of the hut and big enough to hold several large tables and chairs to seat almost thirty. There was some vegetable soup that I ate cold. I was tired and just wanted to rest so I went back to my room and finally managed to urinate. I peed into an empty liter-sized water bottle that I kept in my room for just this purpose. By 7:30 I was in my sleeping bag, feeling tired but with a sense of accomplishment; in a few minutes I was fast asleep.

September 5, 1992 Priutt Hut Elevation: 12,652 feet

I woke at 9:00 a.m. feeling rested. I had a touch of sunburn on my face – the result of losing my sun block the day before, and another reminder of the importance of zippers on pockets. I dressed and picked up my pee bottle to go empty. The foul stuff separated during the night leaving a murky mass floating in the lower third of the bottle. I had the urge to go again and was thankful for the first time the flow-through process was working again.

Since the climb up was now over, I stopped taking the Diamox, but I would continue to push fluids. I joined the others for breakfast and then went outside to sit in the sun where we made the decision to rest here a day. It felt good to sit in the sun; the weather was still wonderful and the clouds that we had hoped would stay away had done just that. Sitting out of the wind beside Pruitt, I took the time to relax. Wearing no coat – just rolled up shirtsleeves and plenty of sun block – I took the time to make entries in my journal.

During lunch we all exchanged more stories; I pulled out my flag and asked everyone who had summited with me that day to sign it. With the permission of the hut manager, it was hung on the top floor of the refuge so all who come here can see it. Toasts were made with chilled Russian water (vodka). After lunch I collected the clothes that I had left outside to dry in the sun and spent the rest of the afternoon writing in my journal while Sasha played his guitar and sang songs.

As I watched the sun go down behind the peaks, the winds reappeared with a chill. It was a beautiful sunset but I was in a solemn mood. My "quest" here was over; it was time to leave, not only the mountain, but the wonderful view you get only while you're on top of a mountain. On a more spiritual note, it also ends or stretches my closeness with God – not to say he isn't always there, but to say that he is within an arm's reach makes it more special.

Tomorrow I'll leave the mountain to return to a more civilized way of life: a hot bath, loud rock and roll, running water and all the other little conveniences that most people take for granted.

11:22 p.m. It's the close of another day; we ate dinner and finished it off by drinking more vodka. Just as he had last year, Sasha took out his guitar and sang the Russian folk songs that he knew so well. Several Russian hikers stopped in at that Refuge; one of them – a girl – she had bad blisters on her nose and face caused by the sun, and she refused to take off the scarf covering. I gave her some antiseptic cream, and we all chipped in a couple of dollars apiece so they could spend the night in the refuge instead of their tent.

The wind is picking up outside, but the sight of the half moon shows that the skies are still clear. In less that 12 hours we will be on our way back to the dacha.

As I lay here in my sleeping bag, I think about how this will be my last night in Priutt, and I think about all the nights I'd spent here last year, trying to accomplish what I did in only 25 hours and 45 minutes this year. I'm glad that I tried again, for without trying there cannot be success.

September 6, 1992 Dacha Elevation: 6,000 feet

The best thing there is after climbing a mountain is getting off it. After our day of rest we packed our gear for one more long haul; even though we were going downhill, it was still going to be a bit of a hike. On this return trip we didn't have the two porters who helped us carry our gear up. We divided Joe's camera equipment and headed down the mountain.

Before leaving I made one last stop in the manager's office at Priutt. Here I looked at my flag hanging on the wall. A lot of effort went into getting it here, and even more getting it to the summit, but for the sake of the ADA it was worth it. I hope it hangs there for a long time, and – who knows – maybe it will inspire someone else to do the same.

My flag hanging in the Priutt Refuge after reaching the summit of Elbrus in 1992.

I left the refuge with no regrets, and I was glad it was not a repeat of last year. Knowing that my job here was finished and that I would probably never return, I bid my farewell to Elbrus and started walking down its side. I turned around periodically to get some last looks at the summit. As coincidence would have it, each time I turned back to look at the summit, I saw clouds – clouds that had been so kind to us by staying away during our climb, were now slowly moving in. I felt bad for the climbers who were just now going up the mountain – the ones I'd passed on the trail; hopefully, their bad weather wouldn't last long.

By the time I reached the top of the chairlift, both peaks of Elbrus were hidden in the clouds. I felt fortunate and thankful that the weather held. I stopped several times along the way down; each time I removed more and more of my warmer clothing. By the time I reached the tram at 12:15 p.m., I was in shorts. We all gathered at the top of the one working tram and road it down together.

Boris was not there with the bus so we killed some time by taking group pictures, but we eventually bribed another bus driver to take us where we needed to go. One beer and one bottle of vodka later we were back at the dacha.

On our return, members of the dacha staff bestowed congratulations upon us, but it didn't last long; the race for the hot water was on. Everyone went to their room and started running water for showers and baths. Water pressure in the dacha was surely down, but baths were taken and odors eliminated. The rest of the day was pretty lax, lunch at 3:00, naps at 4:00 followed by the sauna at 6:00. Boris was kind enough to place two bottles of champagne in the famous KGB planning room next to the sauna. Never before was success so sweet and complimented.

Dinner was at 8:00 and we consumed considerable amounts of champagne, vodka, cognac and Georgian wine. Before turning in for the night, Sasha announced that – should we be willing to pay for it – we could charter a helicopter for an hour for a trip around Elbrus. At a cost of only $75 each, we quickly agreed.

September 7, 1992 Dacha Elevation: 6,000 feet

Today started out an hour earlier than usual, because we had to be on the road by 9:00 a.m. to meet the helicopter. It landed in a field five miles from our dacha and picked up our group as well as some other Russians that I did not know. The helicopter was orange and had *Aeroflot* written on the side. It could seat nearly a dozen people, so we weren't crowded and almost everyone had a window seat.

We quickly took seats inside the noisy thing and took off for a flight around Elbrus. The helicopter flew at 12,500 feet, nearly parallel with Priutt Hut. It took us just minutes to fly to the same altitude it had taken us hours to walk.

One of the pilots came back to the main cabin and showed us how to open the windows so we would not have to look or photograph through the scratches on the glass. Cold air rushed into the cabin as we opened the windows. The peak of Elbrus was still covered by clouds, but looking at the rest of Elbrus in this way was just beautiful. I could see the trails that we climbed and most of our route up to the summit except for the parts that were covered in clouds

As the pilot circled the mountain, I was able to get a good view of the other side. Unlike the side I climbed days before, the back of the mountain was far more treacherous looking with many crevasses and ice flows that ran down this side of the mountain. It would be possible to climb, but it would take much more time than the route we took, and it would be much more dangerous.

The back of Elbrus. This photo was taken from a helicopter during our flight around the mountain.

After circling Elbrus, the pilot flew us past Dagozaroon and Mt. Childa. It was a great trip that lasted nearly an hour; my only regret was that I didn't have more film with me.

For exercise later in the day, I walked down to the mineral spring to show Joe and Sandy where it was. The weather kept changing along the way; first it was windy, then cloudy, then it was warmer and then it rained. At times the wind just seemed to whip down the valley and I saw a waterfall that wasn't here last year.

We had filled our water bottles and headed back to the dacha when we crossed paths with a couple of very intoxicated locals; one of them had a very large knife. They were cutting watermelons and insisted we sit and share with them. They were quite good and since we were Americans, they insisted on giving us several to take back with us. We convinced them that only one would do, which we put in my backpack for the rest of the hike back. We gave it to Lyuba to serve with dinner.

September 8, 1992 Dacha Elevation: 6,000 feet

11:18 p.m. The sound of thunder rolled in as it began raining – not just a drizzle, but a downpour. I'm really glad that I'm not going up the mountain like some of the other people I saw today. I'm in bed now; this was our last day in the valley for tomorrow we head for Patagorskt.

For something to do today we went back up Mt. Cheget. It would be the last time that I would get a good look at Elbrus; its peak was still heavily clouded in. The others in the group kept saying that they too were glad to have been up and off the mountain. Going up now would mean waiting at Priutt for good weather; I have already gone that route. I spent some time on Cheget talking with some of the locals that lived there.

One member was part of a meteorological party; you could tell he was starved for company. This guy spoke well, but in broken English, and wanted to make me tea, show me his photos and hear my life story. I quickly made polite excuses to join the rest of the group.

Through the broken clouds you could barely make out Priutt Hut. The clouds moved our way and Cheget was then covered. Being at 12,500 feet, the temperature quickly dropped. We took the 20-minute chairlift ride back to the bottom.

As I left Cheget and took my last looks at Elbrus, I felt a bit sad. It was like leaving a friend behind. Elbrus had been in my mind for over a year since I started planning this climb, now it was over. I came – even if it was twice – I conquered, and I left. As I rode the chairlift I started to think about when and where my next climb would be. I had been considering Vinson in the Antarctic for awhile; maybe this would be a good time to start thinking about it seriously.

Eight hours from now we will be leaving the Baskan Valley, probably for good. I don't foresee coming back; I have no reason to now, but one never knows. It's very beautiful here and I will miss it, but like all chapters in life this one, too, must come to an end.

September 13, 1992 Lufthansa Airlines Somewhere over Europe

In the days since leaving the Valley the group has split up. We drove to the city of Patagorskt where we would spend the night. Joe, Robert, Sandy, Lyuba and Olga with some other Russian locals took our bus and headed south to the Crimea. Sasha stayed with me and we both went back to Moscow. We arrived very late, after 1:30 a.m. We stopped by the office of Soviet Travels that was in the process of being renovated; from there I sent a fax back home and let everyone know of my success.

I stayed at the homes of Sasha mother and Helen's for the next few days while leading the life of a Russian in a real Russian home. I rode the bus, the subway and even went to the circus. Sasha brought out slides of other trips he had been on, and talked about different clients from previous climbs.

Helen had taken me on tours of the Arsenal and Tussaud's wax museum. It included figures of Peter the Great, Stalin, Tolstoy, Rasputin and Sakarov (the latter being arrested by Sasha's uncle many years ago.) I had learned much more about the country on this trip, but my only regret was that I was barely in Red Square. I was able to cross it only once this year where last year I was able to see it several times.

My last night in Moscow was with my friends. Sasha treated me to dinner because he said, "The reason we are all gathered tonight is because of you." Sasha, Sveta, Helen, Mike and I sat around and drank until the wee hours of the morning. It made sense to stay up from that point because we had to leave for the airport at 4:00 a.m. During dinner we talked about possible future climbs and how maybe someday I would be able to climb Peak Lenin. It is Sasha's wish to someday climb outside of Russia. I hope he gets his chance. His passion for the mountains is greater than mine; I can tell just by the way he talks about them. I said good-bye to Svetlana and Mike before leaving for the airport; boy how I hate good-byes.

On the way to the airport, Sasha gave me one last special treat; he drove me to Red Square so I could have a last look at it. Helen walked with me as I quickly took in the sights that so mesmerized me a year ago. Our chance of walking across it was ruined by the drizzle.

From there it was a 50-minute ride to the airport. I had a 7:10 a.m. flight. The exchange window was closed so I handed all my rubles over to Sasha. He brought me to the gate and – like last year – he said, "This is as far as I go." We hugged and said good-bye. I thanked him again for all he had done for me. I then said goodbye to Helen and thanked her for all the insight she had given me into her country.

I took my bags and moved towards my gate; the last I saw of Sasha was when he was walking out the door of the airport. He stopped there and waved back to me one last time. As I went through immigration, I asked the man collecting visas to stamp my passport for me, but he wouldn't. Again, I was leaving Russia with no proof in my passport. My only proof of being in the country is my flag hanging on the wall back at Priutt Hut and the memories I hold for my Russian friends. In less than an hour I was on a plane flying home.

Looking back, it was a good trip – a successful trip. I returned to a foreign country, climbed to the top of its highest peak and left. I was with friends from the time I first landed until the time I left. What more could anyone ask for?

September 20

I returned home from Russia feeling 10 feet tall. I came back, not with my head in my hands like last year, but with pride and a sense of accomplishment. I didn't fail the American Diabetes Association this time and I didn't fail myself. I set a new goal for them. I reached the peak of Elbrus – 18,510 ft. All of my pledges would be raised to the highest total that could be allowed. I could hardly wait until the next local ADA meeting so I could see how well the other members of the committee had done with their pledge sheets.

Unfortunately, I could have waited; once again I felt defeated. While I was out working to get pledges, as well as training, and working my job at the fire department, the other members of the committee weren't doing their share to help me raise pledges. Of the 460 pledges that were taken, I was responsible for 352 of them, leaving 108 pledges gathered by the seven members of the ADA. My pledges accounted for over 70% of the money raised. I was very disheartened by this; I was helping their charity and I thought that they should've worked harder by getting their share of the pledges. Some members on the board simply made donations and didn't even bother to get any pledges.

But the damage was done; the climb was over, and it was a disappointing let down to a perfect climb.

The final results of the fundraising were $8,405; this was $350 *less* than my summit attempt a year ago. How could I go higher and make less? I learned that I needed more dedication from a Charities Board. Sure the morale they offered was great, but to really make a fundraiser like this work, you have to get more pledges. You need a support group that will work as hard as I did. I did what I could, but it wasn't enough; I needed help getting pledges and getting the word out, and it wasn't there.

Chapter Six
Mt. Vinson

(To one of the farthest ends of the earth)

With the success of Elbrus fueling the fire beneath me, it was time to look ahead to another climb and another mountain. I don't remember what swayed me, but my next choice was Mt. Vinson in the Antarctic. This was a mountain I'd looked at in the past, but decided against because of the enormous cost and adverse conditions; mostly, it was the cost. I'd been in adverse conditions before, even if not for substantially long periods of time, but – like turning on a light switch – I made up my mind to go south, to one of the most barren, desolate and coldest places on Earth. I was going to try to conquer Vinson and make it my biggest and best fundraising event ever.

The going rate for a trip to Mt. Vision was roughly $24,000, not including all the extras, but being a firefighter doesn't allow for that kind of money to be spent on a mountain adventure; still, I was determined to raise that amount. Because this trip was going to cost me so much money, I wanted it to be the biggest fundraising event I had ever done, bringing in more donations than I ever had before. It was early December 1992, and my tentative departure date was November 22, 1993. I had a lot of planning to do.

Like my other climbs, I had to find an outfit that would get me to the Antarctic and to Vinson. My choice was Adventure Network. Most organizations were not willing to go to the Antarctic, and those companies that did go would usually sublet their trips through Adventure Network. (Don't hold me to this though.) The going rate for a trip to the Antarctic, up Mt. Vinson and back was a mere $25,000. I called the Adventure Network people and discussed prices. I told them I was going to climb Mt. Vinson to raise money for a charity. They were kind enough to give me a ten percent discount on my package (a savings of $2,500, and a break I badly needed). Even if I depleted my bank account I still wouldn't have enough money to go, so I started saving every cent I could. If I were to budget everything carefully, I would just have enough to make it, or so I thought.

I had chosen my mountain, but I still needed a charity. My disappointment with the American Diabetes Association, their committees, and their meager fund raising attempts for my last two climbs was fresh in my mind; I knew it was time to move on to another charity. Muscular Dystrophy (the first charity I had raised money for) was the first to come to mind.

Since this would be my grandest expedition yet, I wanted the donation amount to be collected and presented in the grandest way possible. I asked myself, "Who works hardest for the Muscular Dystrophy Association." I thought: firefighters, of course. I wanted every firefighter I could get to be involved. I wanted to make this, not just a local event, but a national one, as well; I wanted to get a $1 donation from as many of my firefighting brothers across the country as I could and have the money sent to the Muscular Dystrophy Association. I was hoping to unite all the members of the International Association of Fire Fighters (IAFF) to participate in a single event.

I was so excited when I thought of this, I was just busting inside to tell the MDA. I called Lynn Deedering (who had laughed at me on my first climb for them) to explain what I wanted to do. Lynn was no longer working for MDA, so I spoke to her replacement, Laura Late (not her real name). First, I explained how I climbed Kilimanjaro and raised almost $5,000 for them in 1988, and how I wanted to do it again. Next, I laid out my groundwork for her; I explained that I would need permission from the International Association of Fire Fighters to contact all the firefighter unions across the country. I would send them a letter explaining what I was doing and how I would like a $1 donation, per firefighter – from those willing to do so – to be sent to the MDA office in Milwaukee. This way, they could keep track of all the incoming funds, and I wouldn't have to worry about handling vast sums of money if this idea worked.

Laura then turned me over to Carrie Hoyer (an associate of hers) to help me with final details. I met with Carrie and gave her the specific details of the climb, and the pledge sheets from previous climbs. I asked her questions regarding what the MDA might need from me. I never heard from Carrie unless I contacted her and asked that she return my call. One thing she did make clear to me: I could not say that *I was Climbing for*

Muscular Dystrophy. I would have to say *I was climbing a mountain with all proceeds going to Muscular Dystrophy*, and with this, I had no problem. Between the months of January and September, most of my free time was spent looking for sponsors to help me pay for the climb. I made phone calls, wrote letters and sent out proposals on what I was going to do – *With All Proceeds Going to Muscular Dystrophy*. While I found very little support for myself, I had already collected $4,900 for the Muscular Dystrophy Association and I was still two months away from the climb. This was more money than I had raised for them earlier when I climbed Kilimanjaro, and I hadn't even left for the mountain.

I was so excited and enthused as I contacted the members of the IAFF across the country. I called Charlie Buss, Vice President of the 5th District of the IAFF. Charlie also shared my enthusiasm and told me to contact Richard Hyatt of the IAFF. In the meantime, Charlie was going to speak to whomever he needed, to get permission for me to solicit IAFF members across the country.

It felt like everything was falling into place, and I was on my way to my largest fundraising mountain-climb, ever. Unfortunately, in another three months all this would turn around. The first week of August something happened I never expected. WITI, a Milwaukee television station, caught wind of what I was doing and asked me for an interview. I quickly accepted, and a date and time was set.

A news reporter named Julie Feldmen came to my home to ask questions about my present climb, my past climbs and about the charities I had helped. I was more than thrilled to do the interview. At last, this was more than just local PR; this would cover all of southeastern Wisconsin. The piece ran later that night. It was the last story of the newscast, and as it started to run, I saw something that put me into shock. In big red letters across the bottom of my television screen were the words: "Climbing for MDA." These were the very words the MDA *didn't* want me to use. I didn't know what to think of it at the time. I just knew there was nothing I could do about it. The newscaster finished the story with: "Anyone wanting to make a contribution to Muscular Dystrophy, call ...," and then they had my home phone number printed on the screen. To my surprise, at 10:35 that night, just moments after the newscast had ended, my phone began to ring and pledges started to come in.

The next day, the MDA office called me. The staff was not very happy with the news story that broke the night before. Actually, they were quite upset with those bold red letters: "Climbing for MDA." I explained to Laura how I'd had nothing to do with the letters, and how I had explained to the reporter doing the interview that I could not say I was "Climbing for MDA." I had made a point of that with the reporter; but nevertheless, it had showed up on the newscast. I called Julie Feldman several times to find out what had happened. She never returned my phone calls.

In mid-August of 1993, while on vacation from the fire department, I was helping an advertising agency out of Milwaukee, Wisconsin, and Jansport, one of their clients. They had a booth they were going to be setting up in Las Vegas at the Clothing Expo. Their booth consisted of a number of their products and an 18-foot-high, three-sided, rock-climbing-type mountain. I went to work for them for several days, showing some of their people how to climb it. I took the job because it was good money for the time I was there, and I needed every cent I could muster to pay for the Vinson trip.

By coincidence, the IAFF also was having its annual convention in Las Vegas. Charlie Buss, IAFF 5th District Vice President, was there; I was to call him when I had a chance. One of the topics of discussion was to be my "Climb up Vinson" to raise money for Muscular Dystrophy. I spoke to Charlie on the phone one night, and he told me some very depressing news. The Milwaukee MDA office had contacted their superiors, and they in turn contacted Al Whitehead, the president of IAFF. They said they were not pleased with what I was doing, and they didn't want me doing it at all. Because of this, I did not get the permission I needed to solicit all the other fire department unions in the country, nor did I get permission to contact them for any other charity.

Not only had Muscular Dystrophy shot down my fundraiser for *them*, but my fundraisers for anyone else. When I returned home from Las Vegas, Laura from the MDA told me that if I decided to still climb for the MDA, they would not accept any money from me, and they would bring legal action against me. At this point, I lost all respect for Muscular Dystrophy. Next, I received a letter from her, which I also found disturbing. I truly liked the last line stating that they would like me to reply.

STAY UP WITH JERRY AND WATCH THE STARS COME OUT!

August 23, 1993

Nick B. Comande
1024 Florence Avenue
Racine, WI 53402

Dear Nick,

While we've discussed your proposal to raise money to benefit MDA by collecting pledges and other donations for your climb of Mt. Vinson (the highest mountain in the Antarctic), it is essential for you to understand that MDA does not endorse or sponsor your endeavor. As I've advised you, since any use of MDA's name requires our prior written approval, and since we have not approved your proposal, you must not solicit any contributions for your climb as benefitting MDA.

Among the many concerns we have with your event is the extremely hazardous nature of your climb. Such hazardous events are prohibited by MDA and by our insurance company out of concern for harm that could happen to you, or you could cause to happen to another participant, in the course of your travels and climb. We also cannot risk that others, who may not be as experienced as you in mountain climbing, may mimic your climb in MDA's name, thereby endangering themselves as well.

In addition, MDA requires that all fund raising on its behalf be managed in strict adherence to recognized accounting principles. We have serious reservations about your ability to maintain to our satisfaction such records of all donations intended to benefit MDA throughout your trip.

Finally, from your correspondence, including your letterhead "Climbing For Causes," it appears that you will make this climb with or without MDA's approval, and that your ultimate purpose is truly for personal benefit and publicity. MDA cannot sanction the use of its name so that you can afford such a lavish adventure.

For all of the above reasons I'm advising you that if you continue to use MDA's name in conjunction with your climb, I'll have to refer this matter to MDA's Legal Department.

I'd apreciate your written acknowledgment of this letter.

Very truly yours,

Regional Director

ss

Muscular Dystrophy Association
2949 N. Mayfair Road, Suite 104 / Wauwatosa, WI 53222 / Telephone (414) 476-9700 / Fax (414) 476-6683

At least in my rebuttal, I was able to vent how they had misled me. This was my letter to them.

Nick B. Comande

September 13, 1993

Laura Late
Regional Director
Muscular Dystrophy Association
2949 N. Mayfair Rd. Suite 104
Wauwatosa, WI 53222

Dear Laura,

In response to your letter of August 23rd, I must admit I was a bit surprised. While knowing that the MDA would not endorse my event to climb Mt. Vinson, your organization has given me several mixed signals as to what they really wanted. I understood that I could not use MDA's name in saying that I was climbing for them. In the months of January and February, Carrie Hoyer said that it WOULD be permissible to tell people that I was having a fund raising climb with all proceeds going to the Muscular Dystrophy Association. That is what I did.

As for the hazardous nature of my climb, I would rather be part of an organized climb rather than run in and out of traffic in busy intersections trying to fill the boot as fire fighters do each year. I had asked to send a letter waiving all responsibilities and liabilities by the MDA. I was told that a letter would be sent to me to sign.

The records that I have kept while planning this climb are accurate. I know what expenses have occurred and have the receipts to prove it. I can even tell you that this year alone that I have made 24 phone calls to the MDA offices. My proposal also stated that anyone donating $100 or more would receive a complete report of the trip, including copies of all receipts, a list of major donators and a summery of the climb. This expense would also come from my pocket. I had ask the MDA office if they would care to handle the finances so they could keep track of records and to provide guidelines to help me be more precise in what I was doing so I would not go against the MDA rules. Your office did not respond with either a letter or with a phone call saying they would not help.

When I called your office to ask for a break down of the MDA expenditures for a party that was interested in donating, you office complied immediately.

In August it was agreed upon by your office that I could have the various union locals from across the country send their donations directly to your office on Mayfair Rd. Your office agreed and said that they would keep track of the amounts and the union local's number for me.

As for my letter head, if I would have had it last year when I climbed Mt. Elbrus for the American Diabetes Association, I'm sure I could have raised more than the $17,000 that I did for them.

The personal benefit that you say I'm going after has cost me over $900 at this point not to mention 11 months of personal time that I have put into this project. I have also put up $20,000 of my money to cover climbing cost. If it would have come to the point to where I would have been able to ask my fellow fire fighters to donate $1 each to the MDA. I would have paid the additional $528.67 for postage, not to mention the time and trouble of typing up all the labels and preparing the letters.

If I was looking for publicity, I would have pushed this project, let you take your legal action and let the courts see my records. Could you imagine how that would look. But because there is no point in it, what would there be to gain on either side. I was out to help the MDA not hurt it.

Everyone who donated to help me pay for the climb, did it because they believed in me and was interested in helping a worthy cause. They also knew that the MDA did not support what I was doing, but came through because they wanted to help.

Since the IAFF (international Association of Fire Fighters) will not let me ask the rest of the union fire fighters of the country for a donation to MDA. All donations sent to me in support will be returned as stated in my proposal. After all, I would then be in conflict with what I had agreed to do. You see, this climb like those in the past have always been on the level. I will explain what has happened as well as a copy of the letter you sent me to all donators. From what I understand the IAFF was in favor of what I was doing until your letter was sent. Thanks to your letter to the IAFF I can't even solicit fire fighters around the country for any other charitable group.

I have supported the MDA since I was twelve years old with my first MD carnival. Since I became a fire fighter, I have filled the boot, participated in bed races, collected money door to door and yes in 1988 I climbed Mt. Kilimanjaro in Africa as a fund rasing event and raised $4,780 for the MDA.

Since that first climb there have been a number of major climbs for charity. Two separate groups have climbed Mt. McKinley in Alaska. One group "Climb for a Cure" raised over $100,000 for aids research and another group raised over $20,000 for the Northwest burn foundation. This group was made up of firefighters who saw the potential in what I have done for others. I know this for a fact because they asked me how to do it. Mt. McKinely is a much more dangerous climb than Mt. Vinson. I have also learned of a group of climbers (mainly women who have survived breast cancer) who are planning a climb up the highest peak in the Andes in 1995. Mt. Aconcagua, it is 22,835 ft. high. Their target goal is two million dollars. It is clear cut that this form of fund raising works.

Most people can't understand why you're so against some one trying to help you. All I wanted to do was raise money for something I believed in. That is why I saved such an impressive mountain for the MDA. For years I have watched Jerry Lewis on his telethon, tell people to give what they can. That is all I wanted to do. Others as well as myself feel the letter you sent to me was not only harsh, but did not explain clearly enough why I had to throw away 11 months of work and over $900 trying to help raise money for the same group that is threatening legal action against me.

On labor day of this year fire fighters donated 9 million dollars to MDA. I was one of those fire fighters that helped to raise it. What is so terrible about wanting to give more?

I realize that this matter is now over and finished with. You can believe me when I tell you that I will not again try to raise money for the MDA. I would like a written acknowledgment to this letter.

Sincerely but hurt.
With the good of the MDA in mind.

Nick B. Comande

I never expected my letter to change their minds about letting me raise money for them, nor would I want to – even if they had wanted me to. My largest fundraising event had ended even before it started. Their reply seemed to dodge any questions that I wanted answered and the MDA would not even be man, or woman enough to admit their mistake as you can see in their return letter.

MDA®

Fighting 40 Neuromuscular Diseases

... a *non-United Way* independent voluntary agency which has never sought either government funding or fees from those it serves.

2949 N. Mayfair Road, #104, Wauwatosa, WI 53222
Telephone (414) 476-9700; Fax (414) 476-6683

September 27, 1993

Nick B. Comande
1024 Florence Avenue
Racine, WI 53402

Dear Nick,

In response to your letter of September 13th, I'm truly sorry that you considered my letter unduly harsh or felt that you'd previously received "mixed signals" from MDA.

As stated in my letter, the primary reason why we can't allow you to use MDA's name in any way in connection with your mountain climbing is the potential liability from this or any such ultra-hazardous activity. I'm told by our Legal Department that a written waiver from you wouldn't be sufficient, as it couldn't deter anyone that might be injured in such event from suing MDA, and if we permitted such hazardous activities to be conducted in MDA's name, our liability insurance would be cost-prohibitive.

We do value your years of support and hope that you will reconsider and continue to work with the IAFF in raising money for MDA.

Very truly yours,

Regional Director

ss

Muscular Dystrophy Association
JERRY LEWIS, National Chairman

The final insult was when I sent a letter explaining everything to Jerry Lewis in care of the Muscular Dystrophy Association. It was returned stamped. "no such person."

Still wanting to make a fundraiser out of this climb, I considered another charity. The American Diabetes Association had already had two climbs and I wanted a new charity. I'm not sure how or why, but the American Cancer Society came to mind.

I called the local office and explained everything I wanted to do, including what had happened with the MDA, and how well climbing for charities had worked in the past. I received a phone call from Ed Lord the following day. He explained what he needed from me and what the American Cancer Society would do to help me in return. In just over 48 hours, I was back in the fundraising business.

To finish all I had started with the MDA, I mailed back all the donations that had been sent to me with a letter explaining what had happened, along with a copy of the letter sent to me by the MDA, and a copy of my rebuttal letter. I asked the patrons if they would consider reissuing their checks in the name of the American Cancer Society. More than fifty percent of the people did, while others thought I might not be legitimate and declined. Still others simply didn't care to donate to the American Cancer Society. It cost me over $1,300 of my own money to send back the $4,900 that had been collected earlier as well as the proposals for both the MDA and the American Cancer Society.

Time - that's what I was really up against. I didn't have the time to promote this climb for the American Cancer Society like I had for the MDA. Even though they were no longer a part of my project, the MDA was still hurting me. I was determined to still do the best job I could. "To hell with the MDA," I thought. Since I was no longer able to contact all the firefighters in the country, IAFF 5th District Vice President Charles Buss gave me permission to solicit the firefighting members of the IAFF in Wisconsin. The turnout was far less than I expected. Out of 57 locals, with a possible $2,600 that could have been raised, only seven responded with a gain of $500 for the American Cancer Society. A lone union local, just south of the Wisconsin border in Illinois, heard what I was doing and donated another $40. Deep down I felt that had I been asking for donations for the MDA, the totals would have been higher.

Meanwhile, my accomplishments weren't going totally unnoticed. In late September, I received a phone call from the Maxwell House Coffee Corporation. They were looking for people who had worked hard for their communities, as well as for others. Out of over 5000 people nominated, I was one of the chosen. Cindy Lessor, who had been so helpful with the printing of my climb proposals and the sending of my fax documents at the local Econoprint, had submitted my name.

Forty-five people from all over the United States, their spouses or their family members (I took my girlfriend, Lisa) were flown to Washington D.C. for an awards ceremony and banquet. The nominees were greeted by Charles Phillips, the President of Maxwell House Coffee, and were decorated with medals by former First Lady Barbara Bush; I was even mentioned in her speech. We were given a tour of the city, and several of us (including myself) were written up in People magazine.

Though it only lasted a weekend, the whole experience was a wonderful time. I was able to meet a number of caring people who went out of their way for others, expecting nothing in return. I was pleased to be in such company. While my accomplishments weren't as great as some, it felt good to be appreciated.

With a little less than a month to go before the climb, I worked hard at getting pledges. Since I had no help like I'd had from the Diabetes Association, I relied heavily on family and friends to help me spread the word and get donations. Even though the bulk of raising donations fell on my shoulders, I appreciated any and all help. I even had the pledge sheets printed on bright yellow paper so they would stand out more and maybe attract attention to them. Anything to get someone to look at it and hopefully pledge.

AMERICAN CANCER SOCIETY®
WISCONSIN DIVISION, INC.

Nick Comande, a firefighter from Racine, will be attempting to climb Mount Vinson for the benefit of the American Cancer Society. You can share in his adventures by pledging money for every 100 feet he successfully climbs.

Mount Vinson at, 16,067 feet, is the summit of Vinson Massif, the highest peak in Antarctica. Nick will begin his ascent on November 15, 1993.

By pledging 5¢ for every 100 feet Nick climbs, your contribution would be $ 8.03. If you pledge 10¢ per 100 feet, your contribution would be $ 16.07. It is also possible to make a flat donation to the American Cancer Society in recognition of Nick's efforts.

Wish Nick luck and pledge what you can!

American Cancer Society
Wisconsin Division, Inc.
6233 Bankers Road
Racine, Wisconsin 53403
552-8022

Mount Vinson - 16,067 foot climb, the highest point in Antarctica

Pledge/foot:	**1¢**	**5¢**	**10¢**	**25¢**	**50¢**	**$1.00**
Total Pledge:	**$1.61**	**$8.03**	**$16.07**	**$40.17**	**$80.34**	**$160.67**

	Name (please print) Address Zip Code	Pledge per 100 ft.	Flat Donation	Total Pledge
1				
2				
3				
4				
5				
6				
7				
8				
9				
10				
11				
12				
13				
14				
15				
16				
17				
18				
19				
20				

Please pledge what you can - All proceeds will go to the American Cancer Society
Pledge sheets MUST be returned by November 25, 1993
Send to: American Cancer Society
6233 Bankers Road
Racine, WI 53403

I was looking forward to this climb more than any of my previous ones. I was going to go to a place that even fewer people go. For me, it was going to be my biggest adventure to date.

In Route

November 21, 1993 Elevation: 200 feet

I'm in a plane on the runway in Puerto Montt, well into the lower third of South America. I'm not sure why I decided to start writing now. I'm on Ladeco Airlines; I missed the connection in Santiago, Chile, by ten minutes, so I ended up waiting for nine hours until the next flight left for Punta Arenas. The plane stopped here to pick up more passengers. I hope I will finally reach Punta Arenas, which is my last stop on the South American continent before leaving for the Antarctic. I made it here by 10:30 p.m. Had I arrived by 1:00 p.m. today as scheduled, I could have used the remainder of the day as a rest day.

I fell asleep right after dinner last night while flying out of Miami, and I slept some seven hours. No real sign of jet lag, but I could use a shower and a warm bed. I met another member of the trip in Miami. His name is Lou Kashiske. He was sitting in the airport when I noticed his bag had a Mountain Travel emblem on it; he had used them before. Lou is 51, a lawyer (but I won't hold that against him) from Dearborn, Michigan, and a very pleasant and knowledgeable man. Lou is also a well-seasoned climber. He has climbed everything I have climbed, and almost everything else. We're about to take off now, so I will finish this when I get a chance.

November 25, 1993 Elevation: Over 20,000 feet

I'm seated in the middle of a Hercules C-130 aircraft. It is hard to believe that after 15 months of dreaming, delays, possible lawsuits and a great deal of work, I'm finally on my way. I stopped writing earlier because the plane was about to take off and I was tired. It seemed to take forever to get to Punta Arenas. Its 14 ½ hours from Milwaukee to Punta Arenas, not including delays and layovers.

I just barely made it to the hotel by midnight. I tried to sleep, but my bed was very, very hard. My room is $99 a night instead of the $36 per night room I signed for. Tuesday the 23rd consisted of a gear check in the morning and a briefing at 5:00 in the evening. The meals here are good and not very costly. The briefing gave everyone a chance to get acquainted while also informing us as to what we needed to know about the flight, including what to do if our plane went down on or before we hit the ice (a worst-case scenario).

It was an informative briefing, and everyone was pumped up and ready to go by the time it ended. Unfortunately, the winds in the Antarctic were over 50 mph – much too strong to land the plane – so the waiting game began. Phone calls were made at 8:00 a.m. this morning and we were told that weather conditions were favorable. We all boarded a large bus to the airport where we made another check of our personal gear, and then once again we waited.

First, there was a refueling delay, then a moving-the-plane-delay, and then talk of another bad-weather delay. During the worst-case scenario presentation, it had been brought to our attention that should thc plane be forced down we would need to be self-reliant against the elements. So, while we waited, we walked around the airport in our climbing gear, and eventually got off the plane in Patriot Hills, Antarctica, dressed in our cold weather and climbing gear

We had been hyped about the flight ever since we knew we were going to leave; it was such a relief to finally be on our way.

There was no customs or immigrations to go through, but Sol, the sister of Anne Kershaw (owner of Adventure Network and wife of the late Giles Kershaw, famous for his piloting skills in the Antarctic), collected our passports and cleared any remaining paperwork. After all we were going to an unclaimed continent – owned by no one and used by many. Before boarding the plane, there were many group photos taken of the crew and all the passengers.

There is a Korean team of four that will be cross-country skiing from Patriot Hills to the South Pole, a distance of some 660 miles. They have a support team that will be waiting for them back at Patriot Hills. It will take them approximately 50 days to make the trek dragging 200-lb. sleds loaded with supplies behind them, and there are three members of the Chilean Army that will be climbing Vinson alongside us. Onboard the plane was also the cook for the Patriot Hills base camp and two gentlemen from Saudi Arabia: Sultan, and his cousin Kaled. I believe they are going all the way to the South Pole and then on to observe the Emperor Penguins. I hear the tour of the South Pole is relatively short and cost another $5,000 to get there. (As much as I would like to be able to say I was at the South Pole, the closest I'll ever come to it is 660 miles away.) There is also some kind of scientist accompanying us to study the penguins.

Another person going to the South Pole is Doug Smith. He is 44 and works with computers. He told me he almost lost his house in the California fires last year. He is a well-traveled individual who is going because he has already been to the North Pole.

The other climbers are Lou Kashiscke, a lawyer, and John Davis III, an investment broker from North Carolina; John is a very nice, intelligent man, but so far everyone I've met has been nice. Rick French will be our assistant guide from upstate New York. All three of these guys learned they were coming here just in the last two weeks. This trip was probably pocket money for Lou and John, and Rick is probably going for free because he is an assistant guide, and then there is me; I'll be paying for this trip for a long, long time. Our senior guide is already in Patriot Hills; his name is Alejo Stoedings, and he has climbed Vinson several times.

Before boarding the plane, members from a Chilean newspaper stopped to take my photo holding my flag; they interviewed me about climbing to raise money for the American Cancer Society. It was windy, so I enlisted John Davis to help me hold it. The photo was printed in the newspaper while we were away.

I had just taken a break from writing and had gone to visit the flight deck, when one of the pilots kindly informed me that we only had four hours left of the six hour flight. Looking out the window, I could see we were over water with small ice flows floating below.

If you were hungry, there were ham sandwiches, soft drinks, orange juice and ½ pound bags of peanuts available to anyone who wanted them. (The commercial airlines could learn something from this airline.) Because of the noise of the four large propellers, earplugs were handed out before the flight. This was not a luxurious airline, but they did have standard airplane seats.

I was advised by the flight engineer that we could have a bumpy landing because of all the cargo onboard; the Korean team has 48 pieces alone.

While I was in the airport, I was fortunate enough to meet Retired Colonel Norman D. Vaughn. He is flying to Patriot Hills on another plane and then traveling by dog sled to climb a mountain named after him by Admiral Byrd some 50 years ago. Col. Vaughn hopes to summit his 10,302 ft. high namesake on his 87th birthday. I wonder if he can do it.

Many people are sleeping now; I should be too, but I'm too excited.

Just a few minutes ago the first large ice flow was spotted; I've never personally seen anything like that. We've been airborne for just over four hours now, with about two to go. Each passing minute we move closer to Patriot Hills. I've heard from the pilots that one's first steps on the ice are the most impressive; I'm sure it will be. To me, it will be like stepping onto the moon.

Looking out the window, I can see low flying clouds; they seem to be just a few hundred feet over the ice fields. I hope they don't interfere with our landing. It has happened – planes have had to turn around and return to Punta Arena because they couldn't land in bad weather. The flight engineer said the longest distance they landed was 11,000 ft.; usually it's only 4,000 ft. I felt a lump in my stomach; I'm sure it's just nerves. I've been excited about this ever since Anne called and told me the flight was on for today. I ran into the dining room this morning when Lou and John were having breakfast, and told them.

I was sure our landing would be fine; it won't be long now.

November 26, 1993 Patriot Hills Elevation: 2,600 feet

A great deal has happened since I last wrote; there has been a plane crash; fortunately, it was not mine. Starting with our landing, the last 24 hours have been very long. My flight landed the second time after 5 hours 52 minutes worth of flying. I was lucky enough to have one of the few window seats onboard, and I could see what was going on outside. There were clouds in the sky but there were also large open spots in which to see through. It was difficult to tell where the clouds ended and ice began.

We circled a bit. I was looking for signs of the ground when suddenly a dark patch of something flashed past my window, and before I could even blink an eye, the wheels of the plane hit the ice. We were pre-warned about the roughness of the landing, but I was totally caught off guard; momentarily, it scared the hell out of me. After a few moments of bouncing around, I heard the engines rev up and the plane lifted off the ice, and we flew back into the sky. Later, we learned that the pilot had landed the plane on the wrong side of the runway markers.

The plane circled again and landed on the proper side of the markers which were fuel drums and large green hefty bags filled with snow so they wouldn't blow away. This was by far the roughest, bumpiest landing I've ever had. The plane stopped, and I couldn't wait to do the one thing that I've been waiting well over a year to do, and that was to walk on Antarctic Ice.

Before getting off the plane the passengers were warned about getting on the ice wearing double plastic boots. We would be stepping onto ice, literally, and would be very prone to slipping. I still couldn't wait to get out of the plane; I felt like this was a momentous occasion. I wondered if this was how Neil Armstrong felt when he took his first steps on the moon.

Looking out of the door of the plane, I could see the ice below. It looked like there were hundreds of divots covering it, which explained why it was such a rough landing. Watching my footing, I stepped out onto the blue Antarctic Ice, and I had been right – it was a very momentous occasion in my life.

I looked out over the ice before me; in the distance – at least a half a mile away – I could see the Patriot Hills base camp. There was a line of flags from various countries marking the last 600 yards to the camp.

The weather was very cold and windy and the sky was overcast; everything was grayish in color. People from the camp greeted us as we got off the plane; others had started to unload all the cargo that we had brought with us. A snowmobile, with a huge sled attached, was used to pull the thousand pounds of equipment from the plane to the camp. We were told to proceed to the camp, and we did so by walking on patches of snow wherever we could to avoid slipping on the ice; the last half of the walk was just on snow.

As I approached Camp, I could make out small tents scattered about; one large white tent laid half in and half out of the snow. There were no permanent buildings here, just tents and bamboo poles sticking out of the ground marking places that needed to be marked.

It wasn't too long after we reached Camp that the Hercules aircraft took off and headed back to Punta Arenas. The entire unloading took less than 30 minutes and the pilot never shut down the engines on the opposite side of the plane where we debarked.

We formally met the staff of Patriot Hills Base. The first person I met was Rachel. She approached me while Lou was taking my picture outside of the Hercules; she got in very close for the picture, as well. The next person I met was Hilda, a cook. Then there is Brydon, Grant, Earl, Max and others. I'm tired now and could use some sleep. It is presently 12:17 a.m., November 27; "Happy Birthday" to me!

The hot meal promised us upon our arrival was truly worth it. It was spaghetti, and either it was great, or I was really hungry. We sat around and talked and set up our tents since that is where we were going to be sleeping. I started to dig a foundation for one of the tents while Lou, John and Rick started to put one of the tents together. After our two tents were up, a snow wall was built around them to block the wind.

I shared a tent with Lou; John took one by himself, and Rick shared a tent with Marcus (one of the ANI people that flew down with us).

It was about 3:10 a.m. when I finally went to bed, but it was still light out. The sun would be up 24 hours-a-day this time of year. If it wasn't for the clouds, the sky would be very bright, instead of this overcast gray.

It happened at 4:30 a.m., or very close to it – something that would change the course of the trip. The supply plane of Norman Vaughn crashed while coming in for a landing. I was sound asleep by then and never heard a thing.

As told to me by members of ANI, the plane flew through a cloud or fog-patch just before touching down; the windows fogged, or the pilot didn't have a good enough view of the landing sight or the surrounding area. The plane hit a high patch of snow that ripped off the landing gear. One of the plane's propellers hit the ground and was jarred loose, cutting its way into the fuselage. Fortunately, the impact tore loose the passenger seats of the plane and thrust them forward, just away from where the propeller entered the aircraft. Otherwise, two people would have been killed by the time the plane stopped moving.

Several people were injured with minor cuts and scratches. One person is seriously injured; his name is Jerry. Someone said he was the veterinarian on board to take care of the sled dogs on the trip.

At the time of the crash, members from Patriot Hills were monitoring the landing. Brydon, one of the pilots for ANI was out by the runway with a radio and saw the crash. He quickly alerted the other members of ANI and then went to help. They reached the site of the crash with two snowmobiles with large sleds tied behind them. I didn't learn about the crash until after I woke up and went into the cook tent. Rachel and John told me about a plane going down, and because of my background as a rescue squad worker, asked if I would help with Jerry.

I agreed and quickly went to Rachel's tent where they had taken Jerry. He was with Earl Ramsey, who is an EMT-II, meaning that with his training, he can do more than I can as an EMT Basic. Jerry was half-in and half-out of a sleeping bag in the middle of the tent and obviously in a great deal of pain. Earl and I spent the next six hours trying to make Jerry as comfortable as possible. To make matters worse, the weather was starting to work against us; clouds were coming in and would delay any rescue flight coming in. We didn't know it at the time, but it would be another 36 hours before another plane could fly in.

You didn't need medical training to know that Jerry was in bad shape. His left leg was broken in at least one spot, his left arm was broken, his chin was split and he must have had a number of loose teeth judging by the blood around his gums. He had a number of punctures and scratches around his face, and his sides hurt from broken ribs or other possible internal injuries.

Earl, to whom I give most of the credit for Jerry's care, did a wonderful job. The only medical items in the Camp were basic first aid kits and one bottle of morphine that one of the members of the Chilean army had in his first aid kit. Earl would periodically radio the team physician back in Punta Arenas while I sat with Jerry.

Jerry was in a great deal of pain; he thrashed around a lot, bringing new pain to his left leg and arm. He screamed, yelled and swore. It was difficult conversing with him in an effort to keep his mind off his injuries, but between Earl and I, we did our best.

Throughout the day we would take breaks in the tent watching Jerry. Many helped, including members of the Chilean army. Rick French helped, and even John Davis was not afraid to get in there and get his hands dirty. I walked around Camp, stretching my legs and looking at the sled-dogs tied up and resting; they, too, had been on the downed supply plane. Out of the 20 dogs flown in one was badly injured and four were missing; they had run off from the plane right after the crash and had not been seen again.

If I understood correctly, this was to be the last dog team to come to the Antarctic. I spent time talking to Mike Diagaspri; he was another person on the supply plane. I cleaned and closed a small laceration on his forehead. We talked awhile and he told me about his experience in the crash. He was glad to be alive and looked forward to seeing his girlfriend again. He asked me why I was here. When I told him I was climbing a mountain to raise money for the American Cancer Society, he insisted on making a donation. I couldn't believe it; here was this poor guy who had almost bought it in a plane crash, and he wanted to donate to a charity in another country.

It's odd what it takes to get some people to appreciate life.

November 27, 1993 (My Birthday) Patriot Hills Elevation:2600 feet

It is 11:49 p.m. and the day is almost over. These entries have been very sparse because it's been difficult to keep up with all of the events of the last few days; it is hard to keep an accurate time line going.

It is 20° F. in the tent and very bright outside. The sun has been shining for the last 24 hours, making it difficult to distinguish night from day. Everyone here must remember to use their sunscreen to protect ourselves against the sun's reflection off the snow. When there's no wind, it's very pleasant out; when the wind blows hard, it's very cold.

Earl and I were watching Jerry early this morning; I was with them for that last three hours before the plane arrived to pick him up. We prepared Jerry the best we could to make him ready for the six-hour flight home. From the tent we could hear the plane land and were glad to know that more competent medical help was on the way. Jerry was hurting; his leg and ankle were really swollen, and blisters had started to form. There was still a lot of dried blood around his face and in his hair that we couldn't clean off. It was difficult not having all the proper equipment that we needed; even rags were scarce.

Yesterday, we were using Tampons to clean the blood off. Just getting hot water was a chore; someone would have to run to the cook-tent and bring it back in a thermos. I found myself missing all those little luxuries I had come here to escape. I never thought that I would be so glad to hear the sound of a plane as I did when the Hercules returned for Jerry. Being in the tent I couldn't see what was happening, but I could hear the commotion of the ANI team getting ready to meet the plane and bring in the people that would take Jerry out.

The snowmobiles pulled the sled to the tent and arrived with the medical team from the still running Hercules. I could hear people talking as they reached the outside of the tent; they were in some type of discussion. As voices started to get louder, I realized they were arguing. I don't know who was yelling at whom, but someone was saying that he wanted the camera crew to go in first so they could film him taking care of the injured man. Someone else was saying that there would be no room and that the tent was already crowded. This went on for several minutes before a bearded man, wearing an expensive snowsuit with patches galore from various sponsors, entered the tent. I later was told that he may have been one of the team physicians

The first thing this person did was take pictures of Jerry; he didn't examine his injuries or take vital signs, but he took pictures! When he realized that his camera lens was fogging up, he stopped to clean it. I could've hit him. I had been with Jerry – on and off – for over 36 hours; I had never stopped, nor had I even considered taking his picture. I felt that this person's first priority should have been the patient, not trying to possibly show off for the National Geographic cameramen covering the Vaughn Climb. I don't think I've ever had less respect for someone in the medical profession as I did for him.

I helped Earl and someone else who came on the rescue plane apply a new type of traction splint to Jerry's injured leg; he was then wrapped in a large insulated-type sleeping bag and we carried Jerry outside to a waiting sled. The National Geographic film crew, which I had seen earlier at the airport, was here filming Jerry's rescue. In the distance, I could see the C-130 Hercules – the one that had brought me down here – sitting on the runway. Yesterday, we had wondered who would be flying down to pick up Jerry; it could've been the Chilean Army or ANI. Apparently, some type of deal was worked out with an insurance company as to who would be paying for the fuel, and ANI had come back down.

Jerry was slowly pulled to the C-130. Earl was by his side giving him comfort, but he did not fly back with him. We all watched as the C-130 revved up his engines and lifted off the runway for the flight back to Punta Arenas. The plane had landed at 2:15 p.m. and was airborne again by 3:00 p.m.

Once Jerry, the dogs, and the rest of the people who flew down on the supply plane were headed back to Punta Arenas, it was time to think about our part of the trip and our climb up Vinson. Because the ANI pilots could only fly if they had so many hours of sleep, our window of opportunity for the day had long since flown by. Brydon Kibbs, our pilot to Vinson Base Camp, had been up many hours since the crash of Vaughan's DC-6. He would have to get some real sleep before we could attempt to leave Patriot Hills. Since we had nothing to do, we boarded the large sled that was used to haul supplies and went out to look at the crash sight.

The plane, owned by Allcot Air, crashed somewhere between five or six miles from PH base Camp. After seeing the plane it was a miracle that no one was killed or more people seriously hurt. It was a terrible sight and the first crashed plane I had seen up close. It lay there on top of the snow, listing to one side.

The D-6 lying on the ice 2 days after it crashed.

A long indentation had been made in the snow where the plane had slid along before coming to a stop. Large holes were dug into the snow where the wheels hit and the landing gear and propellers had all been ripped off. The outside starboard engine was half-off and someone had said it was still burning after the crash. Everyone aboard that plane had been fortunate. The extra fuel it carried had not caught fire, nor had it exploded.

The fuselage was intact except where the propeller cut into its port side; someone had taken an orange tarp and tried to plug the gash to keep snow from drifting in. Everyone took a number of photographs of the plane. We looked at it from all sides, but didn't go in it; we had been warned about that. Someone would be coming down to investigate the crash at a later date.

Dinner tonight was beef and broccoli stir-fry, and for dessert, Hilda made a carrot cake and put a trick birthday candle on it in my honor. The whole group sang *Happy Birthday* to me and everybody laughed when I blew out the candle and it re-lit. Someone asked how I could be a firefighter if I couldn't even blow out the candle on my own birthday cake?

The best part of the evening came when Brydon said, "Hey look, a penguin strolled into Camp." I was beside myself. I wanted to see a penguin so bad this trip, but I knew I wouldn't because we were so far inland; this was my big chance. I ran to the door only to see Alejo – dressed up in a penguin outfit for my birthday. He waddled up to me, shook my hand and wished me "Happy Birthday." I had a wonderful time; this was the first birthday I'd ever spent away from home, but I was far from alone. I had new friends with me.

November 28, 1993 Patriot Hills Elevation: 2,600 feet

I've just sat down in the cook tent; it is a very long tent reaching some 45 ft. in length. Here all the snow is melted into water, meals are prepared, served and eaten. There are makeshift shelves hanging from the upper tent supports; they are filled with paperback books with covers that are warn and curled.

I look across the room. I see a bearded, depressed looking person; he has a slightly reddened nose and some minor traces of sunburn, but soon – too soon – I realize the image is my own reflection in a mirror. Staring back at myself, I wonder what I am doing here, but I know what I'm doing and why: I'm on the adventure of a lifetime. I just wish it wouldn't take so long to get on with the climb. So far, we are three days behind schedule and we're starting to run out of time.

To recap the day's events, I had breakfast, then Lou and I finished packing up our gear and tent; we'll need the tent on the mountain. So far, the weather looks good. Sultan, Kaled and Doug will fly to the South Pole and back today. They'll be flying one of the two twin-engine Otters, piloted by J.C. and we will take the other. They will then fly back to Punta Arenas tomorrow in the C-130 that will be coming back for them. Since I will not be seeing them again, I said goodbye.

Our departure time is scheduled for 1:00 in the afternoon, but I know this won't be so – everything here runs about four hours late.

The four Koreans who are cross-country skiing to the South Pole also left today; they walked past our plane parked next to a fuel cache to say goodbye. They are dragging sleds behind them with over 200 pounds of supplies, and they will be walking for 50 days. We detained them for about 20 minutes so we could take pictures. Everyone wished them good luck, and they wished us the same with our endeavors. Then they walked away from camp, one behind the other, on this frozen sea of ice. I couldn't imagine trying to ski 30 kilometers a day while man hauling those sleds.

After they left, we finished packing our plane. The three Chileans that flew with us are also going to climb Mt. Vinson. There are now eight of us, altogether: the three Chileans, Lou, John, Rick, Alejo and myself, and in charge of the plane are Brydon, the pilot, and Clay, the plane's mechanic. The plane was packed in such a fashion that we could all have a window seat. It was crowded, but still tolerable. We had a quick flight check before take-off (the same kind as with a commercial airline), and then Brydon fired up the engines and we were off.

We left base Camp and flew over the Korean skiers, who broke their uniform stride just long enough to wave to us. As the plane flew low over the crash site of Norman Vaughn's supply plane, our job was to look for the four missing dogs still wandering around out there. We were airborne for about 25 minutes – almost halfway to the base of Vinson – when Brydon abruptly turned the plane around and headed back to Patriot Hills. He told us that the weather was no good. The whole mountain region was clouded in; even their backup landing sight was no good. There was no other choice but to turn back. We may try again in another six or seven hours.

When we landed back at Patriot Hills, we left the plane loaded with all of our gear, tents and supplies. No sense unpacking them unless we have to spend the night here. I think Lou wants a new tent mate; I snore too much for him. He had to give me a shove last night so I would stop.

Unfortunately, I now have the time to catch up on my journal. 5:31 p.m., the same day. I'm sitting outside on a cushioned bench made from the sled that hauls the large piles of supplies to the camp. It is sunny and there is not much wind, the temperature is 21° F. and it's pleasant out. I took a walk alone about a half mile from Camp; when it isn't windy and the spindrift isn't blowing, you can see for miles. From where I sit, I can see the wreck of the DC-6, and that is still five miles away.

At no time was I worried about being lost; I could see the Camp in the distance, and I rather liked being alone. Except for a slight breeze, there was no noise at all – no street sounds of any kind – just nature and all her glory. As I was reflecting on this, someone fired up the generator back at Patriot Hills and I could hear its hum. I thought I heard a dog bark in the distance, but I believe it was just the wind. Grant, the Camp manager, said that the dogs could only last another day or two before dehydrating.

I was enjoying being so totally alone; I felt like walking out to the crash site. I knew it was quite a distance, but I didn't have to worry about it getting dark. All I needed to worry about was the cold. I had my pile jacket on, but not my wind jacket; I'd freeze for sure without that if the weather turned. In this place, wind chill meant just that. Also, in the pockets of my wind jacket were my sunscreen and sunblock to keep me from burning. There was no question about where to go; once again, I let common sense be my guide and headed straight back to Camp.

Before I forget, at 9:00 this morning, Grant came into the cook tent and informed us of a radio call he had received. He told us that Jerry had a shattered left leg, a small bleed in his head, and minor internal injuries. He is stable now and should make a complete recovery. To show their gratitude, the National Geographic Society donated two snowmobiles (the ones that were on the crashed plane) to ANI. Grant gave his thanks to everyone here at Camp for his/her help and patience. Also, it was confirmed that messages had been sent to families back home, assuring everyone that we were all safe.

6:32 p.m. I don't know if I'm just sleepy or bored; I believe Hilda is cooking fish for dinner. No further news on the weather forecast, but the mountain range is still clouded in. If this keeps up much longer, morale will begin to drop. I hope we leave soon. We may try again at 4:00 a.m. tomorrow. Why 4:00 a.m.? I don't know.

November 29, 1993 Patriot Hill Camp (still)

4:00 a.m. came and went; the weather over the mountains is still bad which means another full day's delay. God, I hope not; this waiting is really starting to wear me thin. I believe it's time to get lost in a book or something; I refuse to lie all day in my sleeping bag – like Lou. He may enjoy it, but I'm not one to do that. It just makes everything in the tent wet from condensation.

Yesterday evening, Grant left camp to look for the lost dogs. Well prepared in case bad weather came in, he covered more than 25 miles of area by snowmobile. He would stop periodically to cook bacon, hoping the smell would carry across the ice and bring the dogs to him. He came back an hour ago – no luck. Time is quickly running out for the dogs; they are too far away to reach the coast, and according to Grant, they haven't touched the food left for them at the wreckage site.

Someone said that dogs – if they get hungry enough – will sometimes turn on themselves, but dehydration may set in quicker. Sadly, more than likely they, are gone for good.

Doug Smith took the other twin otter plane to see the Emperor penguins. J.C. is his pilot and Dean is his mechanic. With him are Rachel, Devita (one of the cooks), Marcus, and the Chilean bird specialist who is here to observe the penguins. (I forget what type of -ologist he is, and I don't even know his name because I don't think we've been introduced.)

Patriot Hills base Camp has quieted down a bit since everyone left. There were a total of 39 people here at one time, including the Koreans who are now gone – with the exception of two members of their support team who are still here. Of course, the crash victims are gone and the others are off to see the penguins, so it seems like everyone has left but me. I wish I could start my adventure before I lose my will. It is said that the Antarctic can really test your patience; I can see that now. I'm wondering if there will still be time to climb the mountain before it's time to leave.

I was hoping there would be no delays this trip; boy was I wrong. I'm not a patient person and believe it or not, I think I'm a little homesick. I try not to spend all the free hours I have thinking of those back home and the one's I Love. (Did I ever mention that I think the word "Love" should always be written with a capital letter – no matter where it is in a sentence?)

11:00 p.m., Cook Tent, Temp -11° C. I spent the last 40 minutes talking to Grant about the crash – too many details to write about now. I wish I had a tape recorder with me. If I ever do this again I'll bring one.

We went on an excursion today. Earl, Sultan, Kaled and I took snowmobiles to the hills of Patriot Hills. Roughly 1 ½ miles from Camp, we walked up some of the smaller hills and looked over the ridges. I took what I hope will be some beautiful pictures. It's too bad there were clouds rolling over them. Earl said there was a 50/50 chance of us flying out tomorrow; we'll see.

11:40 p.m. I'm back in my tent but it's not the same tent I was staying in when I first arrived. This tent was unloaded from the plane, along with our sleeping bags and other things we wish we didn't have to unload; it will all have to be reloaded tomorrow. This tent is smaller and doesn't hold heat as well as my earlier Camp Trails tent. There are more ice crystals forming on the roof and sides.

I'm in my sleeping bag now and it's difficult to write. I have bad penmanship anyway, and the cold doesn't help. I can't write while wearing gloves. Sometimes, I just wear my silk liners which makes it easier it to write.

To pass the time I've started to read the book, *IT* by Stephen King. I read this book about five years ago and thoroughly enjoyed it. What better place to read a book that will give you chills, than in a land that is doing the same thing? I'm already a tenth of the way through it. I enjoy reading King and have read his books on the mountains before.

I have to get some sleep now; perhaps tomorrow will be a big day and perhaps I will be sleeping at Camp I on Vinson. I hope I have good dreams tonight – not the nightmares I had last night. I don't recall what they were, I just know they woke me up; maybe I'm afraid of failing to summit.

I know this will be my only chance to come to Antarctica, so I will make the best of it. I might be crazy enough to come back, but I don't know when I would be able to afford it again.

November 30, 1993 Altitude: 3940 feet Welcome Nanatuk Valley

4:12 p.m. Temperature 25° F. I'm getting closer, but I'm still not there. I was awakened by Brydon our pilot; he yelled, "A big early breakfast and we're off!" Well, we had breakfast: peach pancakes and scrambled eggs, juice, cereal, toast and anything else you might want. The Vinson contingent then loaded the plane and we were off. The clouds rolling over the small mountains by Patriot Hills had disappeared. Brydon was confident of reaching the mountain – at least *he* was confident.

After 45 minutes of flying and only 15 more to go, Brydon announced that it was just a bit clouded in; therefore we would have to turn back. But instead of going all the way back to Patriot Hills, Brydon landed the plane at a place called "Welcome Nanatuk." I was told Nanatuk was an Eskimo word meaning, "mountain rising out of the snow." Nanatuk is a lonely little mountain peak, and rounded on the top; it stands all by itself in this barren place.

Welcome Nanatuk. A Lone little peak in the middle of no where. Near where we landed our plane to wait for the weather to clear at Base Camp on Mt. Vinson.

This valley is so peaceful and serene that I just can't describe it. The mountain range is in the distance, but you can't see Vinson through the surrounding clouds.

We dug up a cache left here by some Chileans over two years ago; they repaired a plane that had landed hard and broke its nose off. Since it is so costly to fly everything back out, it was easier to bury it and mark it.

It was like being on a treasure hunt; we dug up two portable Honda generators, a supply of freeze-dried foods, pots and pans, cook stoves, three Scott tents, two Quonset tents and a variety of other things. In case we're here longer than we want to be, we have set up the three Scott tents so we don't have to dig ours out of the plane and build them. We did unpack our own cook stove and made lunch from the stores we found buried in the ice. Some of the food was saturated with cooking fuel, but other boxes were sealed tight and the food was fine.

We had freeze-dried spaghetti with meat sauce from a company called Mountain House. I wasn't sure if I just wasn't hungry or if the food had gone bad, but I didn't like it very much.

Right now, everyone is taking a nap in the tents we put up; it could be a long night if we still fly into Vinson base camp. Rick French is out doing a little cross-country skiing, and I'm sitting here in a thermo rest chair, lent to me by Alejo for the purpose of penning this journal.

Because of the height of the surrounding mountains around us, there is no wind and without the wind there is no wind-chill to drive the temperature down. There also is no sound except my pen scratching along the paper of this book and an occasional intake of air by one of my sleeping companions. So I sit here, peacefully, in the sun, breathing clean air – unpolluted by anything or anyone. There is nothing here but emptiness.

Alejo told us earlier that if we went walking off in any direction for 15 minutes, we would be standing in a spot where no living person had stood before. I did it; if it is true, I may never know, but it was a great feeling to take off alone and enjoy some solitude from our plane and makeshift camp. With my boots compressing the snow – eight to ten inches with each step – I walked for fifteen minutes; I stopped, turned around, and looked at the brightly colored red plane sitting on a sea of smooth white snow. My footprints leading away from it reminded me of the famous first steps of Neil Armstrong when he landed on the moon.

As I looked away from the plane to the virgin snow in front of me, I took the time to look at all the beauty, and I realized – there must be a God; no man could ever produce something like this. Even with all the trip delays, I'm glad I'm here. I wouldn't have passed this up for anything. I would like to take some pictures, but the sound of my camera shutter tripping and the film winding would just pierce the silence like a knife. I just couldn't do that right now. It would ruin one of the most serene moments I've had since I've been here.

Alejo is more than confident that we will reach the summit of Vinson and I want to believe him. Topping off this mountain would really be a feather in my cap. I can't wait to see this place from the top of Vinson.

Now that I have some time to catch up in my journal, I will use it to talk about yesterday's excursion to the other side of the "Hercules Inlet." The inlet is a blue ice runway that is very bumpy when landing on it in a plane; it is like landing on a golf course with millions of divots. On the other side is the Ellsworth Mountains that block a great deal of wind that would otherwise hit Patriot Hills Base Camp.

I was walking out of the cook tent when I met Earl who was going to bring Sultan and Kaled on a sled over to the other side of the inlet. They kindly invited me, so I grabbed my camera and jumped onto the back of the sled. It was being pulled by a Skidoo snowmobile (made by Yamaha). When we reached a pass in the mountain range, the wind began to pick up. The Skidoo's carburetor had not been calibrated to the air in this part of the world; it stalled and could not be restarted.

When it died we were only part way up to the top of a ridge, so Sultan, Kaled and I walked the rest of the way to the top while Earl radioed base Camp for help. The winds coming over the top of the ridge were horrendous. We stayed there only a short while, took some photos and walked back down the hill.

I forgot who came to help us, but they came in another snowmobile to tow our Skidoo back down the ridge to where it would start. It would have been a two-mile walk back if we hadn't been able to restart it.

11:38 p.m., Temperature 10° F. It is almost midnight; the sun is still high in the sky and there are now slight winds blowing over the snow – yet there is no drifting. I'm sorry to say we are still in Nanatuk Valley. The weather is finally clearing and we hope to leave here around midnight. Though we have lost a day, there is an alternate plan. Tomorrow – after some sleep – we will pack our supplies with some of the freeze-dried food we found here at the cache. This will make our packs a bit lighter and we will have less solid or heavy food to carry. We will travel light and climb all the way to Camp II, which will put us all on a tight but doable schedule.

I would've liked to have spent the day on the mountain, climbing and getting closer to my goal. But what can I say? It's just not possible yet. There was an advantage to being here in this peaceful valley; it has given me many hours of solitude, which is something I don't find except when I'm alone and with nature. I took a long walk – always keeping the plane in sight – and sat in the snow, just relaxing. It has been such a very long time since I've had an opportunity like this, and I'm sure it will be a long time before I do again.

It was here in this spot that I thought about God, my life, my future, my past and my worth. I wondered if – in the long run – will my life mean anything to anyone. Will anyone care? Will all this contemplation change anything about me – if it is meant to change anything at all?

Maybe I just enjoy climbing to contemplate. Is all the frustration I've experienced this last week worth the last seven hours of peace and quiet? Yes, I think so, but I feel the pressure of the fundraiser. To come all this way and not even set foot on the mountain because of bad weather would be tragic; I don't know how I could face anyone.

December 2, 1993 Mt. Vinson (finally) Camp I. Elevation: 9,360 feet

1:24 a.m., Temperature 0° F. We finally made it to the mountain base Camp, it was a busy day and I didn't get a chance to write. The weather was exceptionally clear. So after a fast breakfast of frozen fruitcake, cheese and hot chocolate, we packed up the plane, and off we went. We landed at base Camp after taking off from old base Camp where we spent the night.

At roughly 1:15 a.m. on December 1, we took off from Nanatuk to see if we could get in to Vinson base Camp. We couldn't, so it was decided to land at the next closest spot – old Vinson base Camp. Alejo said dinner would be soon and that he would bring it to our tents, where I am now writing this.

Old Base Camp. Located between Base Camp and Nanatuk Valley.

We set up tents and spent the night here. At 3:00 p.m., we again packed the plane, flew to our original destination: new Vinson base Camp. We unpacked the plane again, packed our climbing gear, loaded our sleds and headed directly for Camp I.

I'm trying to thaw out a bit; I'm not very cold, but I'm chilled. I'm trying to warm up my sleeping bag enough so I can put my boot liners in it with me, they are coated with frost; leaving them in my bag with me should help them dry out. I must sleep now – wish I could write more. I just hope I can remember all that has happened.

1:19 p.m. I'm still in the same place, and that means in my sleeping bag. The sun has come up from behind the mountains and it is now 15° F. in the tent. I was cold last night and I must have rolled out of my liner, but from the conversations I heard coming from the other tents, I wasn't the only one that was cold. It is still 0° F. outside the tent; thank God for pee bottles.

Alejo brought breakfast to the tents; it was hot chocolate, freeze-dried instant, and apricot dessert; what a way to start the day. We only walked about four miles yesterday – from where the plane landed – to Camp I, where I am now. There were four of us on a rope; Lou was in the lead; he set an excellent pace whether it was uphill, downhill, or on level ground and he never broke his stride. I wish I could keep such a pace. John was next, followed by me and Rick. Being the assistant guide, Rick was to follow the lead and make sure that none of the regular paying clients got lost. Coming along with us was Brydon and the plane's mechanic. Clay was staying with the plane and would set up the rest of base camp while we were gone. The three members of the Chilean army climbed as their own contingent.

A rope tied all four of us together; if by chance someone were to fall into a crevasse, the others would keep him from falling far. We were carrying heavy packs and dragging sleds loaded with all the supplies we would need. Any loose gear was packed tightly away – or should've been -- so we didn't lose it if we fell into a crevasse. Brydon and Alejo were on skis and were not tied together. Theory has it that your weight is more evenly distributed on skis and your chance of breaking through the snow below you and falling into a crevasse is less.

As we walked in our steady pace up the slight gradient to Camp I, I couldn't believe that we were finally on our way. We stopped periodically for breaks to rest and keep the drinking fluids flowing; dehydration is still a big problem here, and the poor dogs that ran from the crashed plane are probably dead by now.

Everything is white, peaceful and mysterious as Antarctica may be, but I miss colors. I first noticed this in the photo of Lisa (my girlfriend) that I look at every night; how brightly colored the Christmas tree is behind her. Everything short of what we are wearing and brought with us is either white (the snow and ice); gray or black (the rock and distant mountains); or blue (the color of the sky). Those are the only colors in Antarctica. Colors won't enter my life again until I reach Punta Arenas.

Reflecting a moment, if it hadn't been for the plane crash, we would've summited the mountain by now – weather permitting – and would have been on our way back down the mountain.

While we were climbing to Camp I, we heard a long, loud crack; it seemed to echo for miles. Everyone looked around, but we found or saw nothing. Sound carries greatly here on the surface because there is nothing to absorb it.

Once we reached the site of Camp I, we proceeded to set up camp. Once again, we erected the tents – something we have done many times in the last week. While looking for solid ground to put them on, we managed to find a crevasse. It was deep, dark and much closer to the campsite than I wanted it to be. Alejo told us several stories involving crevasses – stories about people being lost in them, rescued from them, or simply being left in them.

One of the advantages of the sun always being somewhere in the sky is that it never gets dark and we can climb, hike, or whatever at any part of the day. Upon arriving here after midnight, we didn't have to worry about darkness as we set up camp. The time it took to get to Camp I from base camp was 7 hours 35 minutes.

I wish we could just storm up this mountain like I did on my last trip to Elbrus, but air quality and difficulties in terrain did prevent this from happening. I think that I'm just getting tired of bundling up so much each time I leave the tent.

December 2, 1993 Camp II Elevation: 10,320 feet

10:50 p.m. Temperature 0° F. I froze last night; so did everyone else. When the sun dipped behind the Vinson Massif, the temperature dipped as well. I wasn't going to crawl out of my sleeping bag until I had to, and I vowed to be better prepared tonight if it gets that cold again.

It took us 4 hours 3 minutes to get to Camp II after leaving Camp I; we arrived at 8:19 p.m. The hike was not as long as it was yesterday. We were tied together in the same fashion as we were on our trek to Camp I. We hiked along a valley between mountain ranges. The ground was not as steep as it was yesterday, so our move through the snow was much quicker. We left Camp I, taking everything that we had brought with us; the only thing left behind were our tracks in the snow.

We made several stops along the way to rest, drink more water and take photos. Once – after taking a break and when we were all ready to go – Rick told us he had to take a crap. We don't know why he couldn't have done this while we were on break. Even Lou said, "Can't you wait until we stop again?" But Rick said that he couldn't hold it. So, we had to wait for him to dig a plastic bag out of his gear, take a crap in it – because we leave nothing behind – and pack it so we could get moving again.

Most of the ground was level so there was less than 1,000 feet difference between Camps I and II, and most of the elevation change was in the last part of the trek. That is where we had to stop to put on our crampons in order to climb the ice hill to Camp II.

We made camp in a little alcove cut out of the snow and ice by the wind; we made this our camp and set up our tents. Because of this little fortress that nature had built, we didn't have to build a windbreak around the tents.

This is really a nice spot. Above us, but not where it would hit us, is a rock sticking out of the ice and slowly working its way out. It stands out so much because it is such a black rock sitting in the middle of the clean white ice and snow.

Tomorrow we will make way to Camp III. Alejo told us to carry only what we need. I will be leaving my journal behind for a day and not take it when we move to Camp III. We will be bringing all our extreme-cold-weather gear, heavy food, fuel and other things that will be needed higher up. The following day we will move the rest of the camp up. As I look at what we have to climb tomorrow, I can see it will be up a very steep side of the mountain.

Alejo showed us the route we will be taking; from here it looks straight up in spots, but I know it isn't. Near the top of the ridge is a crevasse field we must cross; this will make it an exciting day, to say the least. We strung an antenna so we could radio Clay at the plane and the staff at Patriot Hills. I asked the staff at PH if they would pass the word back to Punta Arenas – the next time they talk to them – to send a fax back home and let my family and friends know that all was safe and sound, but behind schedule.

It is beautiful here – very little wind; the weather is great, but I have a slight touch of sunburn. I must be more aware of the danger and prepare myself more efficiently against it tomorrow before we start the climb. My sleeping bag is finally getting warm from me lying on top of it, and it is now time to get in and get some sleep. I feel better that everything is underway and we are making progress to the top.

December 3, 1993 Camp II Elevation: 10,320 feet

9:09 p.m. Temperature 15° F. I have time to kill now and catch up on my journal as I lie back on my sleeping bag. Alejo is sitting in the vestibule of his tent which he shares with Brydon and is cooking spaghetti for our dinner, and making me feel good just knowing that the hundreds of pounds of food we are carrying isn't going to be wasted.

I was cold again last night as I slept. I must write the North Face company when I get back and complain about their Tangerine Dream sleeping bag I bought from them; it was listed to -30° F. It hasn't been that cold yet and I hope it never is. Perhaps it's just damp and needs to be dried out; (which it did, it was fine after that) maybe that's why I'm having strange dreams at night. I must've been snoring loudly because Rick, who is my tent mate now, kept waking me up during the night.

We made a carry to Camp III today. We left about 2 p.m. and I accidentally shut off my stopwatch some four minutes into the trip, so I'm not exactly sure how long it took us. I did look at my watch when we got there and the time was 5:36 p.m., so it took us roughly 3 ½ hours. The climb was very steep in parts, and all of us were roped together – all except Brydon – who did not make the climb. The three Chilean army members will be climbing as an independent unit.

There were several spots along the way where we had to be careful as we jumped over crevasses. Fortunately, no one slipped or fell into any. I really wanted to take photos of some of these, but my camera was packed away. When we reached the spot that would become Camp III, the weather turned, and it became cold and very windy. We wouldn't be spending the night, but we started to work on the snow wall to protect our tents the following day when we moved the camp up. The temperature was -15° F. with the wind chill.

We did our work quickly so we could get back to Camp II. We placed our gear in holes we had dug. Somewhere along the line, I've lost my down jacket, which means summit day could be a cold one if I need it. To add insult to injury, I believe my nose is sunburned again, and I've been trying so hard not to let that happen. My time back down to Camp II took 1 hr.16 min.

The route we took was steep; it involved walking under overhangs and crossing over the same crevasses we climbed over on the way up; they were very deep and ominous looking. Alejo told us that if you fell into one and screamed for help, no one would be able to hear because the sound would not travel up the ice. In my opinion, this has been the most risky part of the climb – so far.

This place is really beautiful; I could have taken some great photos, if my camera hadn't been so secure in my backpack; even then, it would be a bit difficult since we were all roped together. Two of us fell on the 80° incline; I started to fall and yelled falling. In doing that the rest of the guys dug in with their ice axes to keep from being pulled down with me. I slid about five feet before being able to self-arrest with my ice ax. Alejo was behind me on belay, to make sure I didn't slip any further.

About ten minutes later Lou slipped and fell; he slid about 15 feet, but he didn't yell falling. He already was five feet into his slide before I noticed him; I was behind him on the rope and dug my ice ax into the snow like all the others had for me moments earlier. John didn't even know Lou had fallen until it was over. I was Lou's belay until he climbed back to path. It all worked out for the best; no one was hurt and we were all there for each other.

Tomorrow we'll have what I call a grunt day, carrying the rest of the camp, tents, cooking supplies and our personal gear. Our packs will be heavier than they were today. I made the mistake of bringing my camera back to Camp II, and I should've left it up at III. It's a very heavy camera with one lens (a 28 mm, wide-angle to 200 mm, telephoto). It takes great photos, and I could've left it at III; now I'll have to carry it back up. I'm even debating about not taking this journal to spare some weight, but I'm sure I'll take it with me.

If I can get to Camp III tomorrow without too much difficulty, I should be able to reach the summit. I hope to fill in some of the gaps with things I haven't recorded because it was just too cold, or I was too tired to write. I hope to do this on the way home or perhaps back at Patriot Hills.

10:21 p.m. Good night!

December 4, 1993 Camp III Altitude: 12,760 feet.

Temperature -10°. I woke up this morning after a very long night. I wasn't sleeping very well because I kept having bad dreams about crevasses; probably because we will climb through the crevasse field again. It will be the third time through; our final time will be after our attempt at the summit and we're on our way down the mountain.

Today we will all go, including Brydon; he didn't go with us yesterday but today it's necessary since we're taking the tents and everything else with us, and it's another person to help carry supplies. I'm not sure what we had for breakfast; I'm still not a big fan of oatmeal. I think I had dried apricots and peaches in hot water, and several cups of hot chocolate to take the chill off.

We left later in the day, waiting until the sun had reached the tents in their secluded area and warmed them. We then packed our gear and took everything except our sleds and what looked like almost 100 lbs of food. I couldn't figure out why we dragged so much here if we weren't going to use it.

I've learned that the three members of the Chilean Army are part of their mountain rescue division; they have been training for a long time for this. Their packs are exceptionally large and heavy. They walk unroped from each other, except when they are in a crevasse field.

Unlike yesterday, there is little or no wind. This is a much better experience than yesterday. I hated those thoughts of falling into a crevasse in that kind of weather; just looking down into one was scary enough. The bad thing about crevasses is that you could fall into one so far that no one could find you. The worse thing: if you fell into one, and didn't die instantly, you could linger there a long time. But today, with the sun shining brightly it was a good day to climb.

There were six of us tied together on 100 feet of rope – a bit more crowded than yesterday because we had Brydon with us. This so-called lifeline was connected to our climbing harnesses and would, hopefully, keep us from falling too far into an unseen crevasse; these were more dangerous than the ones you could see because you never knew when you might step into one.

If someone was to fall into a crevasse, the man behind him is to literally fall back and take up tension on the rope; this will keep the first guy from falling further into it.

My pack was heavy and I had taken only what I needed: sleeping bag, thermal rest, and the rest of my warm clothing. I couldn't find my down jacket so I assumed it was back at Patriot Hills. I can't believe I did that; I was always so careful about my equipment checks. I left behind my copy of *IT*, so now I was without any type of entertainment. Only my conversation with the others would keep my mind busy.

We continued up the slope and to the crevasse field. My pack was feeling lighter than it had the day before; perhaps I was getting a second wind. The sun was shining and I was in a good frame of mind. Without the weight of all the worries I had yesterday, crossing the crevasse field was much easier. My camera is still secured in my backpack, so I haven't been taking the pictures I should. The only time I can is when we take a break and take our packs off.

Today with the clearer weather, Alejo pointed out the famous pyramid that is usually seen in photos; today I took my own photo of the pyramid.

My physical health on this trip has been excellent, with the exception of not sleeping well. I've been trying to drink regularly, but I know I've been negligent of my hydration. I've been drinking at least a liter of water per hike (during breaks). We also have snacks with us; Rick has been carrying them and when he passes them out, he alternates between cookies and candy bars.

After our third and last break of our climb to Camp III, we cleared the crevasse field. I felt a bit relieved to be past it, but just when I thought the worst was over, I took a step. My crampon and boot – instead of stopping when it hit the snow – just kept going down. I stopped my movements immediately, and fortunately, I was able to keep my balance. I pulled my foot back and looked into the hole, hoping it was just my imagination, but it wasn't; the hole was dark and foreboding, and it looked like it went on forever. I had to warn the others. "Crevasse," I yelled! Surprisingly, without worry or panic, I stepped over it like it was nothing. I was amazed at my calmness; the crevasse hadn't fazed me, and I wouldn't think of it again until later that day when I told Alejo about it.

I told him how nervous I had been going through the crevasse field earlier in the day, but how, when my time came to stare down into one, I had remained calm. He told me that most people are worried the first time they go through the field. He told me not to worry.

Once we reached the site where we had buried everything the day before, we erected our tents in our new campsite. Since the sun was still shining, I took the opportunity to dry out my sleeping bag. To rid it of the built-up moisture, I laid it out across the tent I would be sharing with Rick. There was no wind in the alcove that out tents were placed in. It was actually warm. I took of my jacket and shirt for a few minutes to air out my upper body. It felt great, but with all this light reflection of the snow and being at a higher altitude, I probably could've got a great tan in 20 minutes and a good burn in 30.

We were working on the snow wall when the Chileans came over from their camp about 200 feet below us; they helped us finish our snow wall then talked to Alejo for a while.

From this vantage point, we can't see the summit of Vinson. There's not much left of the day – just enough time to have dinner, lie in our sleeping bags, and rest for tomorrow. It is possible that this time tomorrow I could be standing on the top of another summit.

I'm wishing for a good night's sleep; I tend to loose sleep because Rick keeps waking me when I snore. I don't blame him; he must be loosing more sleep than I. I'm off to rest now. It is about -10° F. now.

December 5, 1993 Camp III Altitude: 12,760 feet.

It was a long night, very frigid and windy, and even with the snow walls protecting us, the entire tent would shake as the winds howled past. I dreaded getting up, leaving the protection of the tent, and going out into the cold.

Today's game plan was set: arise at 5:00 a.m. and be hiking by 7:00 a.m. Rick was awakened at 5:00 by Alejo. He said, "It's pretty windy so we'll hold back awhile." We did and at 8 a.m. Rick – in his infinite wisdom – brought the cook stove into our tent to make water. At the other camps, I could've used this time to get some extra sleep, but today I really needed it.

Not only did I have to put up with the noise of Rick going out to get snow (which was only fair, since I've kept him up many nights with my snoring), but I had to put up with the fumes from the camp stove as well. Rick said, "It's too cold to sit outside and do it out there."

This would be one of those things that would keep me from becoming a guide: having to wait on others. Duties were never really divided up amongst us, so we never worried about them. We finally had breakfast, and while I was eating I overheard Rick and Alejo talking about the food situation; apparently, we are short on food. Either Rick hadn't done something that Alejo had told him to do, or there was a miscommunication between the guide and his assistant guide.

Alejo was saying that we had better hit the summit today, or we would really be short on food. Our other option was to make a trip back to Camp II to get some of the supplies we left behind. I knew there was a lot of food down there; we had dragged more than enough to hold us for a couple of weeks.

Finally, it was time to take a crack at the summit; the weather had let up a little. We filled all the water bottles we had and off we went. We were roped in the following order: Alejo, Brydon, myself, John, Lou and Rick. Alejo asked me to stop him every hour for a five-minute break. The trek was easy at first, but when we broke the first ridge above our camp we could feel the intensity of the wind.

Snow was blowing every which way, and angry clouds hid the sun. We pushed on for an hour before I told Alejo that it was time to stop for our first break. I was doing all right; I still felt strong. The wind would be our greatest enemy this day, but everyone was doing their best as we walked into it.

I walked with my head down, keeping a steady pace and looking up only when I had to. I was doing so well that I forgot to look at my watch; we had marched an hour and a half before I told Alejo it was time to stop. I wanted to keep on going though. During our second break, Alejo decided to discuss our summit bid. The wind was not letting up and my glasses were so frozen I could barely see Brydon's footprints on the ground in front of me.

Because the wind was so strong and blowing so much snow, we could not see the summit or the other smaller surrounding peaks. Brydon said he was willing to go back. John said, "I don't care if we go back." I was hoping for better weather but I didn't think we'd get it today. Then Lou spoke up. He said, "Let me throw my two-cents in. I'm here to climb this mountain, so lets do it." Alejo responded, "If we try today, we will fail…the winds are too strong." I asked to go to the next ridge to see what the weather was like there. Alejo replied, "If the winds are this strong here, they will easily be over 100 mph at the ridge…let's try tomorrow."

Immediately, the food question was mentioned; what would we do about that? Alejo said he would try to dig up Martin's cache of food from last year that had been buried somewhere near Camp III. (I didn't know who Martin was or why he had a cache of food buried.) It was either that or he and Rick would go back to Camp II to get some food. So with the food problem apparently solved, we turned back to camp.

While I was somewhat glad we were going back to camp to get out of the weather, this had its downside; it meant at least two more nights at Camp III. I also had started to realize that I was now going *away* from the very summit I had been fighting to get to for over a year. I had to make it to the top! What would happen if we didn't try again? What would happen if the weather stayed this way and we were forced to turn back as I'd experienced on previous climbs? Unlike Lou or John, I couldn't afford to make this trip again. This would be my only chance to summit Vinson, and it was being put on hold.

On the way back to Camp III, something happened; Alejo fell into a crevasse. I was still the third man on the rope and I just happened to look up to see Alejo, standing up to his waste in the snow. I started backing up to take up slack on the rope. Brydon, who was in between Alejo and me, had a look on his face that said: what should I do? John started yelling, "Back up, back up."

Fortunately, it was not serious; Alejo did not sink in any further and was able to easily pull himself out. He marked the hole with a flag on the end of a small, two-foot bamboo rod (he carried several). Before proceeding back to camp we moved 30 feet to the left of the hole and made sure he was all right before proceeding. Alejo said, "I've never seen a crevasse above Camp III before."

The rest of the trek was uneventful, but very windy. Brydon, being a pilot, estimated the winds to be at least 35 knots with gust up to 50. With the wind chill, he estimated the temperature at -150° F. Our climbing time ascending was 2 hours 39 minutes, and got us to more than a third of the way to the top. On our descent, we ran into the three members of the Chilean Army. We told them that the weather was bad, and the smart thing to do for now was to go back and hope the weather cleared for tomorrow.

Back at camp there was not much to do. Lou, John, Brydon and I simply lay back in our sleeping bags. Alejo and the military went to dig up Martin's last year's cache of food – or at least see if they could find it.

Martin Williams had accompanied the previous group here last year. I was beginning to understand why, whenever we called Patriot Hills on the radio, Alejo would inquire if there was an answer from Martin as to the exact location of the buried cache. So far there was no word from Martin.

Brydon was not feeling well. I could understand this; he had a rest day at Camp II and had pushed for the summit without any previous acclimatizing. If he had never done anything like this before, it would be a real shock to his system. After he mentioned feeling like throwing up while we were trying for the summit, it all boiled down to altitude. It was probably good for him that we did go back down, and I can't help but wonder if that was part of the reasoning of turning back, even though the weather was blamed.

I lay back in my sleeping bag; I was tired, cold and wet. Sleeping here hadn't been easy, with all the perpetual sunlight; and whenever I'd get into some heavy sleep, Rick would wake me up because of my snoring.

I started to wonder again why I was here. I could hear John talking to Lou in the next tent. John had said, "As far as I'm concerned, I made this mountain. Another 6 ½ hours isn't going to make a difference to me." I thought to myself, "Sure that is fine for you, but what about me? I have something to prove; I have a lot of people watching me." I still wanted the summit and I wanted to get the most out of my pledges; I was only going to get here once in my lifetime, and I wanted the top.

I didn't sleep. I thought about going home and saying "hi" to my family and friends. By rights, we should've been off this mountain by now – if it hadn't been for the plane crash and weather delays leaving Punta Arenas.

I thought about music, a roaring fire and darkness. Oh, how I missed darkness. On our first night at Camp II, I pulled out my blinders from my travel pack. I had gotten them from British Airway during my first long over-seas flight to Russia. I kept them just in case I might need them, and now I did. I had never used the blinders before, so I took them out of their wrapper and noticed they were made of cheap vinyl. I tried them; they did seem to work a little once I warmed them up a bit.

Condensation had built up so much in the tent that a single drop of water fell from the ceiling and landed right on my blinders. It hit with a thud and I was instantly awake. I remember sitting up and bumping the side of the tent, next thing I knew it was raining in the tent. It was also very warm; someone had closed the vents, and since it wasn't me it must have been Rick. I would rather have the water freeze on the roof of the tent and dry out later, while we were climbing, than to have everything in the tent get soaked and be useless when we needed it.

My last depressing thought for the day was that we were supposed to be hiking out tomorrow and heading for home, but that is not the case; we still have to finish going up.

Dinner consisted of chicken stew from the stores of the military group. Alejo had never found Martin's cache.

Tomorrow is supposed to be the big day. Rick isn't sleeping well because of his excitement over the upcoming event – at least that's what he told me. I tried to sleep because I know how exhausting a summit bid can be, but the wind whipping around the tent is keeping me awake.

I hope it's not windy tomorrow. If we don't make it tomorrow; I know there will be a trip to Camp II for food, and we will wait until the following day, meaning another delay in going home.

December 6, 1993 Camp III Altitude: 12,760 feet.

The temperature is 5° F. Today was summit day. Alejo woke Rick at 5:00 a.m. so we could have a 7:00 start for the top of Vinson. Breakfast for me consisted of hot chocolate and some more dried apricots and apples; I still didn't want oatmeal. Rick was cooking in the tent again and the gas fumes from the stove were causing my first real headache of the trip. I brought it to his attention, but he made no reply.

I didn't sleep well last night; every time the wind rocked the tent I prayed it would stop; actually, I prayed a lot during the night. I don't see myself as extremely religious, but I'm a firm believer that there is something better than man, and there has to be hope that someone or something is listening.

I remember one of the things that made me a firm believer in God; it was an autopsy. I know this sounds strange and/or morbid, but it's true. Several years ago, I found a body while fighting a fire. I was one of the Department's photographers at the time, so I went with the body to photograph it during the autopsy. As gruesome as it sounds, I was truly moved by it.

As each organ of the victim was removed and studied, I saw things that I had never seen before. Though everyone has a basic knowledge of human biology, to me seeing is believing – seeing how everything is put together, interacting with other parts of the body and making it a living being. I was truly impressed and amazed to see a sight like this; it made me believe that something far greater than man put this all together. So now when I pray at night, I can rest assured that someone is listening.

By 7:25 a.m. we were ready to leave. Brydon was still not feeling well so he was staying behind.

The order on the rope was Lou, Alejo, myself, John and Rick. Lou, whom I officially called the pacemaker, because of the fantastic way he can keep a slow and steady pace, led us off and up the mountain.

The weather was much better today, and with very little wind. I didn't think my prayers would be answered, but they were. During the night, each time a big wind gust came along, I would start to pray again; it also helped to pass the time. Alejo told us that it would take us about six hours to reach the top, but he had lied to us in the past (using his own words) about travel time between camps. He did this to keep us from being discouraged. For example, he told us Base Camp to Camp I would take us four hours; it took us 7 hours 35 minutes. I was hoping he did this for a reason – reverse psychology—but I was wrong; it was going to be *more* than six hours.

The sun was in the sky as it has been since we landed here in the Antarctic, but on this day it was being filtered through the clouds. Looking at it through my sunglasses, I could see a bright white ball that gave no heat.

There were clouds everywhere: above us, below us and beside us. After climbing for two hours the view of the summit was still blocked by clouds. We took a break every hour; once again I was timekeeper.

We eventually walked out of what little wind there was – forever upward, it seemed – with the air getting thinner as we went. Ever since Alejo fell into the crevasse yesterday, I could not stop thinking of what he had said, "I have never before seen a crevasse above Camp III." I would think: "Where there is one – there is probably another."

During one of our breaks, Alejo pointed out the route we would take the rest of the way up the mountain. While he was doing this I noticed the three members of the Chilean Army in the distance. They were going to leave about two hours behind us and they would eventually overtake and beat us to the summit.

Most of the climb so far from Camp III was a gradual ongoing upward slope, but now the terrain was going to change. There was a 350 to 400 foot slope in front of us that angled between 60 and 75°. Since it was so steep there would be no place to sit and take a break, so Alejo said, "We will do it without breaks."

The best chance we will have to rest will be a number of "Davis Steps." These were steps I named after John Davis III, of our group. They were brief stops we took – lasting about 10 or 20 seconds – every ten minutes as we climbed. They meant a lot to John while we were climbing the steep incline between Camps II and III, and I admit, I also found them beneficial. Sure it threw the pace off a little, but it sure did help to get in those extra couple of breaths.

We made it up the steep incline using a number of Davis Steps, and we made it without incident. No one slipped or fell. Everyone had their ice axes ready to stab into the snow to arrest someone in case they did fall. I know I was ready and I would deeply appreciate the same if I were to fall.

Upon reaching the top of the incline we took a well-deserved break; I was tired. The week of resting with no exercise due to delays was taking a toll on me, and I was paying for it. While we were taking a break, Alejo pulled out a surprise for us. Hilda, one of the cooks back at Patriot Hills, had prepared something for us we called "super goodies." Actually, they were Chilean cookies called "Nimilo Bars" and some other dessert she had made while we were delayed in Patriot Hills. The Nimilo bars were filled with chocolate and coconut. They really hit the spot, but 20 minutes after eating them they weighed a bit heavy in my stomach. Alejo also gave us some type of Dextrose candy. I had never had them before and not only did they taste good, they were supposed to give a little lift to the old system.

By now the military group had surpassed us, and they were setting a pace we would not be able to keep. They would surely beat us to the summit – if we made it at all – and when they reached it they would become the first Chilean Mountain Rescue group on the summit of Vinson. But I will be the first firefighter and possibly the first climber to raise money for a charity on Vinson; I just had to make it there first.

Again, we started to ascend the mountain – this time in the tracks of the Chileans. The winds were picking up, and the temperature was beginning to drop. In the back of my mind I couldn't help but think that we should have been flying out of here today, but on the other side of the coin, the summit was within reach.

I remembered feeling this way when I was last in Russia; I could see the summit and I knew I would make it. Elbrus was 18,510 ft. and Vinson was 16,067 ft., but because of its location and the quality of the air, Vinson was the equivalent of a 20,000-foot mountain. It only goes to show smaller doesn't mean easier, and nothing about this entire trip has been easy; from the planning steps to the climb itself, it has been a tough ride. I think I can see light at the end of the tunnel, however, and in a few more hours, I may be able to put another summit behind me.

We came upon a small peak that had to be rounded before our final leg to the summit. The wind was blowing clouds past and over it, so I could only get a momentary glimpse. We would go around this small peak and follow a 20 or 30 foot-wide ledge. There was a slight slant to it so we had to be careful of our footing, and there was a small layer of snow mixed in with the coarse rock; at the end of the ledge was roughly a 1,000-foot drop. We were all roped together still, and needless to say we were all very careful. I can see now why Alejo turned us around yesterday; to have tried to climb this ledge in high wind would've been sheer stupidity.

Planting each foot firmly before taking the next step, we moved slowly, but steadily, past this dangerous ledge. The rope between us was always kept tight in case someone was to fall; this would give a falling person less chance to build up momentum. Last, but not least, it was important to keep looking for a place to plant our ice ax. In most cases if we pushed it into the snow, we were likely to hit rock and our hold with our ax would be no good.

To me, this was one of the most harrowing parts of the climb. Granted, there were many steep inclines earlier – not to mention the trips through the crevasse fields before Camp III – and we still had the return trip in front of us, but this was what I considered the most dangerous.

We kept moving – onward and upward – walking, not just on snow and ice but on rocks as well. Suddenly, we heard a yell or scream from above; it was faint and muffled by the winds blowing over the ridge. For a moment I thought the worst. Had one of the Chileans fallen? Actually, it was just the opposite; they had reached the summit. Looking through the clouds, I could barely make out the figure on the summit waving a flag. They had done it; they had made history for their undertaking.

Now it was my turn.

We pushed on for what seemed like forever, and then we were there – 20 meters from the top. The final pitch before us was roughly 80° and

40 feet up. Alejo wanted us to go around to the backside of the summit the way the Chileans had gone. It would not be as steep, but it would take much more time. Our group was moving slower now, but seeing the Chileans above us gave me some hidden strength. I had been feeling positive about making the summit for the last few hours, but now I was elated. I could see the top, and it was only 40 or so feet above us; I had to make it now. I wanted it, and no one would ever be able to take it away from me. Instead of taking the long way around to the top, the Chileans threw down a rope to use as an added safety line, and up it we went – to the top.

The last 20 feet of the climb was tough, but what I later learned of Chilean philosophy was this: not for one person, but for the entire group to make it. Their team and ours, though climbing independently, were connected as one group because we still went up together. Their belief was to help everyone, in a kind of "all for one, one for all" attitude.

Alejo took the line that was thrown down by the Chileans and hooked it to ours. We climbed and they pulled on the rope. I could feel adrenaline flowing through me, and I felt like the air all around me was charged with excitement.

Lou was the first of our group to reach the top; I followed him with John, Rick and Alejo right behind me. I couldn't believe I was finally here – my third summit; I was successful, and I was so happy. This was the most euphoric moment of my life. Everyone was patting each other on the back and hugging one another; I still couldn't believe I was actually there.

One of the first things that came to mind was my San Diego buddy Wes. He had pledged $1,000 if I made it to the top and nothing if I didn't make it. With a donation like that now under my belt, I had a good chance of reaching my $10,000 goal.

I looked around the summit; the weather was terrible. The temperature was -10° F. according to my thermometer and that was without the wind chill. There were low-lying clouds all around us so we could not see far at all. Any hopes of seeing our plane at base camp were quickly ruled out.

I unhooked myself from the rope; we wouldn't need it here. The summit was 60 feet long by maybe 25 feet wide with an old ski pole stuck into the highest point on this plateau. It was at this highest point that I would take out my flag and have my photo taken with it. Everyone had a camera, and pictures were being taken of everyone and their groups. My big hope was that I would get a decent photo of myself and my flag on the top of Vinson to show everyone back home. I recorded the time I reached "the top of the bottom of the world" as December 6th, 1993, at 3:45 p.m. Chilean time, and according to my Casio watch it took me 8 hours 35 minutes to summit from Camp III.

Nick Comande on the top of Mt. Vinson. December 6th, 1993.

Buried at the top was a small can, almost half the size of a coffee can with a metal reusable lid; inside it was a book with a pencil. We took turns signing it, adding our names to the list of maybe 70 or so, that had already accomplished this task of reaching the summit – the highest point in Antarctica.

We were at the top for almost an hour; I ate a cherry Tootsie Pop while resting. After checking the temperature and realizing how cold it was getting, we decided to head back. Alejo said Camp III was about five miles away, even if it was all downhill. We came down in the reverse order that we went up. I would've liked to have taken photos along the ridge, but again my camera was safely packed away.

We took our first break just past the ridge with the very long dropoff; we rested there because our next move toward Camp III would be down the steep incline and it would be very demanding. There would be no place to rest, and more care and concentration would have to be used descending than in going up.

We safely descended the incline with the help of the "Davis Step," resting at the same spot as we had before going up. This was the place where we abandoned our ski poles and started climbing with ice axes. Never before had I used an ice ax so much, and never before when climbing had I taken such a technical route on a mountain.

The rest of the hike back to Camp III would now be long and boring, not to mention downhill. As I was thinking of this I looked back at the summit. God had played a cruel joke on us, from here I could now see the summit, and all the clouds were gone. If only we had stayed awhile longer, we would've enjoyed an excellent view and taken some fantastic photos. Oh well, I thought to myself; there wasn't much I could do about it, and going back was not an option.

The Summit of Vinson beginning to clear as we were climbing off the peak.

We made it back to Camp III in 3 ½ hours. Brydon congratulated us as we passed his tent; he was eating the Tootsie Pop I had given him to eat on the summit if he made it.

I asked Alejo if they had radioed Patriot Hills to pass the word on or to send a fax back home with the news that we had made it. Since it was late in the day, I went straight for my sleeping bag; Lou and John did the same. Tomorrow we will pack up and go all the way back down to base camp where we left Clay; it seems like we left him there weeks ago.

We will go from Camp III one final time through the crevasse field with full packs, stop at Camp II to pick up our sleds with anything else we left there (save the hundred pounds or so of food we're not going to eat), and then march all the way back to Base Camp. The whole trek is about 15 miles and it will be getting a little warmer as we go down – no more -20° F. nights. If all goes well, we could still fly back to Patriot Hills later in the evening.

As I lay here writing this, with the excitement of reaching the summit behind me, all I can think about now is going home and leaving this beautiful, frozen, desolate, wasteland behind.

December 7, 1993 from Camp III to Base Camp.

Last night was cold, -10° F. according to my thermometer on my pack, which I kept outside the tent during the night. When I brought it inside it only went up to 0° F. We rose about 8:30. The plan was to descend the mountain by 10:30; we had a long way to go today and it would also be our last grunt day. I climbed out of the tent and looked at Mt. Shin, which was across a small valley from us; Shin is the third highest peak in the Antarctic. I looked at it quite awhile when we were camped here. Like the others, I used it to judge the weather; I looked to see if there were clouds around it or if there was snow blowing off it.

As I looked at it this morning I noticed something I didn't think I would ever see here; it was the moon. Just to the left of Mt. Shin was a crescent moon – in an early phase – hanging in the sky. In this land of perpetual daylight, I had managed to find a piece of the night sky. Then I started to think of the darkness I had missed so much. On all my previous climbing trips, I always had a dark night sky, with thousands and thousands of stars above. Since the climbing trips always took me so far from the cities, there was no light pollution to cancel out the stars, but here, there are no stars – for there is no night. How I long to be able to lie down at night, go to sleep and not see the redness of my own blood vessels through my eyelids, or have to resort to pulling my hat over my eyes. I can't wait to experience darkness and the stars above me once again.

With our food supply all but exhausted, Rick took the few remaining packets of freeze-dried food and mixed them together; it turned out to be some kind of melted cheese and butter soup, for lack of a better description. Only Rick ate it, John tried it, but Lou and I both thought it was a waste of the last of our stores.

I settled for the last of my Crystal Light Fruit Punch that I mixed in my water bottle. Camp II was roughly 1 hr.15 min. away. I would get something from the many bags of food we had cached there, or eat one of the several granola bars I left in my supplies.

Since this was the last time I would ever be here – there was no reason for me to come back – I took my last look at Mt. Shin and the surrounding area. I looked up the ridge where our footprints led to the top of Vinson, and I wondered how long they would last. When all our gear and tents were packed and we were again all roped together, we started our descent down the mountain.

Including breaks and a chance to boil some water for hot drinks, the entire trip back to Base Camp took 7 hours, 46 minutes and 42 seconds according to my Casio altimeter watch. We stopped in the same rest spots as on the way up to Camp III and came through what Brydon called "Crevasse Country" with no problems.

We finished the steepest part of the climb without incident. I worked up a bit of a sweat and was glad to rest for a few minutes when we reached Camp II. Here we repacked our gear onto sleds and rested while Alejo and Rick took inventory of all the food we were leaving here. I couldn't understand why we had dragged so much food here. "We must be supplying their next trip here," John said.

Lou and I were ready to go in no time; this even included filling our water bottles for the rest of the day, but because Alejo didn't want us to go un-roped, we had to wait. We wanted to go because the sun was behind one of the peaks, leaving us in its shadow with the temperature dropping; we both had the chills. Once we walked about a hundred yards into the sun we felt better, but the damage had been done. I was soaked with sweat from the climb down from Camp III, and now my clothes were both cold and wet. I think Lou was in the same boat as I.

We walked all the way from Camp II to Camp I, something we hadn't done on the way up. We needed our crampons to get over the ice hill by Camp II, so we just left them on. Several times along the way, we stopped to eat some snacks we'd picked up at Camp II and used the opportunity to take some photos.

The Chilean Army made it to Camp I before we did because they were on skis and made much better time. Brydon, Alejo and Rick were the only members of our party to wear skis. Lou, John and I marched happily through the snow with Lou leading us and setting our pace.

At Camp I we rested again and removed our crampons; we boiled water to make instant soups and to refill our empty water bottles. Twenty minutes later, we decided it was time to push on.

Lou – on the front of our rope – led us down the same trail we had come up a week earlier, setting the pace that John and I would follow. Alejo and the others were on skis, so their weight was more evenly distributed, making them less likely to punch a hole in the snow of a crevasse. Alejo and Rick were cleaning up at Camp I while the rest of us started back. On skis, they would quickly catch up with us.

We were about 150 feet out of Camp I; I was watching Lou who was about 35 feet in front of me, and John who was 35 feet behind me; we were all tied in together. I always watched Lou's steps; it helped me to keep an even pace. He was wearing gaiters that went high up on his leg, and with each step he took, I would watch the snow go half-way up them. Suddenly, I was watching as the snow went past the halfway point and then over the top of his gaiters. Before I knew it, the snow was up to his left knee and his right foot was quickly sinking into the snow.

Lou had found a crevasse. I jumped back as quickly as I could, laid down and dug my feet and ice ax in for traction. By the time I was finished, Lou was in the snow up to his waist. Between my holding on to the now taunt rope and Lou's pack helping to plug the hole, he wasn't sinking any further. Lou carefully leaned back making sure I had a tight grip on the rope.

With me still on my back and John doing the same, Lou pulled himself out of the hole and lay down near it to distribute his weight. Lou looked into the hole and said, "I can't see the bottom of this." Lou probed around the area to find a way across the crevasse. He used his ski pole to tap around the area to find where the crevasse started and stopped. As Lou tapped, I could hear an echo of it coming through the snow where I lay. It suddenly dawned on me that I was on the same crevasse.

From behind me, at almost the same instant, John yelled, "Nick, I think you're on the crevasse that Lou is on." As gently and as quickly as I could, I moved over to my left to clear the crevasse; Lou did likewise. By the time we were finished, Alejo came up from behind us on his skis and found a safe place for us to cross.

After we had all safely crossed the area with the crevasse (the same area we had crossed on our ascent), Lou turned around and said to me, teasingly, "Did you get a picture of that?" He was referring to the many photos I had taken on this trip. "I could have taken your picture or held the rope; which would you have preferred?" I replied with a smile. Lou chose the latter.

For the remainder of the trip back to Base Camp, we were all very careful about where we stepped.

Just before the last half-mile to the plane, there was a thick layer of clouds moving in. Great, I thought; we could get to our plane, but I wondered if the weather would keep us from flying out? I had hoped that it wouldn't, I was looking forward to getting back to Patriot Hills, then Punta Arenas and eventually home. The rest of the walk to Base Camp was uneventful and I used the time to think about how beautiful it was here and how few people have actually been here. I considered myself fortunate to be one of those few.

Rick would serpentine down the valley on his skis; he would ski ahead of us and stop; then as we passed him, he would hand out squares of chocolate to those walking. He called it "a kind of toll booth in reverse."

As we reached the end of the valley we saw a cloud layer between us and our ride out. I took my last photos of the valley. As we entered its mist, the temperature dropped.

We made it back to Base Camp and as we walked in we were greeted by Clay. We noticed all the changes that had taken place since we'd left a week ago. While we were gone, Clay had erected a radio tent, put the covering on the Quonset hut frame that had been standing here when we arrived, and built a kitchen and a latrine. He also had quit shaving while we were gone.

It felt good to get my pack off; from this point on, there would be no more hauling, no more going uphill, no more grunt days, no more acclimatizing and no more thin air. From this point on it should be a more relaxing trip.

We sat in the kitchen where the military group was cooking salami. Not only was it hot, but it also tasted good. We relaxed, talked to Clay and reminisced on our past week. Alejo and Brydon radioed Patriot Hills for a weather update; Brydon said that it was okay to fly out, but I was a little skeptical about it as we sat in this layer of mist.

Within an hour we had the plane packed. Clay took a block of wood and placed it alongside one of the landing skids and then hit it with the back of an ax. This was done to break the adhesion of the skids to the ice which occurred after the plane sat for awhile. When the plane's engines were fired up and warmed up, off we went to Patriot Hills.

Within seconds of taking off, the plane left the low level mist that encased Base Camp and we were soon back to the sunlight. My feet were again wet and cold, but the plane's heater was below my seat. I dried my boots the best I could.

The plane lifted higher into the sky and for the first time I could see the whole of the Vinson Massif. Our flight was short; instead of flying directly back to Patriot Hills, we made a quick stop back at Welcome Nanatuk. With our marks and imprints still in the snow, we quickly dug down to the drums of fuel left behind by the Chilean Army while they were here to fix their damaged plane. Fuel was extremely expensive, roughly $2,500 a barrel, and was treated like gold.

While the plane was being refueled, I took photos of Vinson.

The finally cloud free peak of Mt. Vinson as taken from Nanatuk Valley.

There were no clouds hiding it as before. From almost 20 miles away, I could see the peak better than when I was only a quarter mile away. The whole mountain stood, white, with a clear blue sky behind it. We all took turns having our picture taken with Vinson in the background. This area was as peaceful and serene as before. I could also see where we had parked the plane last time and from there I saw my footprints leading off into the distance and back again. I wondered how long they would last.

With the plane refueled and waiting to go, I took my last look at Vinson. It would be the last time I would see it in person. With no reason to come back here, I said a silent goodbye, and as I've said goodbye to other mountains in my life, I was saddened. I had come, I had done what I set out to do, and for me, the challenging part of this adventure is over.

The twin-engine otter lifted off that great carpet of white, and from my seat in the plane, I could see the plane's shadow getting smaller and smaller as we flew higher. Brydon made one last pass by the mountain so we could see it from the air and then headed back to Patriot Hills.

December 8, 1993 Patriot Hills

Temperature +12° F. We landed at 12:15 a.m. this morning. It wasn't home, but it was one step closer. At least there would be a warm tent to actually sit up in – if you wanted to – and a boom box for music and great food.

When we taxied to the plane's tie down spot, I was surprised to see not some, but the entire contingent of Patriot Hills coming to greet us. There was congratulatory handshaking and hugging. Grant welcomed us back as we stepped off the plane, and Hilda told us there was hot lasagna waiting for us in the cook tent. To top things off, there were two boxes of wine – both red and white – and a couple of cases of Chilean beer. I joked about this, and Clay the Canadian appropriately brought out a bottle of Canadian Club whiskey; needless to say, there was a celebration.

Lou lasted until about three o'clock; I sat up and talked with the others all night. By the time I was ready for bed, it was too late to move my gear into the tent; I didn't want to wake up Lou.

I stayed up and helped in the kitchen for a while. I wrote in my journal of the day's events. I managed to go to bed about 1:00 p.m. and slept until 9:30 p.m. Hilda – bless her heart – left me some dinner to warm up. I was back in bed at 11:30 p.m., and hoping that if I slept all night my internal clock would get back on a more normal schedule. While I lay there in my sleeping bag I hoped that the Hercules would fly in tomorrow and pick us up off the ice. It didn't come in today because weather conditions would not permit. High winds had come in and brought the temperature down to -30° F.; no plane was going to land in this.

December 9, 1993 Patriot Hills

The winds were still blowing, but not as bad as before. We spent the day digging out Max's plane.

December 10, 1993 Patriot Hills

The winds stopped, but the sky was dark with clouds with a ceiling too low for the Hercules to come in and get us. I awoke around 9:00 a.m. for a breakfast of French toast. Since we weren't going anywhere, we helped dig out the Orange Pumpkin, as it was called (a single engine Cessna owned by Max Wenden and the late Giles Kershaw); it helped break up the day.

The plane was placed in a make-shift hanger below the surface of the snow. The plane like the rest of the camp is put below the surface at the end of the summer season and then dug up when the staff comes back in the spring. It would cost far too much to fly out all the equipment and bring it back each year.

I dug more snow than I care to ever remember, but it helped to pass the time. I pulled a muscle or something in my upper back, so I stopped doing heavy work and began driving one of the snowmobiles used to haul away the snow being dug up.

When all the snow was removed and the plywood roofing over the plane was taken off, the plane was pulled out of the ground with a large hand winch. Alejo spent the afternoon getting the winch ready. Doug and I were convinced that Adventure Network International wasn't going to let us fly out of here until the plane was out of the ground. We had heard that ANI had an agreement with the Chilean Government; in exchange for passage to the Antarctic, the military guys that were with us would help dig out the plane.

I formed the MPC (the Mystical Plane Connection), as the plane would come closer to being pulled out of the ice, ANI would say, "the weather was getting better and we would be able to fly out soon".

When we pulled the plane out of the ice, Max was overjoyed. It was great to see him with such a big smile on his face. Max was a very nice guy. On my birthday, he came up to me, shook my hand and wished me a "Happy Birthday" and "many more"; I hardly knew him then.

We had a fine dinner at 8:00 this evening (an hour later than usual because of the plane raising). We had roast beef and Yorkshire pudding with all the extras. It was a wonderful time; Grant even broke open a case of champagne. I think it was supposed to be saved for New Year's, but we had enough reason to celebrate. We had spent a lot of time getting that plane out of the ground, and now it was time to go home.

After we landed back at Patriot Hills after the climb, we were given many reasons for not being able to fly out, including bad communications with Punta Arenas, bad weather coming and no reports from Rothera or Marsh (other bases on the Antarctic Ice).

We were tired of excuses; both John and I felt that we could've been home by now. We pushed Grant; we told him that the weather had been worse when we landed than it was now. Doug and I suggested that John Davis be present in the radio room at the next check-in time.

It was now 10:00 p.m. After Grant's radio call, there was talk of sending the plane at 2:00 a.m. with the plane landing roughly at 8:00 a.m. – if the weather was good.

John said, "It better," and went into the cook tent. Lou was there but he said he was going to bed; you could see by looking at him that he was angry. "I'm mad," he confessed. "When I think about still being here I make myself even madder." With that, he left for his tent.

To break up the boredom from still being here and wanting to leave, John said, "Let's borrow the Skidoos and go for a ride." I thought, "Why not?" I said, "Let me get my camera and I'll meet you outside."

We told Rachel and Alejo that we were going for a ride; they said it was okay as long as we stayed within sight of the camp. With the snowmobiles fueled up and started, John said, "You want to go out to the D-6?"

I replied, "I knew that's where you wanted to go, so that's why I grabbed my camera." In a moment we were off and making a beeline to the crashed plane just as fast as we could.

Neither John nor I looked back at camp to see if anyone was watching; actually, we didn't care. We had the only two snowmobiles they had and we had no radio with us so no one could call us back. There were enough tracks in the snow from all the previous trips out so we couldn't get lost. It was about six miles to the wreck and it took us about 25 minutes to get there. It was a great feeling to be free of the confines of the camp; we felt free as hell or more like a couple of kids on an adventure. What excitement I felt!

We pulled up in front of the plane, and John and I took some photos of each other by the wreck.

The author, Nick Comande in front of the crashed D-6. Notice the snow that has drifted against it since we were here previously.

John leaned over to me and said, "Nick, can you believe that we are here in the Antarctic riding around on snowmobiles looking at a crashed plane"? I said, "No, it's pretty hard to believe, isn't it?" We walked around the plane and looked in the windows and doors. I didn't want to go in because I knew the FAA probably wouldn't like it.

John told me that this plane was over 40 years old and that there were only 52 or 53 of them left in the world. We looked around a bit and decided it was time to go back, returning to Camp much slower than when we left. When we arrived, Rachel and Alejo were waiting for us, and we both received a small lecture informing us that what we had done was wrong, how the Skidoos were for work only, and that we should've stayed in sight of the camp.

The only statement I made was, "We knew where we were going and how to get back." John, having more balls than me, stated simply, "I don't want to talk about it," and walked away. That was pretty much the end of that.

It was now 2:15 a.m. on the morning of the 10th. I was given the news that the Hercules had left Punta Arenas at 1:45 a.m. It would be here in less than six hours, and in less than six hours we would be getting off the ice.

I went back to the tent to tell Lou. He wasn't sleeping, but just lying in his sleeping bag – looking furious. I shared the news I had just learned and he looked relieved to learn that we would soon be leaving.

December 11, 1993 Hotel Punta Arenas

I didn't sleep well; I also didn't have much time to sleep. I talked to Lou until 3:00 a.m., and I told him about the plane venture. Wake-up was to be at 5:45 and breakfast at 6:15 and we were to be packed and ready by 7:15.

Breakfast was bacon and eggs, but I really wasn't hungry. I wanted to leave. As beautiful, mystical, magical and photographic as this place was, I'd had my fill. I wanted to get out of the clothes I was wearing; I wanted a hot shower and a bed at night. I wanted to be doing anything other than what I was doing now.

The time to leave would soon be here. The Hercules would arrive about 7:45 a.m. and then we would be gone. It was quiet in the cook tent; no one said anything about the little joyride John and I had taken out to the plane during the night. Lou and I packed with plenty of time to spare. I gave Rachel my fleece balaclava because earlier in the trip she told me she had forgotten to bring one with her. It would be handy when she was taking other excursions either here or while visiting the South Pole.

She said that it was a sweet thing to do and gave me a kiss; apparently she wasn't too upset about the snowmobile incident last night.

I gave my over boots and new Climb High gloves to Alejo. He had been admiring them since we had returned from the mountain. I didn't think I would need them for at least another year. I told him I was giving these things to him as a tip since I'd spent all my money to get here. Alejo replied, "Nick, my good friend, I feel that you have found the heart of the mountain. You said that you would be a happy man when you made the summit, and I saw how happy you were. You will be my friend always, and I will write to you."

With that he got up and got his address book for me to sign. I was taking a last look around the area when, from out of nowhere, came the sound of the Hercules above me. It circled twice before attempting to land.

Alejo stopped by me with one of the Skidoos with two long sleds tied behind it. They had our gear on them and other things that were going back to Punta Arenas. Lou stood by me and we watched the Hercules land on the blue ice runway. I hoped my pictures would depict how rough that runway really is.

Lou and I started what I called the long walk to the airstrip; it was at least a half-mile walk. During that time we talked about what we liked and didn't like about our trip to Antarctica.

The plane was on the ice for almost 45 minutes and in this time the Patriot Hills staff and the six members of the Hercules crew unloaded 20 drums of fuel, and a large sled full of various supplies. They loaded on our packs, the camp garbage and – last but not least – the camp mail bag. Then the good-byes started all over again.

This time there were sad faces and even some tears. I will miss these newfound friends, as well as the people with whom I climbed the mountain. My Christmas card list is getting longer every year.

I took one long last look at the scenery before stepping onto the plane, watching the spindrift blow across the blue ice; somehow it just mesmerized me. I thought about taking a picture, but I decided against it. This would be one of my personal private memories of Antarctica. Strange as it may seem, in the direction I was looking, the terrain was not a hill, a mountain, a tent or anything else; it was nothing but flat – just a smooth snowy landscape that reached as far as the eye could see. Thinking of it now reminds me of how cold the wind blew and how void the land was – just endless miles of nothing. It's strange how something that big and empty can squash a man's ego.

I wanted to say that I felt alone, but I didn't; I felt just the opposite. I felt at home and content. A long time ago – I'm not sure when, but within the last five years – the dream of coming to the Antarctic called me, and I listened. I don't know if it was the thrill of being there or the chance of seeing one of the last unexplored places on earth, but I do know that I managed to summit a mountain that roughly less than 180 people (according to the staff at ANI) have succeeded in doing; that alone makes the trip worthwhile. I came, I climbed, I conquered and now I'm going home.

Unfortunately, I'm through here. I think of all the times I've said I wanted to leave, and I can't take those thoughts back. My time here was so short in comparison to the amount of time it took to get here. Maybe someday I'll be back; I don't know why, but why should I rule it out?

I stepped on the plane and was fortunate enough to get a window seat, not that these windows are very good for looking out. The pilot fired up the other three engines that had been shut down after landing. (One engine is always kept running to keep the plane warm and is used to start the other three). It turned around, taxed for a bit and took off in the direction of the camp.

As we slowly climbed into the sky, I could see the camp and its personnel waving goodbye. I thought about waving back, but they couldn't see me, or even know it was me. The plane turned north and flew over the wreck of the D-6. I could see the track it made when it flew into the snow. I could see the tracks made by the snowmobiles that went out to the plane and the ones we'd made when John and I walked around it. They would last until the next big wind came and covered them over. Maybe my tracks in Antarctica wouldn't be erased too quickly, I thought.

Even from here the wreck looked terrible, and I knew that Jerry was lucky to be alive after surviving something like that.

As the Hercules rose higher and higher into the sky, the sheet of ice below us grew and grew. I could see the mountain ranges in the distance while Patriot Hills Base Camp and the wreck of the plane disappeared from sight. Then it sank in: I was finally heading home.

I put myself to work by catching up on my journal. I seldom looked out the window of the Hercules; I didn't need to be reminded of what was behind me.

We took off at 8:55 a.m. and landed very smoothly at 2:40 p.m. The flight was downright cold. The pilot informed us that the temperature outside the plane was -40° F, and the plane did not have as much heat in it as when they left Punta Arenas. I had a little trouble keeping my feet warm, so I took off my double plastics boots and put on my camp booties with a heat pack in each of them; it seemed to help.

Once the plane landed you could feel the rush of warm air as the tail hatch and door was opened. Though it was only 50° F. outside, it felt like summer. Anne Kershaw was there to meet us and had our bags taken to the terminal. There was no customs for us to go through since we weren't coming in from any recognized country, so some clerk simply stamped our passports. While in route to the Hotel Jose Nogueria, Doug Smith offered to buy all the drinks we wanted at the hotel bar providing we didn't shower first.

I'm sure we were all smelling pretty bad after working up the lather we had for the last few weeks and not bathing properly afterwards, but we decided to take Doug up on his offer anyway for at least one drink – or until our smell cleared out the bar. Unfortunately, it was a Saturday, and it also was a Presidential Election day in Chile, so all of the city's shops and bars were closed.

Since the bar was closed, John, Doug and I went to John's room and emptied the mini bar. I had not changed my clothing, which was a good thing, because I needed the Swiss army knife in my pocket to open the wine bottles. Lou, unable to handle our smell, went to shower and shave. Rick went to a different, cheaper hotel – which is what I should've done. My credit card bills were going to kill me when I got back home.

John, Doug and I had a good time reliving some events of the trip and discussed the relevance of the Mystical Plane Connection. John said, "There was truth to it; we pulled the plane out of the ground, and suddenly the weather was good enough to fly in the Herc."

With the mini bar empty, Doug and I didn't see the point of hanging around. We thanked John for his hospitality and left for our own rooms. I peeled off my clothes and placed them in a plastic garbage bag until I could get them home and wash them. I then stood in the shower for a considerable amount of time; never before has a shower felt so good. Even putting on clean clothes was a treat. Its funny how we take some things for granted. After cleaning off three weeks of sweat, grime – and who knows what else – in the shower, I went to the lobby and sent a fax back home telling everyone that I had successfully reached the summit of Vinson and that I was finally off the ice.

Tonight, there was a private dinner for all of us. In attendance were the Chileans who climbed with us, the pilots of the plane, Anne Kershaw, Solidad (Giles Kershaw's sister) and a Chilean General. (Though he is a very important and influential person, I can't remember who he is or what he has done.) We all enjoyed the dinner that lasted well into the evening, and the hotel managed to bend its "no alcohol" policy for us because we were the first group of climbers to return from Mt. Vinson. This was also a chance for us to tell the people of ANI what we liked and did not like about the trip.

We said our goodbyes to the three members of the Chilean Army. I felt bad that I didn't speak better Spanish so I could've spoken with them more. I do have their addresses and will send copies of the photos that I had taken with them. Saying goodbye is always the hardest part of these trips. After the party, Lou, Doug and I convinced the bartender at the hotel bar to let us split a last bottle of wine

Early tomorrow afternoon we will head for home. It will be a long trip, but after something as long and exciting as this, all trips seem long. Until I get my photos back, the Antarctica trip will be just a memory to me – just like home is to me now. I'm looking forward to getting back there; after all, home is where the heart is.

January 1994

The trip back to Wisconsin was indeed a long one. From the time I left Punta Arenas until the time I walked into my home, over 28 hours had elapsed. It was the longest return trip I'd ever had. This trip even beat my return from Africa by four hours. One by one at various airports along the way I'd said goodbye to John, Lou, Doug and Rick.

It was great to be home again among family and friends. It was time to unpack and relax, but that wouldn't last for long. I now had the job of collecting the pledges people had made to the American Cancer Society. It took almost a week to realize that what I had worked so hard for was finally over. The Vinson trip was no longer a dream – it was a memory. All the days I'd spent that previous spring and summer sitting in front of my computer, writing letters to would- be sponsors, was over. I had spent so much time sitting in my office while everyone else was enjoying the weather.

Now I would spend the next few weeks in my little, home office completing the fundraising part of my climb. Letters had to be written and mailed, moneys had to be collected and I had to prepare a report to give to those who had helped me with the climb.

The American Cancer Society mailed out flyers to all the people who made pledges. I collected from all my friends and fellow firefighters, saving work for the Cancer society people. When they didn't get responses from some people, they notified me and I gave that person a "reminder" phone call. It had taken a number of weeks, but the payment on the 354 pledges that had been made began rolling in. By the time it was finished, a grand total of $10,672 was raised, including a sizable donation from Saudi Arabia. This was the largest amount of money I had ever raised for any charity. Granted it was a far cry from the $100,000 I was hoping to raise, but it was still an accomplishment; it made me feel that all the delays and hardships that went along with the Vinson climb were worth it.

In May of 1994, Lisa and I took a trip to Minneapolis where I had the pleasure of "meeting" Jerry Vanek, the veterinarian who was injured in the plane crash in the Antarctic. Jerry told me he didn't remember anything of the crash and didn't really recall any of his time on the ice. The extent of his injuries included loose teeth, internal injuries, a shattered left leg and a broken left arm. He told me that he remembered waking up in a hospital in Minnesota five or six days after the crash. He still had pins in his leg from the several places it had been fractured and was still walking around on crutches that he would most likely need for the rest of the year. Jerry said he probably would have another year of physical therapy ahead of him.

He thanked me for helping him on the ice. I told him that most of the credit should go to Earl Ramsey (one of the Patriot Hills staff). He had done most of the work and I had assisted him. Just the same, Jerry was very appreciative.

It was good to see Jerry standing; I had never realized just how tall he was.

Chapter Seven
Mt. Aconcagua Again

(The end of the dream)

The Mt. Vinson adventure was over, but I had no plans to climb in 1994. After all, I was still repaying the money I'd borrowed for the Vinson trip, but I had started to think about 1995. Deciding where to go wasn't very hard. Lou and I – on several occasions while on the Vinson climb and afterwards – discussed going to Aconcagua in South America. Aconcagua was one of the mountains that had escaped me due to bad weather, and I had a great desire to go back and conquer it.

We weren't going with Mountain Travel-Sobek, as it was being called. In the past, Lou had climbed with his friend, Phil Ershler who had his own company, International Mountain Guides; we made our arrangements through him.

I was excited about going back to South America; it would be similar to the time I went back to Russia to climb Elbrus; the whole experience would be somewhat familiar. During the second week of January 1995, I would once again try to climb the highest mountain peak in the Southern hemisphere.

Since my last fundraiser had gone so well, and since I hadn't raised funds while climbing Aconcagua the first time, I decided to do it again. This peak would be my highest, and I would have the chance to increase pledge totals if I made it to the top. My highest climb to date was on Aconcagua back in 1990, where I just broke 21,000 feet, but I hadn't been climbing for a charity at the time.

But who would I climb for? My last climb was for the American Cancer Society so I didn't want to climb for them again so soon, and it would never be cold enough in hell or for me to do another fundraiser for Muscular Dystrophy. So, I went back to the American Diabetes Association.

I spoke with Judy Rupnow of the ADA in Milwaukee. Judy was regional overseer of the ADA in Southeast Wisconsin. I had explained to her what I had done for the ADA in the past – and more importantly – what I wanted from them in the future if I was to climb for them. I wanted help getting the word out; I was tired of doing all the leg work, and I was still a little put-out at some members of the Racine Chapter for their lack of participation in getting pledges for my last Elbrus climb.

Judy did her part, though; she contacted local TV and radio stations, put notices in the paper and made several mailings to various organizations. The ADA was also going to help me in getting donations and collecting pledges. They used an 800 number for people calling in pledges, and later – when the time came – they would send out notices to the people who made donations over the phone. They would take my pledge sheets and send notices to the people who signed them. That alone, would save me a great deal of time and trouble in collecting pledges, which was by far the hardest part of fundraising. They also took care of designing and printing the pledge sheets for this climb.

THE AMERICAN DIABETES ASSOCIATION HAS A MOUNTAIN TO CLIMB IN FINDING A CURE FOR DIABETES.

Nick Comande is climbing that mountain to benefit the American Diabetes Association.
You can help climb that mountain by pledging your support to Nick.

Nick Comande is an outstanding individual in our community, not only does he contribute his time to good causes, he is also a firefighter in Racine. Nick will attempt to climb to the summit of Mt. Aconcagua, the highest peak in South America. He is collecting pledges for his climb and ALL pledges raised will benefit the American Diabetes Association in its effort to prevent and cure diabetes and improve the lives of all people affected by diabetes. Share in Nick's commitment and adventure by pledging money for every 100 feet he successfully climbs or make a pledge just bacause of his effort. The summit of Mt. Aconcagua is 22,835 feet high! It is part of the Andes Mountain Range in Argentina, South America. Comande's ascent begins on January 12, 1995. Nick Comande is an independent amateur mountain climber raising funds for charitable causes. He personally finances ALL trip expenses. 100% of all pledges raised benefit the American Diabetes Association. By pledging a nickel for every 100 feet Nick climbs your contribution would be $11.40, a dime per 100 feet contributes $22.80 to help fund ADA educational programs and research. Join in the Climbing the Mountain against Diabetes.

Your pledge today makes the difference!

If you have any questions contact the American Diabetes Association, 2949 N. Mayfair Road Suite 306, Wauwatosa, WI 53222 or call 1-800-DIABETES (in Wisconsin only) or 414-778-5500.

Mount Aconcagua is the highest point in South America and is a 22,835 foot climb!

Pledge/100 feet:	.01	.02	.03	.05	.10	.15	.25	.50	1.00	5.00	10.00
Total Pledge:	$2.28	$4.56	$6.84	$11.40	$22.80	$34.20	$57	$114	$228	$1140	$2280

Return completed pledge forms by FEBRUARY 1, 1995 to: ADA, 5030 Valley Trail, Racine, WI 53402.

NAME (please print) ADDRESS/CITY/STATE/ZIP	PLEDGE PER 100 FT.	FLAT DONATION	TOTAL PLEDGE
Total Pledges			

Please pledge what you can.
ALL pledges will go directly to the American Diabetes Association.

Film services provided by ONE HOUR MOTOPHOTO IN BROOKFIELD, WISCONSIN

I wished things could've been like this during my first two climbs for the ADA; it would've made things much easier and our fundraising totals much higher.

The other thing I liked about working with Judy was that she was just as excited about my climb as I was; it made raising money for the ADA that much more worthwhile.

Before the climb, I made an appearance on an early morning television show and did a number of radio interviews to help drum up support for the ADA. Each time I spoke, I talked about the mountain, the charity, and how the money would be used locally. More importantly (at least in my mind), was how expenses were coming out of my pocket and all proceeds were going directly to the ADA. I would receive no reimbursement of any kind.

For the two months before the climb, I spent my time getting in shape and getting pledges. Before I knew it, a new year had rolled around and I was once again off to South America. Aconcagua would be waiting for me – right where I had left it.

Hosteria Puente Del Inca Argentina, South America January 13, 1995

I'm back in a journal (once again), so I must be on or near a mountain; it is Aconcagua for a second, and hopefully, a last time. The trip here was hectic, with two days of fog closing Milwaukee's Mitchell Field. The night before I left was stressful, to say the least. I worried that the airport wouldn't open in time; it didn't. I had to race down to Chicago's O'Hare Field and fly from Chicago to Miami, Florida, and from Miami to Santiago, Chile.

There are 11 people in our group, including one man whose flight was late; he will catch up with us tomorrow.

The ride from the Santiago Airport to the Hosteria was roughly 3 ½ hours, including lunch. I napped some along the way. Some of the roads were extremely steep and winding, and there were several times that the group didn't think our overloaded van was going to make it.

We are in Argentina less than a mile outside of Chile. We will be having dinner shortly at the Hosteria, which is a very nice place. The view from here is breathtaking. I hope to get some good pictures tomorrow. I'm too tired to do so now. Even though I slept on the plane and bus, I'm dragging. We'll sort gear tomorrow, so I'll have another day to rest and recuperate.

January 14, 1995 Hosteria Puente Del Inca. Elevation: 8,924 feet

It was 84° F. before the high winds and the thunderstorm came, then the temperature dropped. The thunder woke me just after 8:00 a.m. Until then, I had slept very soundly and stirred very little; I was so tired from the previous days' travel.

Breakfast was continental; I drank a lot of tea. The hydration process has been on since yesterday afternoon, which means whatever goes in must come out. I have felt the change of altitude here which is 8,000 feet higher than it is at home. I had some minor headaches earlier but those have passed; my appetite is still good and I'm drinking lots of water.

Today we packed our gear – both personal and group – for the long march in to base camp; it was weighed and situated into piles that each mule would carry.

After that was finished, Lou and I took a short walk to a nearby Russian church where a warm mineral spring was located, but I didn't drink from it; I didn't want to take the chance of drinking something that might possibly make me sick. It was a beautiful spring, however, surrounded by colorful rock formations which looked like sulfur stains.

Mac (the member of our party who has been detained back in the states due to bad weather), is said to be at the border station; he'll join us shortly. Dinner will be at 8:30 tonight and we will just sit around to kill time until we leave tomorrow.

I'm looking forward to getting started; the sooner we start – the sooner we finish. I'm going to turn in early tonight. It's probably just nerves, but I don't feel as good as I should right now.

January 15, 1995 The Ranger Station in Vacas Elevation: 7,910 feet

I awoke at 7:30 this morning, but I didn't get out of bed until 8:15. I took a long, hot shower, knowing that it would be a long while until my next one. The group got together for the continental breakfast, and many commented on how this would be our last real sit-down meal for a while. I made one last phone call home to tell Lisa, that all was well and that I would call back when I made it off the mountain. Our gear was rechecked, and then we were driven to a drop-off place, which took two trips to get both us and our gear there. Lou and I were in the second group.

It felt good to get underway, and not have to wait for days as we had on the Antarctica trip. We were dropped off at Vacas Del Inca. (Vacas means cow). Our guide, Greg Wilson, gave us a quick briefing before we left and told us what to expect. We started our hike along the chocolate waters – as I named them my first trip. We were alongside them most of the way, but we did go inland, away from the stream, from time to time. We also had a number of ups and downs covering a distance of five miles – give or take a little. The trek reminded me of my first trip to Aconcagua, but it was not the same; this time I was walking in a completely different valley. This route called the Vacas route would take an extra day to reach base camp, but it would be more scenic than the “route normal” which most people take. Unlike the route normal, which I took on my first trip, this valley had just as much green as brown.

As we hiked, Lou and I talked about what we were doing here; Lou said his family was a bit upset because he didn’t go skiing this month. It’s partially my fault that he is here now. Lou wanted to take a later trip, but it wouldn’t work out for me, and we wanted to go together.

We hiked in single file, following the path that had been walked by so many others. The valley was beautiful, and the hike was not very strenuous. The path went up and down in some places, and then it leveled off for the longest time in others. If you looked as far as the valley would let you, you could see snow-covered peaks in the distance. We came to a vast opening where we would camp for the night. To the side of our campsite was another extremely long valley that we would hike through tomorrow.

We’ve stopped for the night in the Vacas valley, near a small stone building that is a ranger station; it’s probably 10 X 10 feet with a small radio antenna in front of it. We are roughly one- third of the way to base camp. We began our hike at 11:53 a.m. and arrived here five hours and 44 minutes later; this included stops to rest and to fill our water bottles.

Three quarters of the way it started to drizzle, and by the time we made it here, it was raining steadily. I hate rain; it makes setting up camp miserable.

We arrived long before the mules with all the heavy supplies, so we were all huddled next to a big rock, waiting for our community gear and our tents to show up. Forty-five minutes later, it did.

By the time camp was set up, out tents were wet; our gear was wet, and it was just a miserable situation. Presently, I’m in my sleeping bag – the most comfortable place I’ve been since I walked out of that hot shower this morning; nevertheless, we are on our way.

I just want to lay back and read awhile, but I’m tired and winded. The walk to this point was as tough as it was long. We gained no real elevation because we lost so much driving down to the place where we were dropped off.

January 16, 1995 Casa Placida (House of Rock) Elevation: 10,600 feet

It is just beginning to drizzle again, and I'm hoping it won't last. I woke up this morning about 7:15. Our departure time was 8:30, but our guide, Greg Wilson, said it would be closer to 9:00; he was right. The rain had stopped early in the night. I knew this because I didn't sleep well, and I noticed the silence as soon as the rain stopped beating on the roof. From the moon's glow on the tent, I could tell the clouds had also disappeared during the night, and the skies were clear.

Last night, the moon was full, but as badly as I wanted to see it, I didn't want to leave the comfort of my sleeping bag. The bag, which is rated to -30° F., had kept me warm – in fact, it had kept me too warm. I remember breaking into several hot sweats during the night, and I had to open up my sleeping bag to cool down.

I wished that today would be a better day than yesterday. During breakfast, everyone was talking to other members of the climb. I will write about them as we get farther into the trip. I was talking to Greg; he told me he had been on Everest several times. He even ran into Robert Anderson, who was on my second trip to Elbrus. He told me that Robert stopped by Greg's tent and rested for a while.

The first obstacle of the day after striking camp would be a river crossing; we crossed it one- by-one while sitting on a horse led by a gaucho on another horse; it took awhile for the 11 of us to cross. Two hours later we had our second of several river crossings; the river was only ten or 12 feet wide – not very deep – but there was an extremely strong current. There were no horses or mules to help us this time, so Greg and Mark Flagg (our assistant guide), strung a rope across the river. Again we crossed – one-by-one – using our ski poles to balance ourselves. If someone should slip, the gear would all get soaked, but they would still be tied to the rope.

It took us 6 hours 6 minutes (by my watch) to reach Casa Placida. I believe someone said it was an 11-mile hike. Halfway here my back started to hurt, and I took a couple of *Advil*; it seemed to help, but I was warm; I felt like I was running a low-grade fever.

The walk through the valley was warm, especially when the sun came over the top of the valley walls. On the higher peaks, you could see snow had fallen during last night's storm. The sun would melt the snow on the lower peaks and that would help supply us with water during the day, but the snow on the high peaks would be there for awhile. We took four or five rest-breaks during the trek and ate chocolate, string cheese, crackers and other snacks we had brought.

Lou is nursing a blister, and so is Mac. Mac Purifoy is from Texas and is a friend and tent mate of Gene McCabe, president of a hospital in New York.

So far, everyone I've talked to has been nice and has had some experience in the mountains. It is 7:45 p.m. Lou and I are in our tent. There isn't a lot to do here. I'm reading Stephen King's *The Stand,* and I'm writing in my journal. (I used to write postcards, but they required too many things for me to carry such as address labels and stamps. It just became a hassle at times, so I'm not doing it on this trip. I know some of my friends back home will be disappointed; they enjoyed getting postcards mailed – at my request – by climbers coming off the mountain.) This trip, they will have to do without.

We will reach base camp tomorrow; it will be good to get there. I wish I felt a little better; I can't shake this fever. I've also been coughing more than usual. I think I need a good night's sleep, and I'll try to get that now.

January 17, 1995 Base Camp Elevation: 13,500 feet

I was the last to make it to base camp. I'm all worn out and I have no reserves left, but tomorrow is a rest day. I have a bad feeling about my health; my chest hurts, my lower right side hurts, my throat hurts and I've been coughing, excessively.

The wind was so strong here at base camp; we all had to help each other set up our tents, so they wouldn't blow away.

I had my first real view of Aconcagua today; it is big and beautiful with much more snow on it than five years ago. When it came into view we decided to rest; this also was an excellent opportunity to take some photos. There are no clouds today, meaning there will be no rain. I'm thankful for that; I hated walking in those drizzles. It has been very windy all day; if the winds don't settle down, it will be a very long night.

I'm so tired; I don't feel like writing. It's a real shame that I feel like this. I just don't have the strength or ambition to put on paper all I saw and experienced today. Maybe it is for the best if my experiences aren't good. I've been struggling this whole day, trying to keep up with the others; I didn't do a good job of it.

I'm going to rest and try to stop coughing for awhile.

January 18, 1995 Base Camp Elevation: 13,500 feet

It is 12:30 p.m. and it was a very long night. I didn't sleep well, my chest still hurts from coughing, and I'm finding it difficult to catch my breath. Two members of our team, who happen to be doctors, came over to my tent and listened to my lungs. One of them says he can hear fluid in my lower right lung.

As soon as he said it, I knew this trip was over for me. I've talked to Greg about my condition and he understands the position I'm in, and I understand his. One of the doctors gave me some medicine to make me feel better. It might make me feel better, but I don't think it will cure me. This feels like the start of bronchitis – again

I talked to Lou about my going down, and I know he's not happy with my decision. He says if I take care of myself, and take only what I need (this means leaving my heavy camera behind), I could still climb. I told him, "I didn't think so."

Today is a rest day – no hiking or climbing, just a day of rest and getting acclimated to the thinner air. I couldn't keep any breakfast or lunch down today. I've decided to talk to Greg about going down the mountain. For me . . . this climb is over.

January 19, 1995 Base Camp Elevation: 13,500 feet

11:30 p.m. I'm still at base camp, and I'm not feeling any better today; in fact, I feel worse, but I'm not the only one. Paul (one of the doctors) is feeling ill. We'll both go down together with Mark, the assistant guide.

The rest of the team made the first carry to Camp I today; I felt miserable and didn't even think about going any higher. I'd just like to start getting lower, so I don't get any sicker. I lost breakfast again this morning, and I feel nauseous whenever I eat anything solid. The weather is good except when the wind blows, and then it becomes chilly.

I told Lou I was going down the mountain. I'm sure he wasn't happy with me, and I don't blame him. I believe he came on this trip, instead of a later one, because of me. But what else can I do? I'm not getting any better – just worse. As much as I want to summit another mountain – this mountain – it's just not going to happen. I've always believed that common sense dictates over all, and I don't plan to walk "further into the lion's den" for that reason, the American Diabetes association, or for anyone.

Hopefully, Lou will someday forgive me for leaving him like this, but as I see it, it's the only thing to do. I don't feel like writing anymore.

January 20, 1995 Casa Placida Elevation: 10,600 feet

There's downhill progress at last. I'm out of base Camp and working my way back to Punta Del Inca. At 12:50 today, Mark (our assistant guide), Mac Purifoy (who was having problems with his knee) and I, left base camp to head for home. Paul (who was not feeling well yesterday), said he felt much better; he is going to continue up the mountain.

Last night was another long one; I woke up several times to find myself sweating and chilling. At this point, I couldn't wait to leave.

There were quick goodbyes said at the camp. I'm sure Greg wasn't pleased to lose his assistant guide; it will make the work load harder for him. It was very hard to say goodbye to Lou. I had asked to climb with him, but I'm not sure what he is thinking about me now. Before leaving I told him, "Now that I'm going off the mountain, you guys will have great weather, a great time, and *you will* summit." I wasn't calling myself a jinx, but they would have a great time, and I would miss it – as my luck would have it. I was the one person climbing for a cause, and I wasn't climbing; that hurt. I had a quick photo taken with my flag to show the ADA.

Before leaving Base Camp to come off the Mt. Aconcagua.

It was very disappointing end to what should have been a great fundraiser and a new personal altitude record for me. Now neither will happen.

The three of us hiked to Casa Placida, where we had camped four nights earlier. It took us just over five hours to get there; we made four river crossings without incident, then we saw a dead mule lying in the river. It was still daylight when we arrived, and we quickly set up camp. We have dropped 2,849 feet in elevation, but I don't know if that is enough of a change to make me feel better. It also took everything I had to make it here.

Tomorrow we will start walking through the Vacas valley. Mark says that it will take us two days to walk out, while camping, where we camped on the way in. Both Mac and I would rather get an early start and walk all the way out, depending on his knee and how I feel. I don't know which feels worse; failing to summit for another charity, or leaving Lou.

January 21, 1995 Hosteria Puentea del Inca

I'm back at Punta Del Inca. Thank God, the ordeal is over! Boy, what a terrible thing to call it; I paid big bucks for this trip. I wanted to summit Aconcagua, and I was hoping to raise a lot of money for the American Diabetes Association. Well, none of that is going to happen now – or maybe ever again.

We awoke at seven this morning. I was tossing most of the night, and Mark said he woke me six times for snoring, which was proof that I was tired and actually sleeping better. Mac and I both told Mark we could do without a hot breakfast, which meant we wouldn't have to break out the stove or get water and boil it. I still wasn't very hungry, so it wasn't much of a problem for me. I kept trying to stay hydrated, but it seemed no matter how much I drank, I couldn't get my urine clear – another sign of a problem.

We broke camp and were on our way by 8:30 a.m. I was feeling a little better, but there was still heaviness in my chest and on my right side. I just wanted to get further down the mountain. Mark told Mac and me not to get our hopes up about marching the rest of the way out today. I assured him that my hopes were not up, but – deep down – they were. The thought of spending another night in this cool air was horrifying; I was also afraid of getting pulmonary edema.

The sun hadn't come over the ridge of the valley, so it was pretty cool for quite awhile, but walking helped me stay warm. When the sun finally did make it over the ridge, it turned the day hot. My thermometer was on my jacket which was tucked away in my backpack, so I couldn't tell what the temperature was for sure, but I bet it was at least 85° F., and much warmer than when we were walking toward base camp.

It had stopped raining several days ago and the small streams we drank from had dried up, so we had to conserve between water stops. The water in my bottles would warm quickly after filling them in this heat. My insulator was packed away with the rest of my cold-weather clothing that I would not be using. Later today, mules would bring out my gear, as well as Mark and Mac's.

While walking out, Mac and I both apologized to Mark for having to bring us all out, and making him miss his shot at Aconcagua's summit. This was a free trip for him because he was working. He said, "I never expected to see the summit; most assistant guides don't. When you have a group this big, someone usually comes down early."

Mac told me that even though his knee was still bothering him, he was trying to keep up a fast pace so when we reached the ranger station (where we camped our first night out) we could march all the way out and not have to camp out again. I agreed with him, and even though my back was beginning to hurt, I kept thinking that the lower in elevation I got, the better off I would be.

It was 1:30 p.m. when we reached the river where we used horses to cross on our way up the mountain. Our first campsite was across the river; we would have to wait until the mules came by to cross on them which would not be until 4:00. What a waste of time it would be just sitting here. Surprisingly, Mark made the decision to cross it without them, and since Mark was in charge and responsible for our safety, Mac and I were all too willing to cross.

With the use of a rope we successfully crossed the river; it was the widest river crossing we had. Being shorter than Mac and Mark, I may have felt the current more than they. It was a strong current, but no one fell in and no one lost any gear. We stopped at the ranger station to rest and sign out. Everyone who was going up the mountain had to sign in and then out again upon their return. The rangers then checked to see if they had brought their garbage out as well; this was part of a big plan to clean up Aconcagua.

Mark then made a grand decision to walk out. Even though Mac's knee was sore, and my back was beginning to get sore from the weight of my pack and my constant coughing, we were willing.

Since we were going out, I suggested that we give some of the food stores we wouldn't need to the rangers. (We called them rangers, although they were just two guys in their early twenties). We gave them the food to lighten our packs a bit, and they reciprocated with something wonderful. They gave us each an orange – a real live, down to earth orange. The only fruits safe to eat in South America, without the fear of getting sick, are fruits that can be peeled. I hadn't appreciated anything orange so much since I'd asked the stewardess for a glass of orange juice as I boarded the plane on my last trip home from Russia. The thing I've always missed on the mountains was orange juice. I ate it all, not caring how sticky my hands got while I ate it.

The last part of the hike out would be about five miles, or so I thought. Mark said it was eight miles, and it turned out to be every bit of that. Once we started our hike out, we would be committed to finishing it; there was no place to camp along the way. The rest of the hike was hot, and streams with clean water were fewer and farther between, so once again we conserved wherever we could.

The rangers were to radio ahead and we would be picked up at the drop off point at 8:00 p.m.; this would give us six hours to march out.

During our trek, hot winds constantly blew over us, and it was not until the sun went behind the valley's ridge that it cooled down. Remembering how cloudy and rainy it had been during most of the hike in, I began hoping for some clouds to block out the sun. As we hiked, I saw a condor soaring high along the rim of the valley, but it was too high and too far away to get a decent photo.

We were all tired and moving a bit slower after the long hike out, but we finally reached the pick-up point at 7:25. My back and chest were still hurting, and my legs were chaffed from rubbing against my pants. Mac's knee was throbbing, and Mark had a huge blister on his foot. Mac said the thought of a hot shower and cold compresses had kept him going. According to Mark, it was an 18-mile trek, and we did it with packs weighing over 50 pounds.

While we waited for our ride, I watched the sun go down. It was getting darker by the minute, and I wondered what the rest of the team was up to on Aconcagua. Today as we were marching out, they were climbing up to Camp I. I could see clouds in the distance, and they were headed in the direction of the mountain; I hoped the weather wouldn't hinder them.

Fernando Rajales picked us up just after 8:00 to bring us back to Punta Del Inca. I emptied the last of my water from my bottles to make my pack lighter; I wouldn't need it anymore anyway. I managed to lift my heavy pack – one more time – and place it into the back of the pick-up with the others. We then climbed in for the ride back.

The last thing I remember of the ride back to the Hosteria was passing the "climbers" cemetery, which was a couple of miles from where we were staying. I remembered that one of the guys from the team had gone to see it before we started on our trek up, but Greg (Wilson) had cautioned, "No, that is something that is done after the climb – never before." It was not a large cemetery; unfortunately, there was room for more.

I checked in a room, showered and managed to keep some solid food down. I still feel miserable but I must be getting better; I haven't written this much in a while. It also helps when you're sitting by a table, instead of lying in a sleeping bag. Mac, Mark and I will head back to Santiago tomorrow, and then home. I wish I were there now.

January 22, 1995

The three of us boarded a bus back to Santiago. When we arrived at the Santiago bus depot, I immediately left for the airport, but Mac and Mark were going to take a few days to relax in the city. We wished each other "farewell" and went our separate ways. I was lucky to get a flight to Miami, considering there were no more openings for the next two days.

My plane was scheduled to leave that night, and I would be home sometime the following afternoon. I still felt winded a great deal of the time, and my pants were loose from not eating anything substantial for the past four days.

As I waited for several hours before my plane took off, I found a quiet corner of the airport where I could sit and not be bothered. Again, I thought of the rest of the group on the mountain and wondered what their weather was like and what they were doing, then I remembered what had been on my mind yesterday while I was hiking out.

I had thought about the past few days on the mountain, the ADA, all the money I'd spent for nothing and how awful I was feeling; I wasn't enjoying myself. On the mountain – while I was striving for the summit or even a higher camp – I was usually having fun. I was proving something to myself, and I was enjoying everything around me from the beauty of nature to its harsh extremes. For the last few days, all of that had been missing. There was no fun in this. There was nothing enjoyable about what I was doing; it was more work than pleasure.

Like a hot wind blowing over me, it suddenly hit me: the enjoyment in climbing was gone. The mystical force that had lured me to the higher altitudes to experience the natures' extremes had left me. The desire to push myself up a mountain was nowhere to be found. Instead, I found myself questioning why I was doing it. Then, like the slamming of a door, the answer was right in front of me. I was able to sum up my entire existence in mountain climbing in four words: *the romance is over!*

February 1995

Still coughing and hacking, I returned to the United States to see my family and friends. They shared my disappointment about not reaching the summit of Aconcagua, but I always let common sense dictate on the mountain. I met with my doctor the day after my return and he and a set of X-rays of my chest confirmed that I had pneumonia, and my right lung was filling with fluid.

It seems I had made the right choice in coming off the mountain. Had I made an attempt, I would've only been endangering myself and risking the rest of the trip for the others, and these were two things I had never intended to do.

I heard from Lou shortly after he returned from South America; the rest of the group reached the summit of Aconcagua. As happy as I was for them, I was bitterly disappointed that I hadn't been there with them. Unfortunately, I had little choice in the matter.

I called the American Diabetes Association, and with my head in my hands, told them about failing to reach the summit of Aconcagua. I told them how I never made it out of base camp. I advised them to base all pledges on the altitude I had reached which was 13, 500 feet. Notices were sent out from the ADA to all the people who had made pledges. Sometimes two and three notices had to be sent to people. I collected from fire department members that had pledged as well as my neighbors and friends; this would help keep the cost of postage down for the ADA.

Sometimes, it hurt to talk about it. Wherever I went to collect, I was asked about how I had done on the mountain. I had to explain about getting sick and having to come off the mountain early. When they asked how the others in the group did, I would say, "They made it."

In the long run, a total of $7,200 was raised for the American Diabetes Association. This was not bad compared to some of my other climbs, considering I didn't summit. Had I made the top, my pledges would have rounded out much higher, but this was not the case. It was not the highest amount I had ever raised, but it was still respectful. It was only $1,205 less than my successful climb up Elbrus and $3,400 less than Vinson.

I had always wanted to raise more money for the charity I was climbing for. Maybe this form of fundraising was getting old in this area. Without more help or national assistance, I don't think I could do much better. I was not a celebrity, nor did I have the backing of any major company to help me spread the word; I'm certain both of those things would have helped.

Epilogue

It has now been several years since I walked off Aconcagua and moved forward with my life.

My souvenir T-shirts – the ones with the names of the mountains I have climbed – have all faded; in fact, they're worn so thin in spots that you can see through them. I've kept my memories of the mountains alive by speaking to numerous Boy Scout troops, civic and outdoor groups. I've relived my adventures – both the highs and the lows – not just on the mountains, but on how and why I made them fundraisers. I still read current articles in newspapers and magazines about what's happening on the mountains and places I've visited.

I was saddened to learn that Priutt Hut on Mt. Elbrus burnt down in 1996, or 1998. The flag I had so proudly hung was probably lost. I'm sure my cairn has fallen over by now, erasing any record showing that I was in Russia. I still correspond with Helen Orzernaja, making her my longest running pen pal since 1991. The Internet has greatly speeded up the letters we write to each other, and since information is now so readily accessible – I was able to learn from Adventure Network's web site that I had been the 188th person to summit Mt. Vinson.

This is not entirely correct because they listed the members of our team alphabetically, and I knew that Lou was in front of me when we reached the summit. There was no mention of the three members of the Chilean climbing team that had summited one hour ahead of us.

I also learned from Adventure Network's records that since Vinson was first climbed in November 1983, until I summited in December 1993, roughly 200 people had climbed it. From December 1993, through January 2002, another 465 people have climbed it. That's more than double the number of people in 10 years. This only goes to show that the world is getting a little smaller; more and more people are climbing and pushing themselves to their limits.

While I don't miss the harsh extremes I endured when I was climbing, I greatly miss the sights and the emotions I had while on the mountains. I have hundreds of photos I occasionally look through, and even though I have numerous scenic photos that come close to catching the wondrous beauty I've seen in the mountains, my two favorites are those taken on my first trip to Aconcagua. They are the before/after group photos. The first was taken on our first day at base camp, and the second was after we spent the day hiking back to base camp after our failed summit attempt. We all looked so wasted; we hadn't shaved or washed for days, and our faces were tanned and burned by the sun – all except where our sunglasses had been.

Right now, I still don't have that burning desire to go back to any of my mountains or even try a new one. The only three mountains I've been on since Aconcagua had the words Splash, Space and Thunder in their titles.

In March of 1995, I married my girlfriend Lisa, whom I had started to date just a month before my first climb on Kilimanjaro. She stood by me between my climbs and worried each time I went away, and when I returned, she was always waiting for me with a smile. In July 2001, we had a wonderful little girl named Rachel who is now my greatest challenge in life. I felt a greater joy on the day she was born than on any of my mountain summits, and that was a feeling I thought could never be topped.

I hope to someday explore the wonders of nature with her – if there are any left by then and we haven't polluted, littered and bulldozed over all of it.

I still keep in contact with some of the people I met on my climbs, some just through Christmas cards. It is always good to hear from them and hear of their other new adventures, or learn that they, too, have hung up their crampons.

I've visited Howard Zatkin and Wes Mudge out on the west coast several times, and I speak to John Davis a couple times a year. He still does a great deal of exotic traveling, which includes successfully cross-country skiing to the North Pole.

Lou Kasischke was on Rob Hall's team on the ill-fated trip up Mt. Everest in May 1996, but Lou was lucky and came back alive after many others on that trip did not. He told me he was only 400 vertical feet from the top when he made the decision to turn around and go back. This only proves my point that *on a mountain, common sense should dictate overall.* This is the same decision I made on McKinley and Aconcagua.

Several people contacted me about my climbs and asked how I raised money for charities, and they in turn did it. In April of 1993 John Stone, a firefighter from Seattle, Washington with 2 of his brother firefighters climbed Mt. McKinley and raised over $25,000 for the Northwest Burn Foundation. In June of 1993 another group called *Climb for a Cure* attempted to raise over $100,000 for AIDS.

A Massachusetts state patrolman from Boston named Mike Coyen called and asked how I went about raising money for charities; he did extremely well raising money to promote AIDS awareness by climbing mountains in Bolivia. He was able to get the word out better than I, and he was successful in gaining corporate backing when I was not. While on his adventures, Mike made the *Guinness Book of World Records* for snowboarding in some extreme places. I was asked to join in one of his climbs, but the timing was not right for me, and I had to decline. This was the closest I ever came to returning to the mountains.

The Jansport Company took a group of breast cancer survivors up Aconcagua to raise money; happily, they were successful. In fact, they were going up the mountain in 1995 as the rest of my team was coming down.

When I think about all the thousands of dollars that were raised by an idea that I may have possibly started back in 1988, it makes me proud. The hurtful actions the Muscular Dystrophy Association took to stop me from climbing still bothers me. How foolish they were for stopping something that could've greatly benefited them. I look at it as their loss.

Though I haven't been climbing for causes I still look for ways to help others. My last big accomplishment was in August of 2003. I was able to change the policy of a major Midwestern Airline to allow infants to wear flight safety vest. For my daughter Rachel I had purchased a Baby B'air safety flight vest that attaches lap children to their parent's seat belt. This remarkably simple device then keeps the child secure to the parent and keeps them from being thrown about the cabin of the aircraft if it encountered unexpected turbulence. When I was denied being able to use it, I wanted to do my part in making air travel a little safer for those who are too young to take care of themselves. Now there is only one other major airline that does not allow the use safety flight vest for children and I am working on changing their minds.

Whenever asked if I will ever climb again, I answer, "I don't know," although I do think about it often. I try to stay in shape, just in case I make that snap decision to once again to challenge myself and subject my body to harsher conditions like I did with Kilimanjaro. Maybe I'll see another picture that will trigger that same something – deep down inside of me

– and give me the motivation I need to go off and conquer a new personal goal.

But until that day comes, I'll be content living with the memories of the mountains I have climbed, the few I have summited, and the adventures I have experienced.

I feel very fortunate to have traveled to all those places I call my mountains, to have been able to experience all that I did, yet still return with all of my body parts intact. I have seen so many beautiful sights and met some wonderful people; I've faced challenges of various degrees and learned to revel while triumphant, and to walk with my head held high after defeat.

I found an inner peace on my mountains, one that I haven't been able to find anywhere else. Those who Love to climb will probably know what I'm trying to say, while others may not understand it, but those are the kinds of experiences that make us unique.

I will always look back on those days and remember the friends I made, the sights I saw and the charities I helped; and I'll think of it as a grand learning experience. After all, that is what life is and should always be – a grand learning experience.

Climb Info.

Mt. Kilimanjaro
Tanzania, Africa
19,340 feet. December 8 to December 16 1988

Tom Ripellino	Nairobi, Kenya	(Guide)
Nick Comande	Racine, WI	
Les (express) Eagle	Columbus, Ohio	
Hugh Grove	Conifer, CO.	
Nancy Grove	Conifer, CO	
Martin Hamberger	Washington D.C.	
Rosanne Hamberger	Washington D.C.	
Blake Sherrod	Birmingham, AL	

Mt. Aconcagua
Argentina, South America
22,835 feet. January 30 to February 16, 1990

Sergio Fitch-Watkins	(Guide)
Ricardo Tores Nava	(Guide)
Augusto	(Assistant Guide)
Cheryl Arnold	Santa Monica, CA
Sidney Bronstien	Denver, CO
Nick Comande	Racine, WI
David Geher	Salt Lake City, Utah
Atanas (Nasko) Katsaerov	Long Island City, NY

Paul	Ontario, Canada
John Moseley	Santa Monica, CA
Wes Mudge	La Jolla, CA
Dick Nawrocki	Dearborn, MI
Charles Pertie	Vancouver, Canada
Howard (Z) Zatkin	La Jolla, CA

Mt. Elbrus
Soviet Union. USSR.
18,510 feet. September 17 to 28 1991

Alexander (Sasha) Morev	(Guide)
Nikolia Savin	(Assistant Guide)
Svetlana Morev	(Tour guide and translator)
Nick Comande	Racine, WI
Dan Weidner	Livingston, New Jersey

Mt. McKinley
Alaska. United States.
20,320 feet. May 9 to May 14 1992

Rodrigo Mujica	(Guide)
Lionel	(Assistant Guide)
Chris	(Assistant Guide)
John Alexander	Geneva, IL
Susan Babcock	Pasedena, CA
Eric Bruce	San Fransico, CA
Nick Comande	Racine, WI
Bob Elias	Redwood City, CA
Roger Kaul	Olney, MD
Harrison Price	Arlington, TX
Neal Swann	Milpitas, CA

Mt. Elbrus
Soviet Union. USSR.
18,510 feet. September 17 to September 28 1992

Alexander (Sasha) Morev	(Guide)
Mike	(Assistant Guide)
Robert Anderson	New Zealand
Joe Blackburn	New Canaan, CT
Nick Comande	Racine, WI
Sandy Willey	London, England

Mt. Vinson
Antarctica
16,076 feet November 21 to December 11 1993

Alejo Steadings	(Guide) Santiago, Chile
Rick French	(Assistant Guide)
Nick Comande	Racine, WI
John Davis III	Winston-Salem, North Carolina
Lou Kasischke	Bloomfield, MI
Brydon Gibbs	(Pilot) Ontario, Canada

Mt. Aconcagua
Argentina, South America
22,835 feet. January 13 to January 22, 1995

Greg Wilson	(Guide)
Mark Flagg	(Assistant Guide)
Nick Comande	Racine, WI
Lou Kasischke	Bloomfield, MI
Robert LeBlanc	Toranto, Canada
Gene McCabe	New York, NY
Paul Mikus	Norwell, MA
Kurt Nellhaus	Wexford, PA
Mac Purifoy	Temple, TX
William Siegal	Studio City, CA

About The Author

Nick Comande is currently a Firefighter-Paramedic living in Racine, Wisconsin. He lives with his wife, Lisa and daughter Rachel.

LaVergne, TN USA
18 January 2011
212927LV00001B/116/A

9 781420 807929